The Life and Times of Margaret of Anjou, Queen of England and France: And of Her Father René "The Good", King of Sicily, Naples, and Jerusalem. with Memoirs of the Houses of Anjou

Mary Ann Hookham

MARGARET OF ANJOU.

RENÉ "THE GOOD,"

KING OF SICILY, NAPLES, AND JERUSALEM, DUKE OF ANJOU AND LORRAIN AND
COUNT OF PROVENCE.

THE

LIFE AND TIMES

OF

MARGARET OF ANJOU,

QUEEN OF ENGLAND AND FRANCE.

BY MARY ANN HOOKHAM.

VOL. I.

LONDON:
TINSLEY BROTHERS, 18, CATHERINE ST., STRAND.
1872.

THE

LIFE AND TIMES

OF

MARGARET OF ANJOU,

QUEEN OF ENGLAND AND FRANCE;

AND OF HER FATHER

RENÉ "THE GOOD,"

KING OF SICILY, NAPLES, AND JERUSALEM.

WITH

MEMOIRS OF THE HOUSES OF ANJOU.

BY

MARY ANN HOOKHAM.

WITH PORTRAITS AND ILLUSTRATIONS.

IN TWO VOLUMES.
VOL. I.

LONDON:
TINSLEY BROTHERS, 18, CATHERINE ST., STRAND.
1872.

LONDON:
BRADBURY, EVANS, AND CO., PRINTERS, WHITEFRIARS.

TO THE READER.

———✦———

IT is not my intention to write a preface to the accompanying work, since I have long felt assured that I may trust to its own intrinsic interest to commend it to the historic reader. The romance of real life, so remarkably depicted in the vicissitudes of Queen Margaret's career, and that of her Father, cannot fail to arouse the feeling heart, and to awaken genuine sentiment : add to this, the broad light diffused over the arts and literature of those times, by King René "the Good."

My sole object, therefore, in this page is to render a just tribute to those who have kindly aided me in a task, which, from the obscure period of which it treats, has been found greater than at the commencement was anticipated. More especially do I seek this opportunity to acknowledge, the valuable assistance rendered me, through the courteous correspondence of that learned historian, the late M. de Barante ; as well as that of M. Grille, Librarian of the University of

Angers, to whom I have been greatly indebted for facts of local interest. To many kind friends and relatives, who have ably assisted me in my undertaking, and foremost amongst them to Mrs. Matthew Hall, I desire also through this medium to express my very sincere thanks.

MARY ANN HOOKHAM.

4, FITZROY STREET, FITZROY SQUARE,
    February 20*th*, 1872.

CONTENTS.

—◆—

INTRODUCTORY HISTORY.

PART I.

PART II.

CHAPTER I.

A.D. 1435.

CHAPTER II.

A.D. 1444.

INTRODUCTORY HISTORY.

PART I.

———◆———

OF THE EARLY HISTORY OF ANJOU.

AFTER the conquests of Charlemagne the Emperor, the great kingdom of France was divided into numerous fiefs, or petty sovereignties.

These were again, after the intervention of that long period called the feudal times, re-united under the French crown. Of these provinces, Anjou was one which took a conspicuous part in the politics of Europe. During 600 years the Angevine rulers were of three separate families or "Houses," originating in, and acknowledging allegiance to, the crown of France.

Some difficulty has been found by writers in marking distinctly the origin and fall of the First House of Anjou; but the dynasty of the "Third House," from which René of Anjou and his daughter Margaret sprung by direct lineal descent, is traced with sufficient perspicuity in all the annals.

FIRST AND SECOND HOUSES OF ANJOU.

In the year 768, Charlemagne bestowed his sister Bertha in marriage on Milon, Count of Maine, giving, as her dower, the territory of Anjou, and conferred upon Milon the title of Count of Angers. From this

768.

marriage proceeded four illustrious warriors, Roland, Thierri, Geoffrey, and Baldwin. After a rule of ten years, Milon was killed in battle against the Saracens in Spain.

778.   His eldest son, Roland, succeeded him in 778. That Roland whose praises have been sung by Ariosto— that famous Roland, who is reported, in one of his hand-to-hand encounters, to have cloven through man, saddle, and horse with one fell blow! But Anjou can hardly be said to have felt his governing hand, since he was killed at Roncevaux, in the very year of his accession.

778.   The title and possessions then devolved upon his brother Thierri, who was destined, during a long reign, to bear the brunt of a cruel warfare, often simultaneously carried on by two fierce enemies, and to witness continual scenes of devastation and carnage overspreading that fine portion of France entrusted to his charge.

The imperial power of Charlemagne was too mighty for the grasp of his son, and, under the mental and moral incapacity of his grandson, it dwindled and narrowly escaped extinction. Louis "le Débonnaire," the son and successor of Charlemagne, had not been

818.   four years upon the throne of France, ere the Bretons rose in open rebellion against him.

819.   The King repaired to Angers, and, joined by his cousin Thierri and the Angevine nobility, marched into Brittany, and speedily reduced that refractory province.

824.   Five years after, a second rising of the Bretons, under their Duke Nomenoé, is stated to have been suppressed

836.   by Louis with equal facility. But, as early as 836, according to some chroniclers, a new enemy appeared upon the soil of France, in the persons of the famous brigand, Hasting, and the Danes, who overran and eventually colonised Normandy; and were, therefore,

often called Normans in those times. No one ever did so much injury to the Angevines as this lawless chief with his pirate hordes.

In 838, the Danes made a descent upon France by the Loire, under the conduct of Hasting. It was not, however, until after the commencement of the disastrous reign of Charles "le Chauve," son of Louis "le Débonnaire," that the Normans on the one hand, and the Bretons on the other, succeeded to any remarkable extent in ravaging Anjou, and dismembering France. In the earliest years of that reign the restless Bretons again took up arms against the new yoke, making their Duke Nomenoé, King of Brittany; and, mindful of the recent loyalty of their neighbours, invaded Anjou, ravaged the banks of the Loire, and destroyed the abbey of St. Florent. They even approached the city of Angers, but, on learning that Thierri was prepared to fight, they hastily withdrew into their own country.

838.

It was about this time, 843—5, that the Danes found their way to Nantes; and, after making a great massacre of the people in one of its churches, established themselves temporarily on a neighbouring island of the Loire. Thence they continued to devastate the province of Brittany, for a length of time, conquering the Bretons in three consecutive battles, till Nomenoé, compelled to sue for peace, loaded them with presents, to induce them to quit his territory.

843-5.

Thierri, meantime, weakened by his great age and the harass of frequent wars, ceased to be formidable to these enemies. The French king therefore resolved, for the better defence of the whole county of Anjou, to divide it for the present into two parts independent of each other.

He permitted Thierri to remain in possession of the city of Angers, and all the territory between the left

bank of the Loire and the Maine, and the right bank
of the Layon, and called from that time "Deça-Maine."
All the rest of the country, thenceforth named " Outre-
Maine," he bestowed on a young captain, supposed of
Saxon origin, named Rostulf or Robert, who was
already distinguished for his bravery and military
tactics. This chief with his companions in arms
shortly arrived in Anjou, and established himself at
Seronne on the Sarthe (now Châteauneuf), which he
made the capital of his territory.

After making peace with Nomenoé, the Normans
advanced up the Loire, entered the Maine, and attacked
345-7. the city of Angers. Thierri sustained the first onset
of Hasting, and even repulsed the enemy out of the
city; but the Normans, after making a feint of retiring,
returned in a few days and took the city by assault.
They massacred nearly all the inhabitants, pillaged and
set fire to the city, and finally burnt alive the unfortunate Count Thierri, a venerable old man of more than
eighty years of age.

From this period the frontier provinces were for a
long time continually the scene of devastation and
849. carnage. The King of Brittany, Nomenoé, bent on
conquest, a second time invaded Anjou, and gained the
capital without striking a blow. He ravaged both Anjou
and Maine for several years, until a violent malady
ended his life.

851. His son Erispoé, who succeeded him, obtained a signal victory over the French king, Charles " le Chauve,"
who was obliged to confirm to him the possessions of
Thierri, viz., Angers and Upper Anjou ; that portion of
Anjou became, in fact, at that period an integral part
of the kingdom of Brittany. Indeed, such was the
deplorable state of the country, that, in order to obtain
peace King Charles conceded all that was required of
him, sanctioning the marriage of his son Louis " le

Begue" with the daughter of Erispoé, and confirming the latter in the attributes of royalty. Erispoé, however, was slain in 857, upon the very altar in a sanctuary to which he had fled, by his cousin Salomon, who then declared himself King of Brittany in his stead. 857

Robert, meanwhile, whose strength and valour had won him the surname of "le Fort," was respected in his territory, and was able successfully to repulse both Bretons and Normans. He remained always faithful to his benefactor Charles, who in return, in 861 entrusted him with the title and authority of Count of Angers and Upper Anjou, to preserve during the minority of his son Louis, the heir naturally of Erispoé. But the French nobility, discontented with the unfortunate government of their monarch, viewed with a jealous eye the favour shown to Robert. They intrigued with Louis, King of Germany, to depose his brother Charles "le Chauve," and at length took up arms with him at their head, and made their rendezvous in Brittany. Upon this, Robert collected troops and took defensive measures against the approach of the rebels. Louis invaded Anjou with a large army in 862, and immediately encountered that of Robert, but the latter succeeded, with inferior numbers, in driving back the enemy into Brittany, killing more than 2,000 of them, and recovering the whole of the booty which they had plundered during the incursion. 861. 862.

The fugitives rallied indeed, and afterwards re-entered Anjou, but when Robert marched promptly upon Louis and gave him battle a second time, the result was the complete victory of the Angevines, and total rout of the Breton and other forces. Finally, both Louis and Salomon, the Kings of Germany and Brittany, took the oath of fidelity to Charles "le Chauve."

In the same year Salomon enlisted on his side the formidable alliance of the Normans in Brittany; but the prudence of Robert dictated to him to buy off the latter at the cost of 6,000 silver livres. Thus, at length, disembarrassed of the pretensions of Salomon in Anjou, the French king confirmed the rank and government of Angers and Upper Anjou to Robert "le Fort" who, in

863.   863, obtained another complete victory over the Normans, entrenched in islands on the Loire, in which he was severely wounded.

865.   Robert attained the climax of his successes in 865, over the Normans, on their return from Poitiers to the Loire after pillaging that city. Taking them by surprise, he killed 500 of them, without losing a single man. In acknowledgment of this especial feat the king created him Marquis of Angers, and gave him the counties of Auxerre and Nivernois. In the following

866.   year he was further promoted to a dukedom of France, with charge of the whole country between the Loire and the Seine. He was not, however, successful against his old foes in this new scene of his operations. The Normans, ascending the Seine as far as Melun, there fell upon a force much superior to their own in strength and commanded by Robert himself, over which

867.   they obtained a speedy and decisive victory. A year or two later Robert returned to Lower Anjou, again to do battle with those insatiable brigands. He encountered, near Châteauneuf, 400 Normans and Bretons, who had despoiled the city of Le Mans. They were led by Hasting himself, who, surprised at this point, retreated within the church of Brissarth with some loss. The church having been speedily fortified, and the night coming on, Robert deferred until the morrow the attack. But, in the night, he was obliged to repel a sally from the besieged, when he was, after prodigies of valour, cut down on the threshold of the church. Ranulph, Duke of Aquitaine, his ally on that occasion, was at the same time mortally wounded by an arrow

from one of the church windows, and died three days after. Their united forces were put to flight, and the whole county fell defenceless under the yoke of the Norman adventurer.

Robert "le Fort," whose just and warlike career thus terminated in battle in defence of his country, was the first ancestor of a long line of French kings, since Hugh Capet, the head of the third dynasty, was his great-grandson, and the little town of Seronne or Château-neuf was consequently the first possession of that distinguished race in France. The peasantry of the country still cherish his remembrance under the homely title of " General le Fort."

At the time when Hasting thus re-appeared upon the soil of Anjou, the people of its capital, who had been peaceably employed for several years in rebuilding their city, had at length learnt to banish all fear of the return of that ruthless scourge, who twenty years before had sacked and burnt it so unmercifully. When therefore they were apprized of the stratagem of Hasting, so fatal to the brave Robert and his ally, the consternation was general. The victor returned with his spoil to his vessels on the Loire. He occupied the banks of that river during five years, living on the pillage of the country.

It is certain that from 869 to 873 the Normans were in possession of Anjou, but about the year 871 their chief resolved to seize upon some important town and make it his abode. 871.

He gave the preference to Angers, and, quitting the Loire, approached that city. The two sons of Robert "le Fort," Eudes and Robert, were too young at his death to succeed to his rule. The title of Count of Tours and Angers was therefore bestowed on the abbot Hugues ; but at his death, a few years after, the trust of the county was confided to Eudes, who was made

Count of Paris and Duke of France. It is, however, more than probable that neither Hugues nor Eudes possessed any but a titular authority over the province of Anjou during that anarchical period. At any rate, on the approach of Hasting, the inhabitants of Angers, despite the strength of their fortifications, fled in terror. The remembrance of his cruelties had so powerful an effect upon them, that neither assurances nor menaces on the part of the authorities could stay the affrighted citizens. They abandoned their city to the mercy of the Normans, who entering, with their leader, established themselves there with their families, and became its new inhabitants.

The French king, aroused into activity by the boldness of this enterprise, at length concerted measures, with the aid of Salomon, King of Brittany, to expel the brigand. In the following year Angers was successfully besieged by the French and Bretons in alliance. It was a protracted siege, and only terminated by means of a stratagem of Salomon.

872-3.

His soldiers dug a wide and deep canal to draw off the waters of the Maine, and thus leave the ships of the Normans on dry ground. The Normans were powerless, or thought themselves so, without their vessels, and, though the canal was never finished, it is confidently asserted that the cause which made the besieged treat urgently for peace was this ingenious undertaking. Hasting found himself compelled to offer a large sum of money for permission to depart the city with his followers. He even promised to quit the French territory for ever, and so completely imposed on the credulity of Charles, that the King raised the siege, and suffered him to transport his vessels into the new bed of the Maine. Thence he reached the Loire once again, when, with a faithlessness natural to a foe of his stamp, he remained, and soon after recommenced

his former system of depredation along its banks with
impunity.

The first person into whose hands the real government of Angers and Upper Anjou was confided, after
the siege of Angers, was one of the foresters of Anjou,
born in the territory of Rennes, in the Armorique,
named Torquat. After Robert "le Fort" and the
Norman anarchy, Torquat was the first governor of   873.
Angers, and was appointed in 873 simply as defender
of the Angevine and Breton frontiers.

He had a son of an aspiring mind, named Tertulle,
who at first filled the office of ranger, but as that
appointment was accompanied by no particular distinction, in order to advance his fortunes he entered
the service of the King and distinguished himself in
the army.

Tertulle became one of the Leudes, or faithful, of
Charles, in the year 875, but at what date he succeeded   875.
his father as governor of Angers and Upper Anjou,
and guardian of the frontiers on that side, is unknown;
it is only certain that between them Torquat and
Tertulle administered that part of the country from
873 to 892. In the year 875, when he had distinguished himself and became a Leude of Charles,
Tertulle won the hand of Petronilla, daughter of the
Duke of Burgundy, which King Charles bestowed on
him, together with a benefice in the Castle of Laudon,
and some lands in Gastinois. Tertulle became Seneschal of Gastinois. The offspring of his union with
Petronilla was a son, born in 876, named Ingelger,   876.
who at an early age attained an historical reputation,
and became the first hereditary sovereign in Anjou, as
well as the founder of a long and powerful dynastic
sway.

On the death of his father, Ingelger was only in his
sixteenth year, too young to be invested with the   892.

important command which Tertulle had exercised, and yet full of promise of a brilliant career. He had been educated under the eye of his father; and endowed with natural genius, a noble physiognomy, and a handsome figure, he had already become remarkable for a skill in horsemanship and in the military exercises, which even compensated for the deficiency of physical strength that years alone could contribute.

It seemed as if already the French King Eudes designed for him the same appointment which his father had held, for though some years elapsed before Ingelger became Governor of Angers, yet history mentions no intermediate possessor of that title, and next after the vacancy created by the death of Tertulle records the name of Ingelger.

893 Meanwhile a romantic occurrence gave rise to his *début*, about a year after his father's death, and contributed in no small degree to his advancement, in that early age of chivalry.

Adèle, Countess of Gastinois, the godmother of Ingelger, had found her husband one morning, dead in his bed by her side. Though respected no less for her modesty than her beauty, the Countess was many years younger than the deceased, and that circumstance, coupled with a greedy ambition on the part of the Count's nearest relative, except herself, named Gontran, made her the subject of an unworthy suspicion. Gontran, in order that she might be disinherited and himself put in possession of the title and estates, published an accusation against her of homicide and adultery. The decision in this matter rested with the crown, but the trial upon which that decision depended was, in those days, one of courage and strength totally irrespective of justice. The French king accordingly came to Château Laudon on a day specified, with his princes and barons, to judge the affair. The Countess was present in deep mourning. Gontran reminded them simply, that some years before, when the King had wished to marry the late Count, the Seneschal of his palace, to the Countess, she had long rejected the offer with *hauteur*, asserting that the Seneschal was born her vassal, and that she had only yielded on the reiterated instances of the King and of all his court; in short, that she had been inspired with sentiments of hatred and contempt only towards this her second husband, and that those feelings had doubtless caused her to commit the double crime laid to her charge. To *prove* his assertions, he immediately cast his gage into the midst of the assembly! The Countess replied only by sobs and tears, for no one dared to take up the gage of combat, and in that age the innocence of the accused was decided by combat alone. At length she sank fainting on the ground, and seemed ready to expire. Unable any longer to endure the sight of the agony of one who had taken so much care of his infancy after he had lost his mother, and had subsequently inspired him with all the generous sentiments which form the hero, Ingelger threw himself at the feet of the King, and besought his permission to fight for the honour of his benefactress. Surprised, yet pleased, the King at length consented, though with regret. On the morrow the same assemblage re-appeared upon the field of battle; the Countess with her ladies was present in a carriage hung with mourning, and, from the raised corner of the sable drapery, her eyes met those of her champion as the signal was given and he loosed the rein to his horse.

The age, strength, and military reputation of his adversary were all superior. At the first shock the lance of Gontran pierced the buckler of the youth, but there rested entangled, and whilst he vainly endeavoured to withdraw it, Ingelger passed his through the body of his opponent, and threw him from his horse; then alighting, he despatched him with his dagger. Amidst the acclamations which followed, his godmother, having alighted from her carriage and embraced Ingelger, petitioned the King to allow her to dispose of all her fortune to him to whom she owed her honour. The royal approval was given, and Ingelger rendered homage for all the lands which the Countess of Gastinois thus bestowed upon him. They were the town of Château Laudon and the Gastinois territory.

The King of France, an eye-witness of this brilliant commencement of his noble career, did not lose sight of Ingelger, and some years after gave him the temporary government of the town of Angers, and of that part of the county which has been called Upper Anjou. This, however, was but the first grade in the ladder of Ingelger's ambition. Before the ninth century, the military benefices granted by the King to his Leudes, or faithful, had been transferable; but during that epoch they existed for life, and before its close became hereditary. Thus, about this date, the French King, for the better defence of his territories against the Normans and others, divided them as heirlooms amongst his generals, with the titles of dukes and counts.

The feudal government, which has been aptly termed a system of organised anarchy, was then established in Anjou; and that province was elevated, in the person of Ingelger, apparently before the year 900, into one of those particular sovereignties which all depended on the principal monarchy, by virtue of faith and homage alone.

Ingelger was created hereditary Count of Anjou "Deça Maine," and as his zeal and talents displayed themselves, he soon after became Viscount of Orleans and Prefect of Tours. He then took the command from Orleans to Andecavi, whilst the Counts of Brittany, Judicael and Alain, completed the chain of defence against the inveterate Normans by undertaking to protect the passage and mouth of the Loire through Brittany. Ingelger's repeated victories over these enemies acquired for him the reputation of one of the first generals of the age, while the wisdom and firmness he exhibited in his administration gained him general esteem. Thus he obtained the notice of two powerful prelates, the Bishops of Tours and Orleans, who gave him their niece, the beautiful Adèle or Aliude, the richest heiress in those countries, in marriage. The Count of Anjou became by this marriage one of the most wealthy and powerful of the nobles of France. The country of Gastinois had for its chief town Château Laudon, and its boundaries were the county of Sens, the territories of Melun and Etampes, the county of Orleans and the Nivernois, including in its compass Courtenai, St. Fargeau, Moret, Puiseaux, and Gien, as well as the territories where the towns of Fontainebleau, Nemours, and Montargis now stand. With all these possessions, Ingelger became the object of jealousy to most of the barons of Gastinois, who had beheld him from being an equal suddenly raised to be their sovereign. At first, indeed, they refused to recognise him; but, either through fear, or out of respect to the King's authority, they all, at length, rendered him their homage.

The last enterprise in the life of Ingelger forms an illustration, almost as happy as his first, of the energy and intrepidity, no less than the love of justice, inherent in his noble character.

It appears that fifteen or twenty years previously, the inhabitants of Tours, in expectation of an incursion of Hasting, removed the body of St. Martin, as their most precious treasure, to Auxerre. The security of their province having been in the meantime established, the people of Tours now desired the restitution of the body of their saint; but all to no purpose. In vain they petitioned the King on the subject; he replied, that, so long as it remained in France, he cared not what town possessed it.

In this extremity they appealed to their Prefect, Ingelger. He collected six thousand Angevine horsemen, placed himself at their head, and marched straightway upon the town of Auxerre; which, no longer able to resist a demand supported in so substantial a manner, restored the venerable deposit without further parley. This incident is referred to the year 912, the same in which Rollo, having married Gisella, daughter of Charles "le Simple," and embraced Christianity, made peace at last between the Normans and French. In the following year occurred the death of Ingelger, whose body was conveyed to Tours, followed by all the barons and nobles of Anjou, and buried according to his desire in the church of St. Martin.

With this commencement of the feudal system, the people of Anjou, who had hitherto always enjoyed certain rights from the time of the Romans, fell into total slavery, and were parcelled out with the lands on which they dwelt. In that state of political annihilation they remained, with little exception, until the thirteenth century.

Ingelger left one son, named Foulques, and surnamed "le Roux" from the colour of his hair. He succeeded his father in the counties of Anjou and Charolais. Foulques inherited almost all the good qualities of his father; but some historians assert that he tarnished their lustre by his dissolute manners. He was certainly brave and enterprising, and always

returned victorious from his wars with the Normans
and Bretons. Foulques became the first hereditary
Count of the entire territory of Anjou. In 914
Charles " le Simple " ceded to him Lower, or Outre-
Maine Anjou, and from that time the two counties
united continued under one head. Foulques " le
Roux " married Roscilla, daughter of Garnier, Count
of Tours, by whom he had three sons : the eldest
Ingelger was killed in battle previous to the year 929,
and the second, named Guy, surrendered himself as
hostage to the Normans to obtain the liberty of Louis
d'Outre-Mer, King of France.

914.

On the death of Foulques " le Roux," his third son
Foulques succeeded him, and the first reign in Anjou
commenced in which the material prosperity of the
Angevine people had obtained any consideration.

938.

This Count was entitled " le Bon," for the worthy
actions of his public life. He was well educated for
his time, cultivated music and the belles-lettres, and
associated with learned men of all ranks, eager to profit
by their talents. His kindness and condescension
towards the poor never varied, and his administration
was remarkable for mildness and justice. In short, he
was a pattern of rulers in his era. He had, besides,
the wisdom and good fortune to live on amicable terms
with his neighbours. The age of Norman and Breton
invasion of Anjou was past. Twenty years of profound
peace intervened before the age of Angevine conquests
in Brittany and the territory of the Count of Blois.

These twenty years constituted the happy reign of
Foulques " the Good," a golden age for Anjou, a
period when that province, already the most enlightened in France, attracted strangers from far and
near to come and share the benefits of its learning and
its prosperity. In that age of feudalism, how much of
all this depended upon the individual character of the

Count who presided over the destinies of that portion
of France.   On his accession, that province presented
the spectacle of towns and bourgs abandoned and
in ruins, of fields left uncultivated, and of a people of
wandering serfs without sustenance and without a
home.   Touched   by   so   much   misery,   Foulques
bestowed his earliest attention upon agriculture.   He
granted permission to the labourers to hew in his
forests all the wood they required for rebuilding their
houses and making their implements of husbandry,
and then made them advances of money to procure
cattle and seeds.   In short, in the course of a few
years, through the wisdom, goodness, and energy of
their ruler, the inhabitants themselves, as well as their
neighbours, were astonished to find the country
abounding with flocks and herds, rich crops, orchards,
and vines laden with fruit.   Foulques "le Bon"
married Gerberge, sister of Thibault I., Count of Blois,
cementing by that union the peace and happiness of
the two provinces, Anjou and Blois, during his time.
Foulques II., who was, besides, extremely pious, was
carried, according to his desire during his last illness,
within the church of St. Martin at Tours, and actually
died there, surrounded by the bishop and monks, A.D.

958.   958.   He left seven children by Gerberge, the eldest
of whom, Geoffrey, succeeded him.

The   character of Geoffrey was much contrasted
with that of his pious, gentle, and humane father.
Geoffrey was surnamed "Grise Gonelle," from commonly
wearing a tunic of coarse grey stuff.   He was warlike
and enterprising.   He rendered some signal services
978.   to Lothaire, King of France, against Otho II., Emperor
of Germany, and assisted in the defeat of the Normans,
Danes, and Saxons whom Otho had led upon Paris.
The King of France, to testify his satisfaction, made
him Grand Seneschal of France, which office he

created expressly for him and his descendants. The life of Geoffrey "Grise Gonelle" was spent mostly in the battle-field. He had incessant contests with William IV., Count of Poitiers; he fought David, Count of Le Mans, and, in compensation for his victory over him, received his estates; he triumphed over the Bretons who had come to pillage Anjou once more; and was besieging one of his vassals in the castle of Marson, near Saumur, when he died of a sudden attack in the year 987.

987.

Geoffrey "Grise Gonelle" had several children by his wife Adèle, of whom two alone survived him, and in turn succeeded to his title and possessions. Of the elder, Maurice, no trace has been left beyond the statement that he ruled one year only in Anjou.

The name of his brother, Foulques "Nerra," who then took the reins, is well known. His good government during a very long reign was of great importance to the province of Anjou, and much resembled that of Foulques "le Bon," despite its warlike character at an early period, and despite the stains with which tradition accuses his private life. But soon after its commencement he experienced a bitter and ambitious enemy in the person of Conan I., King of Brittany, who had married his sister. He had occasion to do battle in person more than once during the year 992 against his brother-in-law, who was as treacherous as Foulques was brave and honest. The last sanguinary battle in that year terminated in the death of Conan, together with a thousand of his Breton followers.

988.

992.

In 994, Foulques laid siege to Tours, then held by Eudes, Count of Blois, and his arms having been there also victorious, a peace of some years ensued, during which he was enabled to give his undivided attention to the administration of Anjou. In his desire to ameliorate the condition of his subjects, and to augment

994.

legitimately the population of the country, he not only built a great number of towns, castles, churches, and monasteries, but placed inhabitants in them, and sought to render them happy by every means in his power. In fact, as the terrible year 1000 passed harmlessly by (when it had been believed that the end of the world was approaching), a surprising change began to operate upon all classes, and in Anjou it especially manifested itself by an era of celebrated architecture, and Foulques became distinguished in history as the *edificateur*. But he was yet more worthy of public renown, for having constantly made concessions to his unhappy people.

1012.   About 1012, he granted lands to the poorest amongst them, and established public markets for the sale of their produce, in order that they might maintain themselves. "Nerra" first brought largely into use the slate with which Anjou abounds. We find him again, 1016. however, in 1016 fighting against Eudes of Blois, and 1025. so late as the year 1025, he conquered and annexed the town of Saumur, which has been called the garden of Anjou. The limits of the province of Anjou were, indeed, considerably extended on each side under his rule, until it comprised about the same area as the department of Maine et Loire in the present day. In 1029. 1029, however, Foulques "Nerra" was unsuccessful in a contest against the Count of Maine and Alain III. of 1036. Brittany; and about the year 1036, his son Geoffrey rose in open rebellion against him. He defeated, imprisoned, and finally pardoned his son.

"Nerra" is reported to have burnt alive his first wife on a charge of adultery. It is stated that her shade appeared to him in after years, and that it was in remorse for this and other similar savage acts of his early martial career, that he made three separate pilgrimages for the Pope's benediction and to the Holy

Land. By his second wife, Hildegarde, he had the son Geoffrey who succeeded him. During Foulques "Nerra's" time, Ethelred II. of England, and many banished Saxons, took up their abode in Normandy.

His son and successor, Geoffrey "Martel," became one of the greatest generals of his age, but inherited none of the qualities which had earned the public gratitude for his father. He was engaged in warfare nearly the whole of his life. After serving in several campaigns under Henry I. of France, Geoffrey "Martel" laid siege to Tours, which was then held by Thibault III., Count of Blois. Thibault, having refused to do homage to the King for his possessions, this monarch had confiscated them, and invested Geoffrey "Martel" with them. In this enterprise, which took place on the 21st of August, 1044, Geoffrey was completely successful, against very superior numbers. The Count of Blois was himself taken captive, and as many as 1800 prisoners, and a considerable booty fell into the hands of the besiegers. From his personal prowess in this victory the name of "Martel," or hammer, was given to him, in allusion to the fatal blows by which he prostrated his opponents. The French King, however, became the mediator for Thibault, who obtained his liberation by ceding as his ransom the towns and castles of Tours, Chinon, and Langeais. From that date, Tourraine was dismembered from the counties of Blois and Chartres. Before he had attained his twenty-second year, Geoffrey "Martel" had twice conquered in battle William V., Duke of Aquitaine.

They contested La Saintonge; and, for four years, there was constant bloodshed between Saumur and Poitiers. On the occasion of his second defeat the Duke was made captive; and, after a confinement of three years, died in his prison. Geoffrey then married his widow, Agnes of Burgundy, who brought him, as

1040.

1043.

1044.

1044-8.

her dowry, the county of Poitou and many lesser fiefs.

1048. The valiant Geoffrey next attacked Normandy, but could make no permanent acquisition within the territory of William the Conqueror. Though always faithful to his sovereign, Henry I., his great ambition led him to invade frequently the states of his neighbours, and, in one important matter, he did not hesitate to employ fraud as well as force to gratify this culpable ambition. He took advantage of the infancy of Herbert II., Count of Maine, to procure his own nomination as administrator of that province during his minority, but never relinquished the sovereign authority over Maine during his life-time. He had, besides, been unscrupulous enough to sieze by force from his nephew Foulques "l'Oison," the county of Vendôme, which he restored only on the King's intercession, after he had

1050. enjoyed its revenue for twenty years. He made great acquisitions to his dominions, but his subjects could have experienced little happiness under his restless rule. Although twice married, Geoffrey "Martel" had no children, either by Agnes or Grecia, to whom to bequeath his great possessions; and with him ended the first branch of the Second House of Anjou, as it is called, or of the direct line from Ingelger. This last of the Ingelgerian Counts in direct descent, resigned

1060. his states in the year 1060, in favour of his two nephews, Geoffrey "le Barba" and Foulques "Rechin," and entering the monastery of St. Nicholas, at Angers, died there on the following morning, in his fifty-fourth year.

Geoffrey and Foulques, the nephews and successors of Geoffrey "Martel," were sons of Alberic, of Gastinois, and a sister of Geoffrey "Martel." The former received from his uncle, Tourraine and the town of Château Laudon, and the latter, Anjou and Saintonge. The inequality of this division was the cause of a bloody feud between the two brothers during eight years, as well as of the most unnatural cruelty protracted over a period of thirty years more by the one brother upon the other.

The surname of "Rechin," or quarrelsome, given to Foulques IV. has, by some, been understood as referring the whole culpability of these disasters to him principally, if not solely. It appears certain, however, that Geoffrey "le Barba" began the feud by claiming a right over his brother's inheritance of Anjou. He was actually master of the whole county of Anjou in 1066. Foulques "Rechin" succeeded in making him his prisoner in the same year, but released him on the command of Pope Alexander II. In the following year, however, Geoffrey "le Barba" renewed the war by besieging the fortress of Brissac. Foulques "Rechin" advanced against him, and took him prisoner for the second time, together with a thousand of his partizans, and confined him in the Castle of Chinon. This incarceration was continued for thirty years, and so terrible was its results, that the unhappy Geoffrey "le Barba" lost his reason. Meanwhile, the whole Angevine nobility had been divided into two hostile camps; and very many had fallen in the civil war. The recent acquisition of Saintonge was, besides, lost to Anjou during these troubles; and to appease Philip I. of France, Foulques "Rechin" was compelled to surrender Château Laudon to the crown.

1066.

1067.

In 1073, Pope Gregory VII. excommunicated Foulques "Rechin" for having married Ermengarde of Bourbon within the prohibited degrees. But although proved to have been a zealous Roman Catholic by his defence of the faith against heretics, and by his gifts to the Church, Foulques "Rechin" seems generally, throughout his life, to have made very light of papal anathemas. He was a second time excommunicated by the same pontiff in 1086, for his lengthy and cruel detention of his brother in prison. But in proof of the

1073.

1086.

utter futility of these anathemas, Pope Urban II., ten years after, favoured Angers, amongst many other French cities, with a visit, to preach a crusade to the Holy Land; and having been magnificently received there by this same Foulques " Rechin," presented him with a golden rose, which had received his blessing.

Geoffrey " le Barba " was as close a prisoner as ever at that very date, though it is true that he was released shortly after, by command of this same Pope Urban II.

Foulques "Rechin" was a very abandoned character in private life. He married three wives, and repudiated them all; but the fourth repudiated him. This last, named Bertrade, was the sister of Amaury of Montfort, and was reputed the most handsome woman in the kingdom; but, such was her frailty, that after living with Foulques "Rechin" four years, she deserted him, and fled to Philip I., King of France.

By his second wife, Ermengarde, Foulques had a son named Geoffrey "Martel," who would have succeeded him in Anjou, but Bertrade was jealous of the interest of her son by "Rechin," named Foulques; and 1106. in 1106, Geoffrey "Martel" was found murdered. It would hardly be expected that Foulques "Rechin" was learned for his time, but so he is reputed. He wrote in Latin a history of the Counts of Anjou, in which, after briefly speaking of his ancestors, he informs us, that the twenty-seventh year of his reign was marked by a great prodigy. He affirms that the stars then fell like hail upon the earth, causing a great panic and mortality in France, 100 persons of rank, and 2,000 of the people having died at Angers alone. Foulques 1109. " Rechin " died in 1109, at the age of sixty-six.

His son by Bertrade, Foulques V., succeeded him. He had been invested with the county of Anjou, by Phillip I. during the lifetime of his father in 1106, after the assassination of Geoffrey "Martel." This Count was destined, in a much shorter reign than that of his father, to attain higher alliances, and to secure wider possessions for his descendants. It was during his reign, that Anjou first became connected with the reigning family of England.

He began by annexing the county of Maine to that of Anjou, by his marriage with Eremburga, daughter of Helie, Count of Maine, who, at his death in 1110, made him his heir. Soon after, the King of France needed his assistance against the English : Foulques V. had maintained that the rank and title of Grand Seneschal of France, borne by Geoffrey ".Grise Gonelle," was a family inheritance in the house of Anjou, and taking advantage of the King's present necessity to plead for a confirmation of that title to him, he gained his object. He next distinguished himself by several victories over Henry I. of England when that king invaded Normandy. His humanity to the prisoners in his triumphs quite won the heart of the English monarch, who finally sought his alliance, and a marriage was celebrated between his son William, and Matilda, the daughter of Foulques. The bridegroom at these nuptials was fourteen and the bride eleven years of age. After William's shipwreck on his return to England, Matilda retired to the abbey of Fontevrault, in Anjou, of which thirty years after she became the Abbess, and died there in 1155.

In 1120, leaving his wife Eremburga with his young children, Geoffrey and Helie, in charge of the county, Foulques made a pilgrimage to the Holy Land, and on his return, as Grand Seneschal, he bore the banner of France, and commanded the *avant garde* of the army of Louis "le Gros." Eremburga was an amiable and high-minded lady. She bore him two sons and two daughters, who were all married to the sons and

1108.

1110.

1119.

1120.

1125.

daughters of kings. She died in 1125. In the same year Foulques re-visited the East; and four years after

1129.

finally returned and settled there, as heir to Baldwin, King of Jerusalem, having accepted the proffered hand of his daughter Melisende.

1131.

In 1131 Foulques succeeded that prince on his throne. He died a violent death in 1144, and was buried at Jerusalem, while his son, Baldwin, by his second marriage, then mounted the throne. Foulques V., who was of a noble and enterprising spirit, was very remarkable for his bad memory; he was known to pass by without recognition persons to whom he had shortly before testified the most sincere marks of his friendship.

When Foulques departed finally for the East, he resigned his rights over Anjou, Maine, and Tourraine to his son Geoffrey "Plantagenet." This name, which served to distinguish a long line of his descendants, was derived from the badge assumed by Foulques, his father, on his way to the Holy Land. The *plantagenista*, or broom pod, when in season, was used to strew the chamber floors, and thence became an emblem of humility, and as such was borne by Foulques in his pilgrimage. Henry II., King of England, afterwards used this badge to show his descent from the House of Anjou, and it was engraved upon his robe in his monumental effigy.

In the same year that Geoffrey acceded, he espoused Matilda, daughter of Henry I. of England, and widow of Henry V., Emperor of Germany. Thus he found himself on the death of Henry I. heir to the crown of England, but not only was that throne usurped by

1135.

Stephen, in 1135, but the Normans also preferred

1137.

Stephen, who was therefore, in 1137, installed in that fiefdom by Louis "le Gros."

For four consecutive years Geoffrey made unsuccess-

ful campaigns into Normandy. Stephen died in 1141, 1141.
but the Normans did not generally succumb to Geoffrey
until the year 1144. Meantime some of his barons 1144.
of Anjou had revolted against him, and even with-
stood his authority until 1147. In punishing one of 1147.
them he sustained the first attacks of the French King
Louis VII., in open war, and braved the thunders of
Pope Eugene III. to the last. He died in 1151, at the 1151.
early age of thirty-eight. He was learned; and beloved by the people at large, and bore altogether a good
character. But twenty years of feudal warfare ruined
and depopulated his three counties of Anjou, Maine,
and Normandy, and the repeated neglect of a due
cultivation of the soil brought on a terrible famine
in 1146.

Geoffrey rebuilt the Castle of Seronne, which, as well
as the town, was from that time named Châteauneuf.
His wife Matilda, lived till 1167, and his son Henry,
eventually became King of England in right of his
mother. Normandy was ceded to him during the life
of his father, at whose death, he likewise took possession of Anjou, and his other territories in France.

Anjou, thus united to the crown of England, was so
held for upwards of half-a-century. Henry II. was
born at Le Mans, in 1133, and was only eighteen when
he succeeded his father in Anjou. Geoffrey had never
intended to unite the possessions of Anjou, Maine, and
Tourraine under the same rule as the kingdom of
England. On the contrary, he had by his will left
those counties temporarily to Henry, upon his oath
that, from the time when he acceded to the English
throne, he should surrender them to his third son,
Geoffrey. An attempt however was made by Geoffrey
to possess himself of them immediately after his
father's death, but having been worsted in battle by 1152.
Henry, in 1152, was forced to succumb to him.

1154. At length, when Henry ascended the throne of England, in 1154, Geoffrey was a captive in the hands of the Count of Blois, Henry's ally, and instead of endeavouring to effect his liberty, and restore to him his rightful inheritance, Henry II. listened only to the dictates of his grasping ambition, and retained possession of the whole of his ill-gotten power.

1156. In 1156, Geoffrey having paid his ransom established himself in Tourraine, but his unnatural brother besieged and speedily vanquished him, and the unfortunate young Count died not long after at the early age of twenty-four.

Henry II. bears a good character in Anjou. It is 1176. stated that in 1176, during a long drought, he had transported from England nourishment for 10,000 men daily for some months; and a clause in his will provided a hundred silver marks for the marriage of the Angevine young ladies. He favoured the works of the Levée, to enclose the Loire within bounds, and they made great progress in his reign. He founded the hospital called "Hôtel Dieu," at Angers, besides other worthy establishments. Henry's administrative talents are recognised in a hundred ways by the people of Angers and Saumur; the communes and other first germs of the liberty of the *bourgeois*, date from him. He had also a great taste for learning, his court was the asylum of the learned men of Europe. In the necrology of Fontevrault, he is called the Solomon of his age. He was eloquent, loved poetry, and wrote verses himself in the Provençal tongue. Above all, having shown himself the substantial friend of the people, he was very popular. His consort, the beautiful Eleanor, the divorced of Louis VII. of France, and daughter of William X. Count of Poitiers, brought him at her marriage in 1152. 1152, the extensive and important province of Aquitaine; she died at Fontevrault in 1204. Henry II. died at Chinon, in July 1189, aged fifty-six.

1189.

Henry II. had four sons, named Henry, Richard, Geoffrey, and John. Henry and Geoffrey died in the life-time of their father, and Geoffrey left a son named Arthur.

Richard next inherited the county of Anjou, together with the other French possessions appertaining to the English monarchy. The short reign of Richard "Cœur de Lion" was entirely occupied in his combats with Saladin in the East, and with Philip Augustus in Normandy. Anjou had little enough of association with its Count during the ten years, 1189—99. Richard

1199.

married in 1191, Berengaria, daughter of Sancho VI. King of Navarre; but left no children. He had designed in 1190, as his heir, Arthur, the son of his brother Geoffrey, and grandson of Henry II.; but finally bequeathed his territories to his brother John. He left, by his will, his body to Fontevrault, his heart to Rouen, and his entrails, in token of his contempt of that people, to the Poitevins.

On the death of Richard "Cœur de Lion," the inhabitants of Anjou, Tourraine, and Maine, declared in

1199.

favour of Arthur, whilst England and Normandy seconded the claims of John, as successor. John, thereupon, accompanied by his mother Eleanor, led an English army to the disputed territory, and laid siege to Angers. Prince Arthur was at this time no more than twelve years old. Philip Augustus, who aspired to concentrate in his own person an absolute authority over the whole kingdom of France, at the same time decided on supporting the cause of Arthur against John, by the arms of France. But a matrimonial expedient saved much bloodshed at that time, although it was fatal to the just cause of the young Arthur.

From the Houses of Anjou we trace all the kings
of France of the Third, or Capetian dynasty; eleven
kings of England, well known as the race of Plantagenet, besides several kings and queens of Jerusalem,
Arragon, Spain, Naples, and Hungary;—so that, at
one period, almost all the crowned heads of Europe
could trace their pedigree by marriage or by conquest,
to the House of Anjou as their great parent source.
Yet, only one hundred years after the families of
Anjou had, in the Third House, attained the zenith of
their prosperity, not a single prince of that far-famed
line survived!

In the person of René, became extinct the last of
the hereditary Dukes of Anjou. At his death that
province was finally re-united to the crown, and
degenerated into a mere appanage possessed by the
younger sons of the kings of France.

With René terminated the Fourth House of Anjou,
according to the division of certain authors, although
in reality there were but two distinct Houses, the
First, Third, and Fourth having proceeded from
Robert "le Fort," and the Second from Ingelger.* The
preceding historical details of the reigning families,
and of the county of Anjou from the time of Charlemagne to that of John, King of France, will be found
explanatory of this subject, and they will also render
intelligible the numerous titles borne by King René,
which only served to emblazon the escutcheon of an
all but titular prince.†

But if, as the last male descendant of a long line of
distinguished characters, René, Duke of Anjou, has a
claim upon the attention of posterity, there is good
reason to hope that when the poetry and chivalry,
the virtues and misfortunes of his long life are set
forth, the history of this king of Sicily and Jerusalem

* Bodin.   † See page 32.

eldest son Charles now first assumed the title of Dauphin, on the occasion of his father's imprisonment.

Louis, First Count of Anjou, the paternal grandfather of King René, was married in 1360,[*] upon attaining his twenty-first year, to Mary of Châtillon, usually called Mary of Blois, the daughter of Charles of Blois, Duke of Brittany. The contract of marriage was concluded at the Castle of Saumur. Mary received as her dowry a great many castles, fiefs, and baronies, and the Count of Anjou added to her jointure the third part of his counties of Anjou and Maine.

Some months later in the same year, while King John yet remained in captivity in England, the Dauphin Charles, as Lieutenant-General of the kingdom, elevated the county of Anjou one degree in heraldry in the person of his brother Louis I., whom he created First Duke of Anjou.

Although Louis belonged by origin to the House of Valois, he has been more generally denominated from this and subsequent occurrences the head of the " Second House of Anjou-Sicily." [†]

The treaty of Bretigny, between England and France, bore the date of the 1st of May in the same year, and from that period the name of Louis, Duke of Anjou, becomes of frequent repetition in the history of his country. By the articles of that treaty King John was, at length, released from his detention, under certain important conditions. His ransom was fixed at three millions of golden crowns, to be paid by instalments to England in the course of six years. But Edward III. required numerous hostages, meantime, for the performance of these stipulations, foremost among whom were to be the King's brother, the Duke of Orleans, and his second and third sons, the Dukes of Anjou and Berri. These princes voluntarily

---

[*] Moreri ; Godard Faultrier.   [†] Moreri ; Bodin ; Godard Faultrier.

John embarked at Boulogne, on the 3rd of January, **1364.** 1364, and there is some reason for suspecting the strong displeasure of the father towards his son from the mere circumstance, that, during the seven complete intervening months Louis did not present himself at his court, and in fact, did not come to Paris until after his departure. He then, however, aggravated the flagrancy of the dishonour by boasting publicly, that when his father learnt the motive of his escape he would excuse him! Perhaps it will be found a safer judgment, after following to the end the selfish track of this most unworthy ancestor of the "Good René," to adjudge as his motives, not any amount of patriotism nor even of marital affection, but a sordid and ambitious desire of preserving his bartered castles, even at the expense of his solemn bond.

King John died in exile in the hotel of Savoy, in London, in the year 1364, and the Dauphin succeeded him on the throne of France as Charles V.

The surname of "the Wise" has been perpetuated in history in connection with the name of the new monarch. It is objectionable, as exhibiting only one side of his character. In his own time he was called Charles "the Learned," but he was acknowledged to be the most pusillanimous being in the kingdom. It may be difficult to reconcile to modern ideas that the height of wisdom can consist in a series of the most disgraceful retreats before inferior numbers, and in ever refusing battle. Yet such was the successful policy by which Charles V. regained, under his rule, nearly the whole of France of that age.

Ever timid, ever sickly, he was rarely seen out of his palace, while his presence was felt in the country only through a course of timid, revengeful, or despotic edicts, issued from time to time for the rigid performance of his servants. Hated by most of his and by his loss after the death of Charles of the inheritance of Brittany.

In Languedoc, Louis governed with tyranny; and his exactions were to the utmost limits of toleration. The sums which he thus raised were employed by him in prosecuting his wars against the English in Spain and elsewhere. Louis revenged himself on the King of Navarre for permitting the army of the Black Prince to pass through his territories, by seizing the lordship of Montpellier, which adjoined his province of Languedoc. He also, by the aid of the brave Duguesclin, invested Tarascon, and penetrating Provence, laid siege to Arles, belonging to Joanna, Queen of Naples; but in this war he was arrested by the interference of the Pope, and by his means reconciled to his cousin, Queen Joanna. These unjustifiable wars could only be maintained by the exactions of Louis on his province of Languedoc, over which he again presided in 1368, to obtain fresh supplies.

1368.

There was in the character of Louis a selfishness of purpose, and a deep seated revenge, with a hastiness of disposition singularly at variance with the wonderful self-control of his brother Charles V. To this monarch alone must be ascribed the wise administration of his country, and the concealment of his designs until the very hour for the declaration of war with England had arrived.

Upon Louis may with justice be charged the glory of having precipitated the new war, by espousing so warmly, in the first instance, the cause of Henry against Peter of Castile. To these testimonies of weakness of character, events from this date add those of unbounded cruelty, the total lack of military talents, and the possession of a very limited share of personal bravery.

The sanction of Parliament had been sought and

ical court at Avignon, displaying always great
for, and obedience to that Pope. To him had
confided the government of Dauphiné, where he
led Gregory in his cruel efforts to exterminate
audois. Almost the entire population of these
s was in prison, preparatory to being conducted
stake. Gregory even complained to Charles V.
period that there were not prisons enough. But
g after, in 1376, he was compelled, to the great
n of both Charles V. and Louis, to remove his
rom Avignon to Rome.

he year 1374, King Charles V. issued an edict 1374.
le his son, born on the 3rd of December, 1368, to
pon the administration of the kingdom at the
fourteen. At the same time he appointed, in
f his own death before that period, Louis of
to govern the country in the interim, and passing
le Duke of Berri, bequeathed the guardianship
children conjointly to his Queen Jane, his
, Philip of Burgundy, and the Queen's brother,
Duke of Bourbon. These provisions were
ed in Parliament on the 21st of May in the
ling year, in the presence of the Duke of Anjou.
time, Louis governed in Languedoc as if he
s sovereign. He assembled the states there
but it was in order to have voted to him, under
of the defence of the country, subsidies which
sed of arbitrarily. That province was now in
us a condition, and its population had been
to so great an extent in the course of his ad-
tion, that although the hearth-money, or tax
es, had been raised to two francs instead of one,
ced no more than had been collected by the
e formerly. A day of reckoning was ap-
g for the selfishness, as well as great harshness,
ich he exercised the extraordinary powers

war, by which they had already profited much;
accordingly we find the latter employed in
thening the French interests in various ways;
either he nor Philip of Burgundy re-appeared at
s in April, as expected, to renew the pacific
iations.

he following year Louis invested the fortress of
ellier once again, without experiencing any
nce. He next resolved to besiege Bordeaux,
a English fleet arriving at this place with suc-
effectually put an end to his project.

sovereignty of Louis over Languedoc was
ibly independent and absolute. Charles V. never
osed so long as the people were passive, and
orbore to revolt while it was possible to hope.
ouis's exactions became insupportable, and in
ginning of this year (1378) Nismes first resisted,
fused to vote the new taxes; but being un-
ted was compelled to succumb, and Louis, in
learning a lesson, thought no more of so trifling
llition. Accordingly in March, 1379, he is found
ng the heaviest fire-tax yet known on the in-
ts of Languedoc, the fires having been already
l in the course of the last thirty years by means
famine, and tyranny from 100,000 to 30,000.
ouncil of Montpellier refused to collect this tax,
people, driven to despair, rose on the 25th of
r, and massacred the Duke's officers and eighty
suite. Clermont-Lodêve followed the example
tpellier, and the whole province seemed ready
lt.

d been well if the Duke of Anjou, then in
r, had hastened into Languedoc, to enforce or to
w the obnoxious tax; but although in his fury
atened nothing less than to put all the in-

rthiness of Joanna for the high position she occu-

He well knew both the weakness and cunning
r disposition, and justly suspected her intentions
ds his nephew, Charles of Durazzo, who was
earest relative and the rightful heir to her
tions.

us of Hungary therefore negociated with Urban
or the deposition of Joanna, and furnished his
w with a small army to establish himself on her
. Urban fulminated a pontifical bull against
id favoured the march of Charles through Italy,
9, to depose her.

Urban VI. had so strongly identified himself
his cause, it was but natural to expect a counter
on, and a new claimant to issue forth from the
ee of Avignon. In fact an intrigue had been
g for some time past between Joanna of Naples
ement, by which the former proposed to exercise
ageance upon the family of Anjou-Hungary, by
ng Charles of Durazzo of the succession, and
ter found a superior kingdom for his especial
te, Louis of Anjou, without the trouble of adju-
g upon his claims to that of Majorca.

ie commencement of May, 1380, the Duke of
quitted Languedoc for Avignon, to pursue his
es for the monarchy of Naples; and at length
minaries having been arranged, Joanna adopted
s her heir and successor on the 29th of June
g.*

ights of this question cannot be better defined
vords than by citing the language of Sismondi,
s,—"It has sometimes been allotted to a king,
ry to every principle of legitimacy, to have the
of disposing by will of his crown, when the title
ession appears so uncertain that it is necessary

es. History; Daniel; Moreri; Hallam; Godard Faultrier.

r ingots. It had probably transpired that the
ure lay at Melun, and thither went the Duke of
u, and commanded the attendance of Philip of
isy, the treasurer of Charles V. Lavoisy readily
ssed that he had been made the depositary of the
t, but added that his master had imposed upon
an oath to reveal it only to his son, when he came
e throne.

e Duke appeared to yield to this just plea of an
st man. He gave orders for the coronation of his
ew at Rheims, whither he dispatched him, attended
e princes, peers, and the whole court. Louis him-
however, lingered behind, and with him the obsti-
Lavoisy, who still declined to betray his secret.
1 again closeted with him, the Duke without
er scruple, sent for the executioner, and at once
anded him there, in his presence, to cut off the
ppy treasurer's head. No one at all acquainted
the savage character of Louis could for a moment
the fell determination of the man at that crisis.
sy doubted not that he was in the power of a
blood-thirsty animal, and hesitated not to pro-
him.

bars of gold and silver had been built into the
of the Castle of Melun as stones, and the
ers who had placed them there had been
ed of, as workmen who knew the secrets of
s usually were in those days. It is needless to
hat the whole treasure was extracted, and
ned to the keeping of the Regent; who,
d with this last cunning plunder of his nephew's
, hurried away to the solemn ceremony of that
w's consecration and coronation.

s highly probable that this and the previous
eous conduct of the Duke of Anjou, since he had
e Regent, were the source of a movement now

of forty-five. But the bitterness of his last trials, upon
such a temperament, cannot be omitted in enumerating
the combined causes of his early death, since it has
even induced some historians to ascribe it erroneously
to a broken heart. Immediately upon his dissolution
his army was scattered abroad in a confused and igno-
minious flight. Most of its soldiers, however, met their
death upon the Italian soil, while some of the proudest
knights of France were seen to traverse all Italy on
foot, their clothes in shreds, and begging their bread.

Thus ended this vain-glorious expedition to establish
an hereditary monarchy in the person of a weak, selfish,
avaricious man; thus all the hoarded treasures of the
" wise " King of France were lavished by his ignoble
brother, and the lives of tens of thousands of French-
men were sacrificed to render only the more secure the
right of Charles III. over the kingdom of Naples.

While the remains of the unfortunate army of Louis
begged their way back to France like walking skeletons,
Peter de Craon had the audacity to re-appear at court
with a magnificent train.

Louis had entrusted to his consort, Mary of Blois,
the government of Anjou in his absence, as well as the
guardianship of his three children, Louis, who was then
but five years old, Charles, and Mary.[*]

With the spirit and resolution which characterised
Mary of Blois, she proceeded immediately to Paris, and
there in her own name as the widow of Louis, and in
those of her two sons, now styled Louis II. of Naples,
and the Prince of Tarentum, summoned Peter de Craon
to appear before the Parliament of Paris, and to restore
to her the 100,000 ducats of gold which she had
confided to his charge. She prosecuted the baron for
robbery and felony, and demanded, as the just penalty
of his crime, that the barony of Craon, and his other

* Lobineau ; Bodin ; Moreri ; Guicciardini.

property, situated in Anjou, should be confiscated. Craon did not appear, although summoned four times.

The Parliament, therefore, pronounced him convicted of felony, and ordered the forfeiture of all his estates to the duchy of Anjou. He was condemned, besides, to restore the sum of gold he had withheld, and to submit to perpetual banishment; but his high rank and influence with some of the French nobility, enabled him to escape the just punishment of his crimes.

The enterprising Mary of Blois occupied herself at this time also, in seeking the assistance of the Dukes of Berri and Burgundy, to preserve for her son Louis the sovereignty of Provence. In this undertaking she was unfortunate. All Provence, with the exception of the towns of Marseilles and Arles, had revolted to Charles III., unfurled his flag, and installed in Aix the Governor Spinola, whom he had dispatched there.

The body of Louis I. was buried in St. Martin's at Tours, and his heart was deposited in the Cathedral of St. Maurice at Angers.*

His character has been shown by his actions, already recorded, to have been one of the worst. In summing up the annals of his life, scarcely one virtue shines forth to modify the indignation inspired by his vices and crimes. Happily, his whole career affords a complete contrast with that of his grandson, and will thus serve to display only to the greater advantage the heroism, amiability, and benevolence of the " Good René." So insatiable was his love of wealth, that he created "letters of protection" which passed current in his chancery, and with the riches thus acquired, he purchased the county of Roucy, and the castleward of Rochefort; but Parliament annulled the contract of

* Berlin; Godard Faultrier; Sismondi; Hallam; Lobineau; Villeneuve Bargemont.

sale, and he was compelled to restore those lands to
the family of Roucy. He also adopted a method of
raising money employed in Italy, by selling at an
extravagant rate "letters of familiarity" to all those
who wished to engage in his service.

He was so utterly devoid of true magnanimity, that,
although always restlessly fomenting new quarrels and
campaigns, he was personally concerned in no single
act of physical bravery during life. When to the long
list of his evil qualities he added the no less certain
evidence of his morose disposition, exemplified in his
unrelenting resentment against Charles V., and his
quarrel with his brother Philip, it might be truly
affirmed, that, however miserable his end, his punishment was inadequate to the injuries he had inflicted.
He seems not even to have enjoyed the reputation of
counterbalancing virtues in private life, for it is expressly
affirmed, that he evinced but little regard for his consort.
An ordinance was made by Louis "the First" during
his last hours, expressly to appease the remorse of his
conscience; and this, while it makes some trifling
amends, is confirmation also of the bad character
assigned to him.   By that last enactment he distributed
to the shop-keepers and peasantry of Anjou and Lorraine the sum of 20,000 livres, (or 145,000 francs,) to
reconcile them to the taxes and imposts which he had
so unjustly levied.   His title to the kingdom of Naples
and Sicily was as empty as to that of Jerusalem; and
his descendants only inherited as possessions, *de facto,*
the counties of Anjou, Maine, and Provence.*

The events in connection with the rival claim to the
throne of Naples should here be retraced, to make clear
the causes of a protraction of the struggle in that
kingdom after all hope for the Angevine standard
seemed to have been utterly annihilated. A little

* Sismondi ; Lobineau's Bretagne ; Gaufridi ; Godard Faultrier ; Bodin.

episode in the history of Hungary, and of great moment in the affairs of Naples, explains how, after the death of Louis I. of Hungary, the enthusiastic people elected his daughter Mary to succeed him, crowning her *king*, contrary to their law, by which the throne was hereditary only in the male line. The rightful claimant to the throne of Hungary was Charles III. of Naples; who, after the death of Louis of Anjou, was no sooner established in peaceful possession of the Neapolitan territory, than he prepared to assert, by force of arms, his rights over Hungary. His enterprise was successful. He compelled "King Mary" to abdicate, and was himself crowned, by the nobility, in her place. This prince, who was in the prime of life, and had been not merely exercising a sound policy in all the personal matters of his rule, but whose knowledge of military tactics had kept at bay, for so long a time, his rival of Anjou, was generally applauded. The life of Charles III. was, however, shortened, through the intrigues of an ambitious and bad woman, Elizabeth, the widow of the great Louis of Hungary. She first employed assassins who failed to dispatch him, and then, as it is believed, administered poison which caused his death.

1385.

Summary justice was inflicted on the unprincipled Queen Dowager, who was seized and thrown into the river, by the Ban of Croatia.

Her daughter Mary was also cast into prison, and detained there until the 4th of June in the following year, when she was released and married to Sigismund, brother of Wenceslaus, King of the Romans. Sigismund and Mary then mounted the Hungarian throne.

1387.

Had it not been for these occurrences, Southern Italy and Sicily might probably have enjoyed under Charles III. a protracted reign of peace; and the Angevine family might not, after their utter defeat in the person of Louis I., have again enforced their pretensions.

Charles III. left one son, named Ladislaus, only ten years of age at the date of his death, to inherit and protect, under the tutelage of his widow, Margaret, the interests he had found so difficult to defend from spoliation. The eldest son of his rival, Louis II. of Anjou, was even a few months younger than Ladislaus, and under the guardianship of his mother, Mary of Brittany. It might have been inferred from this circumstance, that the cessation of hostilities would endure, at least during the minority of these princes. To calculate thus was, however, to lose sight of the unbending firmness and dogged perseverance of character of Mary of Brittany, evinced by her sometimes to such a degree, as to make her unscrupulous and utterly indefensible in the means she employed.

Ladislaus was acknowledged King of Naples without loss of time under the regency of his mother, Margaret; the form was fulfilled, but the fact was hollow, and the struggle of the two mothers for their children was even then impending. For before Mary of Brittany and her son Louis II. had even left France to countenance their party, it was already disputing with the adherents of Ladislaus by force of arms, both in Naples and Provence, for the claim of Louis.

Mary of Brittany had determined to contest her son's pretensions even during the lifetime of Charles III., and she repaired with him from Angers to the court of Avignon immediately after her husband's death, and there easily prevailed on Pope Clement to espouse the interests of Louis II. Secure of the papal support, she then hastened to Paris to present her children Louis and Charles, who are styled by the annalist of Anjou " the most accomplished princes in the world," to their cousin Charles VI. Accordingly on the 9th of February, 1385, the title of Louis II. to the kingdom of Naples and the duchy of Provence was acknowledged by Charles of France, and in May following recognised publicly by the Pope.* On the 10th of December, 1385, Mary and her two sons entered Arles, and confirmed its privileges, a stroke of policy which won her the future hearty support of that town.

The intelligence of the death of Charles III. in June, 1386, gave at length the signal for a general revolt throughout Provence against the House of Durazzo. When established at Avignon, Mary devoted herself, with all her zeal, to the prosecution of her son's interests, and was enabled before the end of the succeeding year, 1387, to reckon with certainty on the allegiance of entire Provence.

Meantime, at the instigation of Clement, Otho, the husband of the late Queen Joanna, had entered the Neapolitan territory soon after the death of Charles III., and had occasioned a rising at Naples in July, 1386, which, after a sanguinary battle, obliged Margaret and Ladislaus to fly to Gaëta.

Louis II. was then formally proclaimed there, under the regency of his mother Mary, and at that epoch his cause seemed equally prosperous and hopeful both in Naples and Provence.†

Southern Italy might be styled peculiarly the battle-ground of the Popes in this era; they fomented all the discords, and encouraged all the battles of that unhappy country, because each beheld in the aspirant whom he seconded, a vassal and a temporal ally whose propinquity to the Eternal city made him all important as the conservator of the chair of St. Peter. Thus on this first success of the adherents of Louis II., the Gonfalonier of the Roman pontiff, Raymond des Ursins, was

* Godard Faultrier.
† Moreri; Villeneuve Bargemont; Godard Faultrier; Sismondi; Bourdigné.

chased out of Naples with the same ardour as were
Margaret and her son, Ladislaus. For on either hand
the rival Popes had taken sides in the quarrel for their
own ends only, and Mary and Otho had taken oath to
drive Urban VI. out of Rome in the event of their
permanent success, just as Margaret, and in good time
Ladislaus, were sworn to preserve the temporal power
of Urban in Rome, if needs be against all Europe.

At this critical juncture the good fortune of Mary of
Brittany was arrested on a sudden by her own hand.
The Duchess of Anjou was not ignorant of the fickle
enthusiasm with which the Neapolitans frequently acted
before their conquerors of the hour, and fearing lest the
husband of Joanna by the late success of his arms
might become a new pretender, she now at once
deprived him of his charge of captain general. This
act proved her keen foresight, no less than the great
enterprise of her character. That it was not, as at first
supposed, impolitic, that on the contrary it was an act
of true wisdom, will be sufficiently clear to the minds
of many from the circumstance that Otho immediately
placed himself under the banner of Ladislaus. The
man who would be guilty of tergiversation so rapid and
complete, of the abandonment in a moment of the
entire principle for which he had fought, even for the
sake of a slight practised on him personally, might
well be suspected of the unworthy ambition for which
he was displaced.[*]

1389.   In the year 1389 Charles VI. of France, having attained his nineteenth year, resolved to bestow the Order
of Chivalry upon his two cousins, Louis and Charles of
Anjou. That fête was celebrated on the 1st of May,
at St. Denis. The young knights passed through all the
forms of the institution; and a tournament of three
days' duration followed, ending with a *bal masqué*.

---

[*] Eccles. History; Hallam; Godard Faultrier.

The coronation of Louis II. by the Pope, Gregory XI., took place six months later at Avignon. Charles VI., with a brilliant company, was present at this ceremony. Provence had already declared unanimously in favour of the young Louis, then only twelve years of age, who was on the first of November duly crowned and anointed King of Sicily with great magnificence. The court broke up soon after; Charles VI. returned to Paris, and the King of Sicily proceeded to Anjou, where great rejoicings were made in his honour.

Mary of Blois appears to have exercised an admirable perseverance and adjustment of designs towards the goal of her ambition, her son's advancement. She had undoubtedly, before the date of his coronation, been in treaty with John I. of Arragon concerning a project for marrying him advantageously. The Arragonese fleets were among the best of that era, and keeping in view the disputed question of succession in the sea-girt island of Sicily, and the Neapolitan peninsula, an alliance with such a power was peculiarly desirable for the pretensions of Louis. On the other hand the King of Arragon could hardly be adverse to a match which offered to his daughter the prospect of a throne, with many other advantages.

In the course of the winter the young King journeyed to Barcelona, and there was united to Yolande, daughter of John I., King of Arragon. Louis was not yet thirteen years of age, but the espousals were in unison with the matrimonial custom of the age. On the occasion of this ceremony, Mary announced publicly the next step in her projects for her son's aggrandizement; viz., that he should set out in person in the ensuing summer to Italy, to assert his rights.*

Louis II. of Anjou did in fact set sail from Marseilles on the 20th of July, 1390, with a fleet of twenty-

1390.

---

* Moreri; Godard Faultrier; Sismondi; Bodin; Villeneuve Bargemont.

one ships, and landed at Naples on the 14th of
August.* He there met with a triumphant reception.
The feudal government, first introduced into the
kingdom of Naples by the Norman kings, had been
strengthened by the Angevine princes, and at the close
of the fourteenth century the government of Naples continued altogether feudal. Extensive domains had been
bestowed by way of appanage on the princes of the
blood, and these were at one period numerous. The
greatest part of the kingdom was the principality of
Tarentum, and the rest belonged to some great families,
who exhibited their power and their pride in the
number of men-at-arms they could assemble under
their banner. Thus it was that at the coronation of
Louis II., the Sansaverini appeared, attended by 1,800
cavalry completely equipped.

The supporters of Ladislaus had become discontented,
by reason of the exactions which his mother had been
compelled to levy to prosecute the war. The people of
Naples, as well as the feudal lieges of great part of the
surrounding territory, had changed sides; and it was
not perhaps wonderful, that the child who had never
yet taxed them for his necessities, and who now for the
first time presented himself before them, should succeed
under these favourable circumstances in winning their
present homage and support.

He was well escorted and received in Naples; but
at first, all the forts around were in the possession
of Ladislaus, and it required time, especially with the
superior military tactics then practised in Italy, to
1391.   besiege and capture them. A year later, we find Ladislaus still at Gaëta, and in secure possession of the
northern provinces.

It would appear, at first sight, that Margaret of
Durazzo laboured under a great disadvantage as com-

* Bourdigné ; Sismondi ; Eccles. Hist. ; Hallam ; Godard Faultrier.

pared with Mary of Blois, in being compelled to draw largely upon the resources of the country itself, for whose dominion she was contending. A reaction had, however, already begun in the affairs of the latter, and it became evident that the dissatisfaction of the other countrymen, over whom Mary ruled and whose resources she drained, could prove as detrimental to her cause as any difficulties upon the Italian soil itself.

It is remarkable, that neither Charles VI., who had professed so staunch a partizanship for the cause of Louis, nor France, of which Anjou was an integral part though an appanage, did anything whatever for him in this enterprise, from the date of his coronation. To Mary of Blois alone was due all the praise for the vigour and perseverance with which Naples had hitherto been attacked and maintained, for she was the soul of those strenuous efforts by which the Angevines had been numerously and continually pressed into the service of Louis II.; but upon her also rested the entire responsibility of having taxed and levied arbitrarily and exorbitantly, for the same purpose, the people of Provence, totally regardless of the privileges she had confirmed to them four or five years before. In consequence, although the ever loyal province of Anjou continued in tranquillity, the old civil war between the factions of Anjou and Durazzo broke out again with renewed vigour in Provence, and raged there at the same time and with the same intensity, as at Naples. Upon the head of Mary of Blois rests the odium of having kindled anew these flames; of having foiled, by her unscrupulous excesses, the masterpiece of her previous talented career; and of having ruined the brightest hopes which her maternal pride and affection had built up, by disregarding the happiness of her subjects and the solemn pledges by which she had sworn to protect them.

By the time that Louis II. had attained the age of eighteen, his own mediocre capacity, combined with the bad faith of his mother in violating the capitulation by virtue of which the Provencaux had submitted to her, and the greater talents and energy of his rival, had nearly disinherited him of Provence as well as of Naples. Count Raymond de Turenne, a partizan chief of the House of Durazzo, had, by the year 1395, subjected anew nearly all Provence to Ladislaus.

Mary of Blois, at length, relinquished in despair the task of directing her son's cause, and quitted the neighbourhood of the struggle altogether. She now alternately employed herself in the government of her loyal subjects at Angers, and frequenting the grandeurs of the King's court at Paris; while Louis continued at Naples in the enjoyment of a very limited sway.

The Angevine cause was shortly after arrested wholly by the Pope at Avignon, the Seneschal of Provence, and the Bishop of Valence. The disputed territory of Provence was fearfully laid waste, for the civil war raged most violently there at this period; and so numerous became the bands of adventurers who crossed the frontier from France, to join the camp of Turenne, that Benedict XIII., who had succeeded Gregory XI. at Avignon, sued for, and obtained an edict from Charles VI. to interdict and restrain that practice.

Mary of Brittany, when devoting herself to her rule over her attached people of Anjou, in some of her enactments exhibited much wisdom and piety. There had existed for a long while among the Angevins a tax called *Tierçage*, which consisted in allotting to the clergy a third of the value of his household goods, on the death of an individual.

This tax had an immoral tendency, and was a subject of great affliction. Perceiving how dangerous to religion was the struggle which this impost occasioned, Mary contrived to reconcile the inhabitants of Anjou to their curates, by converting the *Tierçage* into a tribute of *fouage* or hearth-money, which, less arbitrary in its nature, only obliged them to pay one penny as an oblation for each fire on the sabbath-day, and the curates were then expected to inter without any other remuneration. The poor besides, were exempted from paying this tax altogether. This act, which redounds so creditably to the memory of the Duchess, was finally confirmed by Parliament.*

Again, we are constrained to admire the strength and pertinacity of character of Mary of Brittany, when devoting herself to a good purpose, for it was not out of a weakness for the gaieties and luxuries of the court of France that a woman of her mould resided at repeated intervals in the French metropolis. She was engaged in the pursuit of justice; she had been plundered, and she watched her opportunities for bringing the culprit into court, that she might obtain a reimbursement of her due. Doubtless she had watched the dawn of a broad ray of hope out of the iniquitous attempt made upon the life of the Constable Clisson by the same Pièrre de Craon, who, ten years before, had failed to appear before Parliament in answer to her charges of robbery. The patronage of the Dukes of Burgundy and Brittany had sheltered him from the execution of the sentence then passed upon him. Mary had, however, entered a new cause against him before Parliament, for the restitution of the late Duke of Anjou's 100,000 ducats of gold; but Craon dared not to appear, on account of the greater crime of which he had since been guilty. Even this difficulty was at length surmounted by the Duchess, who solicited and

* Godard Faultrier.

obtained for him letters of abolition or exemption for his greater crime of attempted assassination, in order to compel him to appear in answer to her accusation. A trial in due form ensued, and Pièrre de Craon was sentenced to refund immediately to the Duchess the whole amount in question, or to be imprisoned until such time as her claim should be satisfied. Mary formally returned thanks to the assembly, and Pièrre de Craon was at once seized, and imprisoned in the castle of the Louvre.[*]

1400.

In the course of his long contest with Ladislaus, Louis II. had, at length, drained all his resources; and although by the year 1400,[†] Provence was once more beaten into submission to his rule, and although he never omitted to style himself King of Sicily, his generalship and personal administration of affairs would appear to have alienated from him, during the same period, the kingdom of Naples. He had besides, before this date, lost the support of his spiritual chief by the blockade of Benedict XIII., at Avignon, by the arms of France.

At Tarentum, on the 13th of July, 1400, he learnt that the city of Naples had opened its gates to his rival, and that his brother Charles was besieged in the Castello Nuovo. His partisans were still very numerous, and he was yet in possession of half the kingdom; but, unable to bear the straits of poverty, he hastily relieved his brother, and then abandoned the country altogether for which he had been so long contending.[‡] This circumstance is sufficiently demonstrative of the mediocre talents of this prince, as well as of a total absence of ordinary energy, perseverance and judgment in his disposition and character. Like his cousin, Charles VI. of France, he had been prematurely, as a child, invited to a throne; even, perhaps,

* Bodin; Sismondi; Godard Faultrier. † Bodin. ‡ Bodin; Sismondi.

before he had learnt to wield the sceptre, which he thus hastily suffered to escape his grasp. It might be, however, that he relinquished it to attend the ceremony awaiting him in Provence; viz., the celebration of his nuptials there with Yolande of Arragon.

That event took place with the accustomed rejoicings not long afterwards, and thence the royal couple proceeded to Avignon, where they resided for two or three years; during which time, no effort was made to revive the hereditary claims of Louis on the kingdom of Naples.

The consort of Louis II. brought to him as her dower, her right to the crowns of Arragon, Catalonia, and Valencia, and by her marriage received that of Sicily; therefore was she usually styled "The Queen of the four kingdoms." Yolande subsequently inhabited the castle of Angers, and took pleasure in embellishing it. To her, as well as to her mother-in-law, Mary of Brittany, has been attributed the construction of the chapel which forms part of the castle, and the roof of which is raised above its towers.[*]

While Yolande dwelt at Angers, she exhibited great partiality for the promenade of Lesvière, a priory near Angers, surrounded by cornfields and vineyards. Bourdigné relates a curious anecdote of Yolande. He says that—" during one of these walks, diverting herself " in the company of her ladies and gentlemen, she " reached the priory of Lesvière, and there seated her- " self upon the ground, and contemplated the sports of " some young spaniels belonging to the party. Sud- " denly, a rabbit sprang from a neighbouring bush, and, " frightened at the barking of the dogs, took refuge in " the lap of the queen. She fondled the animal, which " evinced no desire to escape and remained in its new " quarters for some time, apparently forgetting its natural

* Moreri; Bodin; Daniel; Godard Faultrier.

"wildness. Queen Yolande construed the circumstance
"into an omen favourable to herself, and commanded
"the bush to be dug up whence the rabbit had sprung;
"when, to the surprise of all, a subterranean vault was
"there discovered, containing an image of the Virgin
"holding an infant in her arms, with a glass lamp in
"front of her. In her satisfaction, Yolande caused a
"little oratory to be erected on this spot, which, like
"similar endowed edifices, had its visitants and its
"miracles from that time." *

1403. The schism in the papacy had endured so long, and
so many fruitless efforts had been made to terminate it,
that a kind of public opinion had been raised against
it, which, shortly before the beginning of the fifteenth
century, had displayed some activity upon the question. Benedict XIII. had refused, in opposition to the
Dukes of Berri and Burgundy, who then directed the
destinies of France, to resign simultaneously with his
rival and submit to the decision of a council. He had
been, consequently, besieged during five years in his
palace at Avignon, as a fomenter of the schism, by an
army sent in the name of the French king. The king's
brother, the Duke of Orleans, still supported Benedict,
perhaps chiefly because whatever party received the
favour of Burgundy was certain to engage his cordial
hatred.

Louis II. also, from other motives, countenanced
Benedict. This pope had sustained his pretensions to
the kingdom of Sicily, and if he succumbed, his Italian
interests must suffer seriously, for the new pontiff
elected by the council might favour the rights of Ladislaus, and the anathemas of a pope exercising a spiritual
autocracy over the millions were not to be lightly estimated in that age. Louis therefore determined to act
in opposition to the government, court, and army of

* Bourdigné ; Godard Faultrier.

France, and upon this occasion he evinced symptoms of energy and vigour. Early in 1403, he went to Avignon, and gained easy access to the pontifical palace; he rendered his homage to Benedict, offered him his protection and assistance, and concerted with him for his liberation. Not long after, Benedict escaped in disguise to Château Renard, a fortress belonging to Louis, where a guard of safety awaited him.

Unworthy indeed must have been the subject of this solicitude, for within one short year after he had thus obtained his freedom, both the King of Sicily and the Duke of Orleans were utterly disgusted with the pride, selfishness, and obstinacy of this elect of half Christendom. 1404;

On the 12th of November, 1404, Mary of Blois, the queen-mother of Sicily and Duchess of Anjou expired at Angers; and was interred in the Cathedral of St. Maurice in that city.* 1404.

As long as she lived she had governed Anjou and Maine as a patrimony out of which to make her profit. She had amassed there a treasure of two hundred thousand crowns, which had been accumulating even during the period when her son was in distress in Italy, and was constrained, at last, to abandon the kingdom of Naples for want of money. Her maternal solicitude seems to have undergone a serious change from the date of her son's reverses. There was no great expression of public lamentation in Anjou on the occasion of her demise.

The life of the King of Sicily from this period becomes rather closely identified with the history of the court and government of France. He occupied the third rank in the royal council, which ruled the kingdom; but as minister he did not, whether from want of

* Moreri; Godard Faultrier.

G 2

talents or ambition, distinguish himself in his new and exalted position.

It was much in that age not to have rendered himself notorious for his vices, not to say crimes, like his father and his uncle of Berri did before him, and like some of his contemporary relations, who did disgrace and brutalize themselves a little later, as it were, in his presence and company.

If he never signalised himself by the practice of great and exalted virtues, at least, he can never be charged with the exercise of gross vices, or even of petty crimes. It has even been affirmed that, whilst in Italy, he had learnt by heart, as a lesson of faith, the necessity of making himself beloved, in order to win and preserve a crown. It is asserted of him, that at Naples, and still more in Calabria, he had gained credit for good nature, amiability, and a degree of liberality which partook rather of prodigality.

In this new character the King of Sicily became adverse to intrigue and unambitious; not the leader of factions, but the mediator between hostile parties on many occasions in the course of the terrible and tedious ordeal of civil feud to which France became subsequently exposed.

Louis II. assisted at the funeral obsequies of the Duke of Orleans, as well as at the subsequent reception of his widow, the Duchess, whom he led into the King's presence to make her formal complaint of the inhuman murder of her lord by the Duke of Burgundy.*

It must be remembered that the French court was at this time the most dissolute of the age, and that the French people were sunk in misery and deprived of the shadow of liberty; thus we may more readily comprehend the strange dereliction of duty, and the fatal

* Sismondi ; Monstrelet.

display of imbecility, immorality, and injustice which supervened. When the formidable and unscrupulous Jean "sans Peur" appeared before the capital in hostile array, no one remained near the imbecile monarch bold enough, or sufficiently talented to oppose the designs of this insurgent, and the council contented themselves with praying him to grant a conference ere he advanced on the city.

It is observable, as delineating the more accurately shades of character, that while the King of Sicily and the renegade old Duke of Berri could so far tolerate the triumphant murderer of Orleans as to meet him at Amiens for a parley, the upright brother-in-law of the late king, the only member of the royal family of France in those times whose character remains wholly unsullied at the bar of history, the Duke of Bourbon, seeing only disgrace in this unjust compromise, retired in disgust to his duchy. The good service which the moderate Duke of Anjou thought to render to his king and country by that compact was, in fact, a deliberate surrender of the nation's, the king's, and his own honour.

Following then, an invariable rule, innocence and truth having first conceded, there was no end to the impudent encroachments of guilt, until it became evident at last, that France would have ‚been in a better position if every other member of the royal council had followed the example of Bourbon. Early in February, 1409, a pretended reconciliation was effected with the Duke of Burgundy at Châtres. The King of Sicily was one of those present in close proximity to the king. •

The scene is once again changed from the court and civil contests of France to the soil of Italy. Here, in May, 1409, Louis II. found another opportunity for contesting the Neapolitan dominion. The Council of Pisa had deposed the two popes, Benôit XIII. and

1409.
Sismondi.

Gregory XII., and had elected Alexander . But the chair of St. Peter and the Papal States were forcibly subjected to the temporal power of a refractory and ambitious king, to wit, Ladislaus of Naples. This monarch, now verging on the prime of life, and having been successful through his talents, energy, and perseverance, aspired to the Imperial crown and adopted for his device, "*Aut Cæsar aut nullus.*" He rejected, therefore, as a matter of course, the Council of Pisa, and declared in favour of the easy Gregory XII., who was indeed nothing better than his paid and passive instrument. He had already made war on the Florentines, because they would not acknowledge him legitimate sovereign of the states of the church. On the other hand, the Florentines and their allies had recognised the council and the new pope. They desired to expel Ladislaus from Rome, and fixing upon Louis of Anjou as a worthy coadjutor, in consequence of his claims to the throne of Naples, they offered him the command of a joint expedition against their common enemy. They accordingly influenced the Council of Pisa to acknowledge Louis, King of Naples, and he in turn, thus supported, undertook to establish Alexander V. in the papal chair. With this view he embarked 1,500 Provençal cavaliers on five vessels at Marseilles, and arrived at Pisa by the end of July.

Alexander there invested him with the kingdoms of Sicily and Jerusalem, and with the Gonfalon of the Church; and Louis, having joined the Florentine army, entered the pontifical states. The Florentine army was commanded by Braccio di Montane, Malateste di Pisaro, and Ange de la Pergola, all celebrated generals, and better versed in the art of war than any Frenchman of that period. Some of the cities of the Papal States opened their gates to them without opposition, and this emboldened Louis with Quixotic valour to push his army to the siege of Rome, where, however, he soon suffered a repulse from the Count de Troya, who commanded the city for Ladislaus. Thus the campaign of Louis terminated for that year. He could not patiently await in camp in person beyond November, when he crossed again to Provence, and hastened back with all speed to Paris. Before he reached that city the army he had abandoned had been admitted into Rome, and Paul Orsini went over to the Florentines with 2,000 horsemen.[*]

The intelligence of the success of his army, *malgré lui*, did not induce the King of Sicily to retrace his steps to the scene of action. An interval of four months elapsed before he returned to Italy. That period was employed by him in seeking an alliance with the Duke of Burgundy; and it does not redound to his credit that he was at this time conveniently oblivious of the murderer's confession addressed to his own ears, and that he testified no sense of degradation in the step he was taking in the bethrothal of his son Louis to Catherine, the daughter of this powerful Duke of Burgundy. This proposal being accepted, after the espousals, the young princess was consigned to the charge of Queen Yolande, to be brought up at Angers along with her future husband. This lady's dower, ten thousand crowns, was paid at the same time by Burgundy to Louis, and was of vast utility to the latter in the preparation of a new armament with which to invade the Italian shores once again. Arms, men, and ships were from that moment, by his orders, levied and prepared with the utmost dispatch in Provence; so rapidly was this expedition organised, that in a month's time, by the beginning of May, Louis actually set sail from Marseilles for Porto Pisano, with sixteen large ships and numerous smaller vessels.

1410.

[*] Daniel; Sismondi.

Circumstances of an unexpected nature, however, interposed to convert his triumph into defeat, and to punish him with remorse for having bartered his child's and his own honour for gold.

Six of his larger vessels were, in the first place captured by the Genoese. The others arrived in safety, and disembarked the remainder of his army at Piombino; but on his arrival there, Louis was apprized that Pope Alexander V. had died at Bologna, on the 3rd of May, and that John XXIII. had been appointed his successor. He proceeded at once to Bologna. On this occasion of the arrival of Louis of Anjou with so large a force in support of the council and the papacy at so inopportune a moment, it was not unnatural that he should be met by a numerous clerical deputation. There were present twenty-two cardinals, two patriarchs, six archbishops, twenty bishops, and eighteen abbots, all handsomely equipped. Monstrelet adds to this account, that "the King of Sicily himself was clothed in scarlet, "and his horse's furniture was ornamented with small "gilt bells, and his attendants consisted of fifty knights "arrayed in uniform." On the 6th of June, Louis did homage to John XXIII. for the kingdom of Naples, but was compelled to postpone his operations until the autumn, in order to concert afresh with the new pope, and the Florentine republic.*

1411. The army of Louis of Anjou seemed formidable, for besides his Provençal troops, there were the emigrants from Naples of the Angevine party, and the companies of Braccio di Montane, of Sforza, paid by the Florentines, of Angelo de la Pergola, retained by the Siennese, and of Paul Orsini in the pay of the Pope. There was, however, a scarcity of money and ammunition, and much time was lost in reconciling the generals, who were ever readier to turn their arms against each other

* Godard Faultrier; Monstrelet.

than to unite in a common cause. At length, the
Florentines having seen the Pope re-established in
Rome, seceded from the compact, and made peace with
Ladislaus. Louis accompanied the pontiff to Rome,
determined to prosecute the war, although he had not
money enough to maintain his 12,000 soldiers, the
bravest warriors of Italy, during even a short campaign. He then conducted them at once to Ceperano;
Ladislaus took up a position at Roccasecca, on the
other side of the Garigliano, and awaited him with
forces nearly equal in number. After passing the
river, Louis attacked the enemy with impetuosity. It
was the 19th of May, 1411, and Louis of Anjou then
obtained a great victory, which went by the name of
Roccasecca. Almost all the barons in the army of
Ladislaus were taken prisoners, and the baggage, and
even the King's table utensils fell into the hands of
the conqueror. Ladislaus fled, but rallied his troops
at St. Germaine. Then, strange as it may appear,
the extreme poverty of Louis's soldiers caused them
to sell to the large body of their prisoners both their
liberty and their arms; and Ladislaus apprized of this,
dispatched from St. Germaine some trumpets and
money, and thus, in a few hours, he regained his
army.

Louis of Anjou had indeed employed his victory to
so little profit, that when he would have advanced, he
found all the defiles which led to the kingdom of
Naples occupied by hostile troops, while his own men
were in want of the necessaries of life, a prey to sickness, and even more untractable on account of the
booty they had seized. Three days after the battle of
Roccasecca, Louis was compelled to retreat before
Ladislaus. In the month of July he reconducted his
forces to Rome, and in the following month abandoned
the struggle altogether to return to France. This was

the last bold attempt of Louis II. to retrieve what he considered his hereditary and rightful possession. He never again returned to Italy.[*]

At the time that Louis II. was thus, for want of resources, compelled to evacuate the kingdom to which he had aspired as rightful heir, his consort, Yolande, "the Queen of the four kingdoms," was endeavouring as fruitlessly, for the same reason, to assert her more genuine rights in Spain.[†] On the death of her father, John of Arragon, in 1395, his brother Martin had possessed himself of the crown. Martin died in 1410, having no children; therefore the right of Yolande, as John's daughter, to one of her four kingdoms seemed incontestible. A pretender to the succession, however, appeared in the person of Don Ferdinand, Infante of Castile, the nephew of King John. The rival claims of Yolande and Ferdinand were brought before the Parliaments of the different States of Arragon. Queen Yolande appeared personally at Barcelona in defence of her rights; and the Count of Vendôme, with other ambassadors, repaired thither from Charles VI., to further her cause. These negotiations lasted three months, when the claims of Yolande failed, and Ferdinand obtained a peaceful recognition as king. The court of France was glad to procure a confirmation of their former alliance with Arragon, and Yolande was forced to content herself with the promise of 200,000 crowns in compensation, a sum afterwards reduced to 200,000 francs.[‡]

The last failure of Louis II. in Italy seems to have been generally considered final. In the following year, 1412, Ladislaus was duly invested with the kingdom

1412.

---

[*] Monstrelet; Sismondi; Daniel.

[†] Jean Michael of Beauvais, who for his talents became secretary and counsellor of Louis II., and afterwards of Queen Yolande, drew out for her a genealogy to prove her rights to the crown of Arragon.—Godard Faultrier.

[‡] Daniel; Sismondi; Eccles. Hist.

of Naples, and Louis returning to France, engaged in the intrigues of that court, and had soon to raise troops in Maine and Anjou to defend his own states against the attacks of the Counts of Alençon and Richmont, and the Duke of Orleans.

A change had taken place in the opinions of Louis II., and since the treaty of Bourges he had openly espoused the faction of Burgundy's enemies. Hitherto Burgundy had perhaps taken small heed of this, for his daughter Catherine, who had been affianced to Louis, eldest son of the King of Sicily, had already lived three years at Angers, and was still under the guardianship of Queen Yolande.

On the 20th of November, however, the Lady Catherine was sent back, with a good escort, to the city of Beauvais, and thence to Lille, to her father, who uttered furious imprecations at this treatment of his daughter, and took a solemn oath to be revenged upon the Duke of Anjou. He regarded this act as a deep personal insult, and his resentment continued throughout his life. It is difficult to assign the motive of Louis for this extreme proceeding, since it was not because Burgundy had been branded with the crime of murder, which had happened before these espousals were proposed.

The useless advances of the Duke of Anjou a little later, with a view to an accommodation with Burgundy, exhibited only his usual instability of purpose, and encourages the inference that the dismissal of Catherine could have arisen from no high-minded cause. It is probable that Charles VI. may have asked at that date for the hand of Louis's eldest daughter, Mary, for his third son, Charles, since their pledges were exchanged two years after. Louis, the intended of Catherine of Burgundy, was at the same time espoused to Margaret of Savoy. Poor Catherine, who was as amiable in disposition as she was tender in years, did not long survive the ignominy of this occurrence. She died unmarried, not long after, at Ghent.[*]

1414.

The King of France supported by his princes entered upon a campaign, in 1414, against the Duke of Burgundy; but, after some success, a recurrence of the King's malady and sickness in the camp obliged them to conclude a treaty with the rebellious duke.[†]

In the year 1414 died Ladislaus, Louis's successful competitor in the kingdom of Naples. His sister, Joanna II., succeeded; who, surrounded by unworthy favourites, passed her time in licentious fêtes, utterly neglectful of the cares of government. Many princes, however, sought her in marriage, and feeling the need of support, she, at length, decided in favour of Jacques de Bourbon, Count de la Marche, hoping, by an alliance with a prince of the House of France, to protect herself from a recurrence of any active pretensions on the part of Louis of Anjou.

She secured to herself an undivided monopoly of the regal power, allowing her husband only the title of Count and Governor-General of the kingdom. The marriage took place in 1415.

1415.
Sismondi;
L'Abbé
Millot.

Soon afterwards Jacques de la Marche, not content with the semblance of power, and besides resolved to reform the manners of his wife and her court, cruelly put to death one of the Queen's favourites, and confined Joanna herself within her palace, out of the sight of her people, appointing as guard over her an old French officer. She was, however, soon rescued by the Neapolitans from this captivity and re-established in her authority, while Jacques de la Marche was, in his turn, thrown into prison.[‡]

[*] Mezerai; Bourdigné; Barante; Monstrelet; Daniel; Villeneuve Bargemont.

[†] Bourdigné; Mezerai; Barante; Monstrelet.

[‡] Sismondi; Monstrelet; Eccles. Hist.; Daniel; Mezerai; l'Abbé Millot.

The wars of Henry V. of England at this period wholly absorbed the attention of Louis II. On this invasion of France by the English, Louis joined the large army which King Charles VI. led on in person against Henry in Normandy. In the disastrous defeat which followed, Louis of Anjou was present, and must have saved himself by flight; but his relatives, Sir Robert of Bar, and Edward, Duke of Bar, who, with the Duke of Alençon commanded the main army, were numbered among the heaps of slain.

From this time little more is recorded of Louis II., whose life was drawing to a close. At this juncture he felt ill, and retired to Angers. While under this indisposition, he sought an accommodation with the Duke of Burgundy, but his overtures were treated with haughty contempt by Jean "sans Peur," whose vengeance could only be appeased by the life of the King of Sicily; nay, this was even at this period augmented by two unforeseen events: first, the death of the Dauphin making way for the next son of the King, as heir to the throne, and who was wholly Burgundian; again, by the death of the profligate old Duke of Berri in 1416. This same year a conspiracy was discovered amongst the Burgundians, affecting the lives of the Queen of France, the King of Sicily, and others; also a similar attempt was made on the life of Louis in the following year.[*]

1416

The fury of the Duke of Burgundy against Louis had not yet been goaded to the utmost. On the 4th of April, 1417, his son-in-law and *protégé*, John the Dauphin, died suddenly, apparently poisoned by the Armagnacs. Again, and for the last time, the rage of Burgundy was evinced, and this branded ally of the foreign invader, this absentee from the patriot field of Agincourt, whose success in life had been achieved

* Daniel; Monstrelet; Barante; Mezerai; Villeneuve Bargemont.

by the impudence of his crimes, whose hirelings had
twice attempted to assassinate the Duke of Anjou as
they had of old the Duke of Orleans, had now an
audacious public clamour ready to ascribe the death of
the young Dauphin John to the agency of Louis II.,
because by that event his son-in-law became Dauphin
and heir to the throne of France.

There was no real index to the author of this crime,
if such it was.   But, ere its authorship can be assigned
for an instant, even by innuendo, to the instrumentality
of Louis, some evidence of crime in his former life
should at least be charged against him, and some consideration must be allowed for the well authenticated
moderation and want of energy in his character ; and
in common justice also, some examination should be
made into the respectability of his accusers.   Besides,
in twenty-five days after the decease of the Dauphin
John, the King of Sicily himself was no more. Louis II.
died in Paris, at the early age of forty, on the 29th
of April, 1417.

1417.
Moreri ;
Monstrelet.

With how much greater appearance of truth might
the death of Louis have been ascribed to the machinations of the criminal Burgundy !

"This Duke of Anjou," says the annalist of Anjou,
" was in great triumph and lamentable honour carried
"to Angers, and interred in the cathedral, near the
" great altar."   Charles VI. and many of the princes of
the blood were present at his funeral obsequies.

Louis II. left to his children the possession of Anjou
Maine, and Provence.   They also inherited his pretensions to the kingdom of Naples, and his hatred to
the House of Burgundy.

From an engraving inserted in the Parnassus of
Angers, we have a portrait of Louis II.   His features
were regular and imposing.   He is represented with a
jagged turban on his head, and in a robe of great

richness embroidered with flowers, with a cope of fur.[*]

Such was the father of René. He was certainly a great improvement upon the grandfather, and there was reason to hope that the race might perfect itself in the next generation.

The children of Louis II. were of a more estimable and high-minded character than their relatives who had preceded them; Louis III., René, and Mary, Queen of France, were not more distinguished by their position in life than by their virtues and excellent qualities.

Louis III. was born in 1403, and at the age of fourteen succeeded to his father's titles and estates; his mother, Yolande, undertaking the government during his minority. The nobility of Provence united their tribute of respect to the memory of Louis II. with that of the court of France, and framed an address to his successor to testify their fidelity. They also deputed some of their nobility to wait on Queen Yolande, and renew to her the oath of obedience in the name of their states. These were so graciously received by Yolande, that, it is said, she even conceded on this occasion her son's rights over Nice and the Valley of Barcelonnette, to the Count of Savoy, in liquidation of a large sum of money furnished by Amé VI. to Louis I.[†]

1417.
Villeneuve
Bargemont

The memory of Yolande is fondly cherished by the Angevines to this day, for her good works in their country. The writers of her time praise her benevolence, and the wisdom of her administration. One fact may be cited, corroborative of this view of her character.

---

[*] Moreri; Daniel; Monstrelet; Sismondi; Bourdigné Mezerai; Godard Faultrier; Villeneuve Bargemont.

[†] Villeneuve Bargemont; Godard Faultrier.

The fortifications of Anjou had fallen into ruin, and required, as an imperative necessity in those days of walled cities and frequent sieges, to be almost completely rebuilt, in 1418. A considerable sum was needed for this undertaking, and the people, already heavily taxed, were alarmed at the project. Yolande accordingly published an ordinance, fixing the impost of these repairs at a tenth of the tenanted value of all the houses of the city; and this, without exception even of the clergy, who were too often, through their great influence in those times, exempted from the operation of taxes which it was their duty to have borne equally.

1418.

Further, this princess authorized the people of Angers to assemble, and fix for themselves the value of their dwellings. To encourage also the citizens who usually bore alone the burden of public offices, and who might have been intimidated before the privileged classes, she caused the members of her council to preside at the meetings, in order to effect both a prompt execution of her ordinance, and to invite the free discussion of its interests.[*]

On the 10th of September, 1419, another of those great crimes occurred, which at intervals afflicted France at this period of her history. This was the foul murder of the Duke of Burgundy, upon the bridge of Montereau, where he came by appointment to ratify a treaty with the Dauphin Charles, in whose presence he was assassinated. The consequences of this base act were long after of grave import to the rival arms of France and England. Philip of Burgundy, the son and successor of John " sans Peur," had vowed ven-

---

[*] This ordinance, made by a woman, is remarkable for its wisdom; and after the lapse of more than four hundred years, it has been restored amongst the Angevines, who, in its observance, still honour the memory of Queen Yolande.—*Bodin.*

geance against the assassins of his father, and gone
over directly from France with all the renowned wealth
and power of his house into a close alliance with the
English, and by the treaty of Troyes, in 1420, 1420.
Henry V. and his heirs were declared legal successors
to the throne of France after Charles VI., to the total
exclusion of the Dauphin Charles; Henry was als⟩
appointed Regent of the kingdom during the life-time
of his father-in-law, Charles VI.

The Dauphin Charles thus beheld on the one hand
his father, his mother, and his sister Catherine, Queen
of Henry V., strenuously bringing to bear against him,
the arms of France and England united; it appeared
at least strange, that, on the other hand, his cousin
and brother-in-law, Louis III. of Anjou, should first
studiously cultivate a good understanding with his
enemies respecting his French provinces, and then
wholly desert his cause for the rest of his life, in
order to pursue the conquest of the kingdom of
Naples.

Louis III. departed in the summer of the year 1420, 1420.
with a great number of warriors and a large amount
of munitions of war and money, to assert anew his
right to what might almost be called, the hereditary
calamity of his family;[*] but he never returned to
France. The events which led to his adoption of this
course may here be briefly related.

When Martin V. had been acknowledged Pope, he
concluded a treaty, in 1419, with Joanna II. of Naples,
on very advantageous terms, since she was induced to
flatter his nephew, Antonio Colonna, with hopes of the
vacant succession to the Neapolitan throne. At his
request she also released her husband, Jacques de la
Marche, after a captivity of four years, and he returned
to France, and died there in a convent.

[*] Sismondi; Villeneuve Bargemont.

Joanna was then crowned Queen of Naples in the name of Pope Martin V.; but ere long that pontiff took offence, because she did not realise his expectations in nominating his nephew her successor, and he resolved to withdraw his alliance and to second the pretensions of Louis III., Duke of Anjou, to the kingdom of Naples.*

The discontent of the nobility of Naples, and the hatred of Sforza Attendolo against his rival Caracciolo, added to the fact that there was no true heir to the crown, although Joanna was now advanced in age, seemed to prepare the way at length for the elevation of the House of Anjou.

The Queen, troubled by the contests of Sforza and Caracciolo, who, even with arms in their hands, disputed for her person, willingly gave up the former, with all his devoted followers to the Pope, and Sforza repaired to Rome. There Martin confided to him his secrets, hoping he would assist him to take revenge on Queen Joanna and her favourite Caracciolo.

It was not without some compunction that Sforza abandoned the party of Durazzo, to which he had sworn fidelity; but at this period, ambassadors from Louis III. arrived at Florence, and advancing to him considerable sums of money, engaged him in their master's service. By these means Sforza assembled a new army, and marched upon Naples. When he approached that city, he restored to Joanna his bâton of Grand Constable, declaring that, to escape from the caprice of Caracciolo, he renounced her service, and revoked his oath of fidelity. After that declaration, considering himself no longer under obligation to her, he at once proclaimed Louis III. of Anjou, King of Naples, asserting his hereditary rights, founded on the

* Monfaucon ; Moreri ; Sismondi ; Monstrelet ; l'Abbé Millot ; Daniel ; Godard Faultrier.

adoption of Joanna I. He then invited the Angevine barons, and all the partisans of Louis, to join his standard, and in the month of June, 1420, he invested Naples. 1420. Sismondi.

A deputation of Florentines and Genoese, with fifteen galleys, about this time entered the port of Marseilles, which then belonged to Queen Yolande. She gave permission to them, but, as we are told, " not without heavy sighs," to transport her eldest son, Louis III., to Rome, in order that he might be crowned there by the Pope. As she did not entirely confide in the loyalty of the deputation, she demanded as hostages for her son, eight of the chief nobility of Naples, who had accompanied it from that kingdom. Accordingly the young Louis embarked at Marseilles, and sailed to Rome, where the Pope solemnly invested him with the kingdom of Naples; and although not actually crowned, he ever after obtained the title of king, as his father had done. Louis brought with him to Naples an armed fleet of nine galleys and five transports, with which he arrived on the 15th of August, 1420. He immediately seized on Castellamare, while Sforza made himself master of Aversa, which was afterwards the head-quarters of the Angevine party.* 1420. Sismondi.

This new enterprise had originated with the Pope, but he now affected neutrality, and engaged Louis and Joanna to submit their rival claims to his arbitration.

To defend herself against Louis, the Queen of Naples applied to Alphonso, King of Arragon, for succour, offering to adopt him as her son, and that prince dispatched to her, eighteen galleys and three of his best generals. When these approached Naples, the fleet of Louis, being inferior in strength, retired; and the Arragonese (although opposed by Sforza,

* Sismondi ; Hallam ; Monstrelet.

who, with Louis, was besieging Naples) effected a landing.

Alphonso's generals were received with great honours by Joanna, who assigned them the Castello Nuovo and the Castello dell'Uovo, to hold for Alphonso, who was now proclaimed the adopted son of Queen Joanna II., and presumptive heir to her throne.*

1420.
Sismondi.

Calabria and almost all the eastern boundary of the country had declared for Louis of Anjou. The feudal lords committed ravages from time to time in the territories of their enemies, but it was at the gates of Naples that the war was really carried on. There Alphonso appeared early in 1421, and was joined by the celebrated Braccio, who was honourably received by him, and created Prince of Capua, Count of Foggia, and Grand Constable.

1421.
Sismondi.

No important event, however, resulted as yet from the near approach of the two hostile kings and the two great generals; and at length Louis, wearied by such inaction, returned to Pope Martin at Rome.

Braccio succeeded in seducing one of the generals of Sforza, Jacques Caldora; but another, named Tartaglia, was arrested and put to death by Sforza.†

The court of Joanna meanwhile was agitated by the secret plots of Caracciolo, who beheld with distrust the increasing power of Alphonso. Fearing for himself the fate of the other lovers of the Queen, he prevailed upon her to negotiate with Louis. Alphonso, who was not ignorant of these intrigues, resolved to secure his fortresses even against the Queen herself, while Braccio

---

* Sismondi; Hallam; Monfaucon; Godard Faultrier; Monstrelet; Villeneuve Bargemont; l'Abbé Millot.

† Sismondi.

was intent only on extending his own principality of Capua. Sforza was fully occupied in supplying his troops at the expense of the Neapolitans, for his army was almost destroyed, and required considerable expense to restore it. Martin V. had besides now grown weary of furnishing subsidies to Louis of Anjou; and alarmed at Alphonso's threats that he would acknowledge Benedict XIII. in all his kingdoms, and thus revive the schism in the Church, he prevailed on Louis to restore to the papal dominions the cities of Aversa and Castellamare, which alone remained faithful to him, while on his part, Martin surrendered to Queen Joanna the strongholds which the Angevine party possessed in the kingdom.

Upon this Louis III. retired to Rome, to live in obscurity. The interests of the House of Anjou were still cherished in secret by Sforza, but being no longer able openly to espouse them, he was again received into the Queen's favour, and he was employed by her to oppose Alphonso.

The Spanish monarch soon made himself independent of Joanna, and filled the fortresses with his troops. Disgusted at beholding the Grand Seneschal ruling the states and armies of the Queen, he refused to submit, as others did, to his commands; and feeling sure of the attachment of Braccio di Montane, he resolved to assert his own claims to the throne. His intentions were perceived by Caracciolo, who, desiring to preserve the equilibrium between the rival aspirants to the throne, and for the better security of the Queen, formed a secret alliance with Sforza. Already had Joanna repented of her adoption of Alphonso; for had she chosen Louis, she would by that act have united the Houses of Durazzo and Anjou, and have ended the civil war in her kingdom.

It now became more and more evident that the

1422.
Siamondi.

Arragonese faction was the stronger of the two, and Braccio, who supported it, was daily making new acquisitions, and at length, in 1423, his authority extended almost all round Rome, seeming to block up the pontifical court. He needed only the conquest of the Abruzzi, and this he was attempting with 3,000 horse and 1,000 infantry. Martin V. beheld his increasing power with dismay, and exhorted and encouraged the people of Aquila to defend him. He next sought the protection of Queen Joanna for the besieged, and endeavoured to persuade her to deprive Braccio of his command.*

1423.
Sismondi

The unexpected arrest of Caracciolo by Alphonso occurred on the 22nd of May, 1423, which gave reason to believe that the arrest of the Queen was likewise intended, had not her guards prevented it. Joanna, finding herself besieged in the Capuan castle, sent for Sforza, who hastened to deliver her, and a pitched battle ensued, which lasted six hours, with equal intrepidity on either side. At length Sforza triumphed, and Alphonso was in his turn besieged in the Castello Nuovo.

A fleet from Catalonia soon brought a considerable military armament for the relief of Alphonso; and Sforza, unable to prevent the landing of this force, was obliged to conduct the Queen from Naples to Aversa.† Queen Joanna, while separated from Caracciolo, had abandoned herself to despair, and would have resigned even her crown to procure the freedom of her lover. His liberation was effected without loss of time, and twenty of the most distinguished of the prisoners taken at the late battle of Formelles were exchanged for the Seneschal.

From this time the Queen resolved to look for

* Sismondi ; Eccles. Hist.
† Sismondi ; Eccles. Hist. ; l'Abbé Millot.

defence to the party of the Angevines. She invited Louis III., who resided still in poverty at Rome, to repair to her at Aversa, and wrote to the different courts of Europe to make known the ingratitude of Alphonso, to revoke her adoption of him and to substitute in his place Louis III., Duke of Anjou, whom she declared Duke of Calabria and presumptive heir to the throne. She even permitted him the title of king, that he might not be inferior in dignity to his rival.[*]

It is not a little to the credit of Louis III. at the early age of twenty-one, that his naturally mild character, perhaps further modified by the ordeal of his previous misfortunes, never allowed him, when he had grown powerful again, to raise his pretensions beyond that which Queen Joanna willingly granted him.

The Pope supplied him with such troops as he had at command, and at their head he repaired to Naples, in obedience to the summons of the Queen. The Genoese and the Duke of Milan also furnished him with soldiers, and thus Louis was soon enabled to retake all that the ambitious Alphonso had gained in the kingdom; and he preserved these acquisitions till his death. He remained but a short time at the court of Queen Joanna, and then withdrew into Calabria, where the mildness of his administration and his amiability made him beloved by all his subjects.[†]

Alphonso, alarmed at the combination formed against him, returned to Catalonia, leaving his brother, Don Pedro, at Naples, with some Italian condottieri. In his passage he surprised Marseilles, and pillaged it, to

1423.
Sismondi.

---

[*] Sismondi ; Eccles. Hist. ; Moreri ; Hallam ; Villeneuve Bargemont ; Godard Faultrier ; l'Abbé Millot.

[†] Sismondi ; Eccles. Hist.

revenge himself on Louis of Anjou. Enriched with the spoils of that city he proceeded to Spain, carrying off the body of Saint Louis, Bishop of Toulouse, his relative.[*]

1424.
Sismondi.

The following year witnessed the death of the two hostile generals, Sforza and Braccio di Montane. The former was succeeded, both in the army and in the Queen's favour, by his son, Francesco Sforza. The principality of Braccio was destroyed on the death of that general.

Of the generals left in support of Don Pedro, one went over to Braccio, and another, the notorious betrayer, Jacques Caldora, once more changed sides, first entering into treaty with his enemies, and then opening to them the gates of Naples.

On its return to the capital the Queen's army exercised no cruelties towards the inhabitants, and Caracciolo, now once more in the enjoyment of the supreme power, would not suffer the siege of Don Pedro and his small force shut up in the Castello Nuovo, in the politic intent of retaining Louis III. in submission through fear of his rival. Louis became, however, at this time virtually as well as in name, King of Naples; during the life time of Queen Joanna, he had, in fact, won more than his father or his grandfather in that kingdom, since his inheritance was no longer actively disputed.[†]

As Caracciolo advanced in age, the passion of love, to which he owed his elevation, gave place to ambition. In his sixtieth year he continued to rule the Queen, whose passion had made her his slave, and he was never satiated with power, riches, and honours. His demands became exorbitant, and excited the jealousy of the courtiers. At length Joanna, distressed by his importunity, to console herself, admitted to her confi-

---

[*] Sismondi; Eccles. Hist.; l'Abbé Millot.   [†] Sismondi.

dence the Duchess of Suessa. Through the instigations of this lady, the Queen gave orders for the arrest of Caracciolo, and her servants, exceeding her commands, murdered him.*

1432.
Sismondi.

Louis III. had been suffered to reside at Cosenza, in Calabria, an exile from the court of Queen Joanna, in order that she might without restraint resign herself and the government of her kingdom, into the power of Caracciolo.

When, therefore, Louis was apprized of the death of the Grand Seneschal, he flattered himself that he should be recalled to court, and at last enjoy the prerogatives of the presumptive heir to the throne. It was not so, however, for the Duchess of Suessa, who now in her turn became desirous of maintaining the sole influence over the Queen's mind, would not suffer his return. In fact, Joanna, incapable of having a will of her own, was from this time governed by her *confidante* as she had formerly been by her lover.†

Louis did not resist the intrigues of the court; he was content to live in Calabria. He had been united on the 22nd of July, 1431, to Margaret, the daughter of Amé VIII., first Duke of Savoy, and this princess came to him at Cosenza in the year 1434. On her progress thither, she rested at Bâle, where the Diet was then being held, and where the King of France was receiving various high personages.

1434.
Villeneuve
Bargemont.

" The King treated her very courteously," adds the historian, "and came after supper, and after that the " said Princess had made reverence to the King, they " danced a long time, and afterwards they brought spices " and served the King," &c. After the entertainment, Princess Margaret took her leave of King Charles, and was received at Avignon with much liberality by the

---

* Sismondi. † Hallam; Sismondi.

Cardinal de Foix, the Pope's vicar. Thence she journeyed to Tarascon, where she was lodged in the fine old castle which was now her property. The Governor and chief nobility of Provence welcomed her there, and provided her with 50,000 florins, while each town presented to her a vessel of gold or silver; and a grand fête was given in her honour which lasted three days. She then went with her attendants on board her galleys on the Rhone. On leaving Nice a furious tempest arose, but they succeeded in reaching Sorento in safety; the Princess, however, having been much indisposed by the passage.

At first, Queen Joanna wished her to come to Naples with her husband, Louis of Anjou, in order that they might there receive the honours due to their rank; but she was again dissuaded by the Duchess of Suessa from inviting them, and contented herself with making some presents to Princess Margaret, who proceeded to Cosenza.*

Louis III. did not long enjoy the sweets of wedlock and the genuine attachment of his people. Ever obedient to the caprices of the Queen of Naples, he undertook, by her command, in the year 1434, a war which he considered to be unjust.

He was required to reduce the most powerful of the Neapolitan feudal lords, Giovanni Autorico Orsini, whom the Queen's favourites desired to despoil of his wealth. Orsini was in danger of losing all his estates, when besieged in Tarentum by Louis of Anjou and Jacques Caldora.

Suddenly these proceedings were arrested by an attack of fever; and Louis III., like his grandfather Louis I., was cut short in the midst of his career by

* Moreri; Sismondi; Villeneuve Bargemont; Mezerai; Monfaucon; Rapin; Monstrelet.

this virulent malady, of which he died on the 15th of November, 1434, in the thirty-first year of his age.[*]

1434.

This prince left no children by his wife, Margaret of Savoy. His remains were interred at Cosenza, in Calabria, excepting only his heart, which was deposited in the Cathedral at Angers, the sepulchre of his ancestors.[†] By his extreme mildness of character, Louis III. had won the affection of all who surrounded him. He had lived long amongst the Calabrians, and in his person commenced a genuine and firm attachment on their part to the House of Anjou, which never failed during the civil wars that succeeded.[‡]

The condescension of Louis, it may be said, even amounted to a weakness, in having surrendered Queen Joanna to her bad counsellors. For to his long exile from the Neapolitan court must be attributed, in some degree, the loss to his family of the rights he had acquired by his adoption, as well as the long wars, which, after his death, once again devastated the kingdom.[§] His death was generally and deeply regretted: it is even said, that his enemies shed tears for the loss of one so respected for his amiability in private life, and so justly celebrated, considering his years, for his talents as a military commander. The Queen of Naples especially, seemed to be inconsolable at his death.

It is pleasing to observe, that amidst the wars with the English and the expeditions to Naples, the attention of Louis III. and of his mother Yolande, who was the practical ruler of Anjou during his absence, had been nevertheless directed towards an establishment of

[*] Sismondi; Monfaucon; Moreri; Eccles. Hist.; Monstrelet; Villeneuve Bargemont.

[†] Moreri; Godard Faultrier.

[‡] Sismondi.   [§] Sismondi.

lasting utility to the people of that province. Until that period, degrees in the law only could be conferred by the University of Angers; but, through their united solicitations, it acquired from Pope Eugene IV., the right of completing its studies by the addition of the three new faculties of medicine, theology, and the *belles lettres*.

1434.
Godard
Faultrier.

At the request of Yolande also, on the death of her son Louis III. in 1434, Charles VII. granted to his mother-in-law, letters patent for conferring degrees in all four of these branches of public instruction.*

1435.
Sismondi.

Queen Joanna herself died in the ensuing year, 1435, in her sixty-fifth year. All her recent efforts had been consistently directed towards ensuring the succession of Louis III., and his premature death did not change her project regarding his family. Shortly before she died, she executed a will, nominating as her heir to the kingdom of Naples, René, Duke of Anjou, the brother of Louis III. This testament was confirmed by the unanimous voice of the people, who were then so devoted to the memory of Louis, that they felt a gratification in declaring themselves for his untried and unknown successor, René of Anjou.

To maintain her people in their fidelity to this prince, Queen Joanna left behind her a treasure of 500,000 ducats. She also appointed a Council of Regency, composed of sixteen lords chosen by herself; and with these were associated twenty deputies selected from the nobility and people. By these lords an embassy was dispatched to their new monarch, inviting him to come to Naples, and take possession of the kingdom.†

* Godard Faultrier; Villeneuve Bargemont.

† Sismondi; Bodin; Moreri; Eccles. Hist.,; l'Abbé Millot; Godard Faultrier; Hallam.

Joanna II., following the example of her brother Ladislaus, had assumed the title of Queen of Rome. She was the last individual of the " First House " of Anjou.*

* l'Abbé Millot.

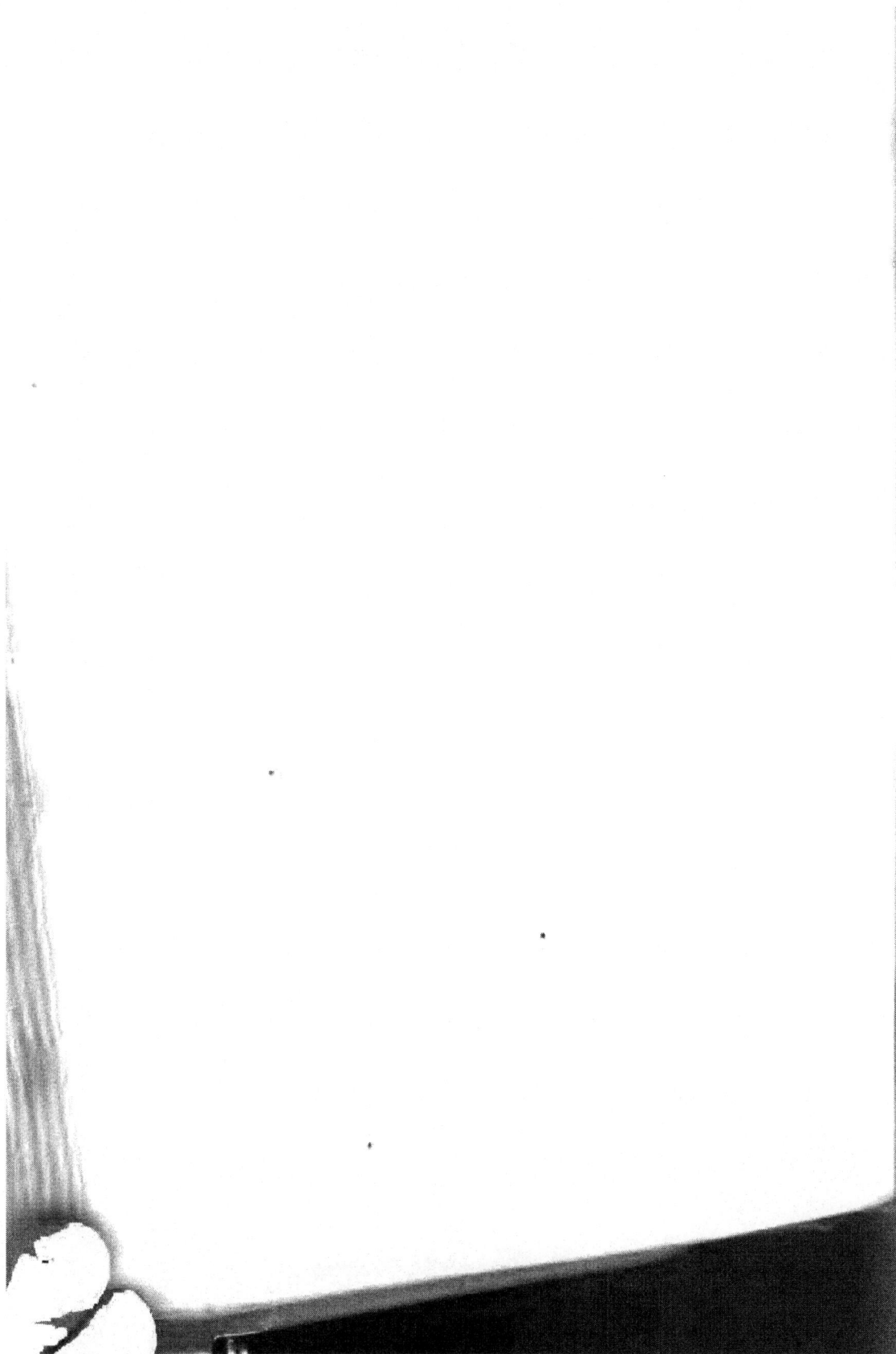

1st wife, BONNE, dau. of John of Luxembourg, Ki Count
of Bohemia : 4 sons, 4 daus.

MARGUERITE, a nun.	ISABELLA, m. Visconte Galeas, 1st Duke of Milan.	JEANNE, m. Charles "The Bad," King of Navarre.	MARY, m. Robe Duke of

CHARLES,
Count of
Maine.

CHARLES.

BONA, Countess of St. Pol.	MARY, Countess of Namur.	YOLAND, Queen of Aragon.	HENRY, Lord D m. Ma Countes

ROBERT,
Count
Soissons
Agincou

CHARLES.	RENÉ.

Died young.

walls and circular towers, eighteen in number, with the
deep moat and two drawbridges leading to its Gothic
and machicolated portals, gave it a truly imposing
character. Within these barriers stood the ancient
ducal palace, the residence of the Angevine princes,
and at this time inhabited by Queen Yolande, who
evinced a strong attachment to Angers and its vicinity.

The winter of 1408 was one of the most remarkable
for its severity ever recorded in history. The Danube
was frozen over, and Provence suffered extremely from
a continued frost, but its inhabitants rejoiced greatly
on the birth of the young prince, as though they anticipated the fortuitous events which would pave the way
for his exaltation, or entertained a secret presentiment
of the permanent affection which would hereafter be
felt for them by their future sovereign.

It was while René was yet in his cradle that those
dissensions originated, which during his whole life prevailed throughout France. The civil warfare which
they caused,* added to the invasions of foreign armies
and the desolation consequent on the victories of the
English, reduced this kingdom† to a deplorable condition, which has been aptly depicted by the annalists of
that period.

We are not informed who undertook the sacred
charge of sponsorship at the baptismal font for René;
but he received his name, a very uncommon one before
his time, in memory of the holy bishop, St. René, much
respected by the people of Angers, and who, according
to a pious tradition, was resuscitated at the end of
seven years, whence he was called Re-né, or twice
born.‡ The title of Count of Piemont had been be-

---

* Just before the birth of René occurred one of those prominent events
in the history of that kingdom which paved the way for its misery, viz.,
the cruel murder of the Duke of Orleans by John "Sans Peur," Duke of
Burgundy.

† Moreri; Bodin; Villeneuve Bargemont; Godard Faultrier; Monstrelet.
Biographie Universelle.

‡ On the banks of the Loire, in a charming situation, stands the Château

stowed upon René at his birth. The care of his infancy was entrusted by his mother, Queen Yolande, to a virtuous nurse named Theophaine la Magine, who was a native of Saumur, and had already fulfilled the same duty for his sister Mary. The solicitude of this poor woman was ever after remembered by her foster-children, who did not neglect her in after life, but loaded her with benefits, and evinced their gratitude for her tenderness and care.* The infancy of René passed under the eye of his mother and her ladies at Angers,

de la Possonnière, and near it the ruins of another more ancient edifice, with the Chapel of St. René. St. René has been cherished among the pious Angevins, though forgotten by the world ; and the history and miraculous legend of this saint are too important in the annals of Anjou to be passed over in silence. St. René was born near the end of the fourth century, in the villa of Possonnière, of illustrious parents. He preached some time at Chalon, and on the death of St. Maurille, was elected Bishop of Angers. After filling this office twenty-two years, he went to Rome, and thence repaired to Sorento, where his fame caused him to be advanced to the dignity of bishop. He died at this place in the year 450 ; and his remains being claimed by the Angevins, were conveyed into Anjou, and deposited, first in the Church of St. Morille, and finally in St. Maurice, at Angers. The shrine of St. René has been much celebrated. Leo X., in 1513, and Clement VII., in 1533, granted edicts in favour of the institution of the brotherhood of St. René, whose members of both sexes then amounted to more than 7,000. Some of the kings of France inscribed their names at the shrine of this saint, amongst whom were Louis XII. and Henry III.

The legend of his second birth runs thus :—"The parents of St. René having no offspring, addressed themselves to St. Maurille, the Bishop of Angers, promising to dedicate to God their first-born. Bononia became a mother, but her joy was transient;—her son, being carried into the Cathedral of Angers, died before his baptism. After this event St. Maurille went into Britain, and after an exile of seven years returned to Angers. The illustrious lady of Possonnière then besought this bishop to restore her dead son. St. Maurille approached the tomb—caused the stone to be raised—sprinkled it with holy water—and then, throwing himself on the ground in an attitude of devotion, he offered up aloud his supplication, upon which the tomb opened and the child was restored to the world and baptized. This miracle may be doubted by many, but the existence and episcopacy of St. René are not to be contested. The legend passed through the Middle Ages, and even in these times, the country people may be seen carrying a banner over their heads while descending the hills or passing the Loire on their way to the Chapel of Possonnière to implore the aid of St. René. It is a pretty sight this march of young mothers, some praying for deliverance, others offering their newly born." One author adds, " it is remarkable that the people of Angers, our ancestors, have had a great veneration for mothers and children."—*Godard Faultrier ; Villeneuve Bargemont.*

* René even composed her epitaph, which still may be seen on one of the

and in occasionally visiting the French court, where
Louis II. chiefly resided. In his early years the Count
de Piemont is described as " remarkable amongst the
children of his years, for an agreeable figure, a sweet,
intellectual and precocious disposition, and great aptitude to learn."

The father of René, Louis II., in the year 1409, engaged in a new expedition into Italy, to regain the kingdom of Naples. He returned, however, the same year
to Provence, where he was rejoined by Queen Yolande
and her three children. The object of this journey was
to gain plenary indulgences, granted to the ancient
abbey of Mont-Major; the pilgrims of both sexes, who,
together with the Duke of Anjou and his family, resorted thither on this occasion, amounted to 150,000
persons.*

When he had attained his seventh year René passed
from the control of the women of Queen Yolande into

---

pillars in the Church of Notre Dame de Nantilly, at Saumur. On a block
of stone is the following inscription :—

"Cy gist la nourrice Theophaine
"La Magine, qui ot grant paine
"A nourrir de let en enfance
"Marie d'Anjou, royne de France
"Et apres son frère René
"Duc d'Anjou, et depuis nommé
"Comme encore Roy de Sicile
"Qui a voulu en cette ville
"Pour grant amour de nourreture
"Faire faire la sépulture
"De la nourrice dessus dicte
"Qui à Dieu rendit l'âme quiete
"Pour avoir grace et tout deduit
"Mil cccc. cinquante et huit
"Ou moys de Mars XIII. jour
"Je vous pry tous par bon amour
"Affin qu'elle ait ung pou du vôtre
"Donnez-lui ugne patenôtre."

Beneath this epitaph, which was anciently in the choir, on a stone monument was represented Theophaine reclining, and holding in her arms her
two foster-children, Mary and René of Anjou. The verses remained entire
in the year 1840; but the monument was destroyed in the civil wars of the
sixteenth century.—*Bodin; Godard Faultrier; Villeneuve Bargemont.*

* Villeneuve Bargemont.

the hands of the men; and although the heir of a sovereignty, he was, like the son of a private gentleman, submitted to the guidance of certain old barons and knights of high reputation and experience, under whose instructions, enforced by noble examples, a manly and severe education succeeded to the tenderness of maternal care. The effeminate games of childhood also gave place to violent and painful, and sometimes dangerous exercises. It was thus that the youth of that period were inured, even in the bosom of the palace or castle, to the fatigues and perils of war.*

It was about this time, upon the occasion of Queen Yolande's visit to the capital with her little son, that the good disposition and extraordinary application to study evinced by René first attracted the attention of his uncle Louis, Cardinal of Bar, who began, when his pupil was only seven years of age, to direct his studies. He had frequent opportunities of observing his character, and delighted to behold in him those inestimable gifts with which nature had endowed him, and which his parents had most assiduously cultivated. It was indeed to these that René owed the unexpected change in his destiny which the notice of the Cardinal procured him, and which paved the way to his subsequent distinction. Being only the second son of the King of Sicily, René had no hopes of any inheritance beyond the title of Count of Guise. It was not, however, his fortune to be throughout life only a titular prince; yet, while seeming to delight in overwhelming him with unlooked-for favours, this same fortune granted him not one of these without subjecting him to some new adversity.†

The relationship of the Cardinal of Bar to René was

1415.
Godard
Faultrier.

---

* Godard Faultrier.

† Dom Calmet; Bodin; Biographie Universelle; Villeneuve Bargemont, Godard Faultrier.

that of great-uncle on the maternal side. He was fourth son to Sir Robert of Bar and Mary, daughter of John, King of France. Sir Robert, who was both learned and valiant, died in 1411, and having lost his two eldest sons, he bequeathed the duchy of Bar and castlewick of Cassel to his third son Edward, Marquis of Pont. This duke, with a younger brother John, lord of Puissage, and Robert their nephew, Count of Marle and Soissons, all three perished on the field of Agincourt; and thus the Cardinal became sovereign of Bar, although this inheritance was claimed by his sister Yolande, Queen of Arragon, and their dispute only terminated in 1419, when the Cardinal gave up his rights in favour of René of Anjou. After the death of so many relatives, the Cardinal, seeing his name about to be extinguished, and having already felt some affection for René, gave him the preference over his other nephews; and, as his attachment increased, he took upon himself the charge of his education, under the *surveillance* of Jean of Proissy, to whom René had been entrusted by his mother Yolande.[*]

Prelates of the fifteenth century lived like sovereigns within their own dioceses with great magnificence. They did not always find the thunders of the Church sufficient to defend their temporal rights, and were sometimes obliged, as Monstrelet tells us, " to carry a helmet for a mitre, a breastplate instead of a cope, and for a cross of gold, a battle-axe." The breviary was not more familiar to them than the sword, and Louis of Bar, surrounded by examples of glory, had, as it were, imbibed in his infancy the hereditary valour of his race, while at the same time he possessed in the highest degree the virtues which honour the Church. He united to the most extensive information a taste for literature; and his love for the arts, of which he was

* Dom Calmet; Monstrelet; Villeneuve Bargemont.

the enlightened protector, induced him to extend his
munificence to most of the artists of his time, whom he
attracted to him, either to the old palace of Bar or to
Paris, where he often prolonged his stay.

It may be presumed that this prince neglected no
means to perfect the rising talents of his pupil, and it
is probable that in these visits which they made together to the French court, René received his lessons
in drawing and painting of the brothers Hubert and
John Van Eyck.   The latter, better known by the
name of John of Bruges, had passed great part of his
youth near Charles V., who had conferred on him
many favours.   It is believed that it was to these celebrated masters, or to their pupils, that René was
indebted for his first instructions in an art which he
constantly loved, and cultivated at all periods of his life.

It is in childhood, when the imagination is susceptible and the senses are awake to every impression
made on them by external objects, that the strongest
tastes are formed, and the outlines of future character
are observable.

René's taste for painting was not more surprising
than his inclination to engage in all that related to
chivalry.

In the Middle Ages the institutions of chivalry
formed the best school for honour and moral discipline,
and were very influential in promoting intellectual improvement.   Hallam, who has so ably written of these
times, says, " Chivalry preserved an exquisite sense of
honour as effective in its great results, as the spirit of
liberty and religion on the moral sentiments and ener-
gies of mankind."

There were notwithstanding amongst the members
of the chivalrous orders, many individuals more conspicuous for their vices than for the virtues they
professed.

At the same time that René was taking his first lessons in the art of drawing, he probably beheld the commencement of a chivalric institution, in which no doubt, although so young, he was permitted to take some part. This was the "Order of Fidelity" which Thiebaut, the fifth Count of Blamont, desired to found; but of which, in order to confer *éclat* and durability, the Duke of Bar was declared the supreme chief. It was at Bar that this order was recognised, on the 31st of May, 1416. Forty knights of Lorraine, some of them very young, were associated together during five years, bound by oath in love and unity to support one another in every reverse of good or bad fortune.* It may be well to notice here, that one of these knights who thus pledged himself with others, was Robert de Sarrebruche, called the Damoisel de Commercy, afterwards much distinguished by the frequent violation of his engagements to René.

Time was rapidly passing with the young pupil while occupied in his new exercises and delightful employments. He had just entered his ninth year when his father, the King of Sicily, died. On being informed of his dangerous condition, René hastened to him, and received his last farewell. He then beheld the tender interview between this dying monarch and his son-in-law, Charles VII., who was counselled by him especially " never to trust the Duke of Burgundy, but to employ every means to keep on good terms with the formidable John 'Sans Peur.' " It had been well for Charles had he obeyed these counsels.

René, who became by his father's will, Count of Guise, continued to reside with the Cardinal. By his happy disposition and attractive qualities, he so far confirmed the good opinion of his patron, that he began to regard him truly in the light of a son, and

1417.
Rapin.

* Dom Calmet ; Monstrelet ; Villeneuve Bargemont.

did not hesitate to name him as his heir in the duchy
of Bar. He initiated him in the affairs of his state,
and associated him in all the acts of his government.
He even desired that René should be considered by
his subjects as their future sovereign. In 1418, this
young prince first acted in concert with his uncle in
the government, and addressed letters in his own name
to the different officers of Barrois.*

At this time the greater part of Lorraine was in-
fested by brigands, deserters, and vagrants, who upon
being repulsed from the interior of the kingdom, and
from the fortified cities, dispersed themselves towards
the provinces on the borders, where they pillaged,
committed murders and all kinds of violence. Such
were the sad results of the long wars which had desolated France. More than once the Cardinal of Bar
had been compelled to take up arms, and go in
person to defend his states; but he resolved at length
to put an end to these evils by forming a league with
Conrad Bayer de Boppart, Bishop of Metz, another
martial prelate like himself. They attacked together
several lords, who were even more culpable than the
brigands themselves, inasmuch as they had sheltered
them from justice in order to profit by their plunder.
René of Anjou accompanied his uncle in this rapid
expedition which might be said to be the first
campaign of this young prince, and it proved successful.†

1418.
Villeneuve
Bargemont.

Discussions were at this time entered into between
the States of Lorraine and Bar. Their proximity to
each other caused their interests sometimes to clash,
and involved them in dissensions and bloodshed. A
furious war had been recommenced in 1414, under

* Dom Calmet; Biographie Universelle; Villeneuve Bargemont; Godard
Faultrier.
† Villeneuve Bargemont.

Edward, Duke of Bar, which had brought destruction by fire and sword on these unhappy states. Two years later a treaty was concluded between them; but they were again apprehending a speedy rupture, when the Cardinal of Bar proposed a means of establishing peace between these duchies on a solid basis.

After nominating René of Anjou to succeed him in his own states, the Cardinal did not rest here, but further evinced his solicitude and the interest he took in his welfare, which, added to political considerations, induced him to propose an alliance between his young relative and Isabella, the daughter and heiress of Charles II., Duke of Lorraine, and Margaret of Bavaria. Thus he hoped to form a lasting union between the States of Bar and Lorraine, and to restore unanimity and peace.*

It might naturally have been expected that much opposition would have been raised to this marriage, although many lords of Lorraine openly expressed their desire that it should take place.

Charles II. had been a long time devoted to the Duke of Burgundy, who had in a manner protected him in his youth. His consort, Margaret of Bavaria, was a near relative of the Duchess of Burgundy; and besides that, he had entertained a personal enmity against the princes of the blood, and was at variance with the Duke of Orleans at the time of his death.† Great manœuvring was required to negotiate for the hand of this duke's daughter, since it was on the part of an Angevine prince, but the Cardinal triumphed over all obstacles; Duke Charles readily consented to the marriage, and appointed an interview with him on

---

* Villeneuve Bargemont; Monstrelet; Dom Calmet; Biographie Universelle.

† Duke Charles of Lorraine had in his will, made in 1408, even forbidden that his eldest daughter should be united to a prince of the House of France.

the subject. They repaired to the Castle of Foug, near Toul, which belonged to the Cardinal, on the 20th of March, 1418 ; and it is remarkable that Charles of Lorraine, besides the lords of his court, should have brought with him Antoine de Vaudemont, his nephew, to countenance by his presence the articles of this marriage, since he ultimately became the most powerful opponent of René.

1418.
Dom Calmet ;
Villeneuve Bargemont.

The Cardinal was accompanied by his young *protégé*, of whom it was said, that his prepossessing appearance, his courage, of which he had already given proof, and his rising reputation charmed the Duke, and contributed, as much as policy, in deciding him to bestow on him the hand of his daughter. The agreement * was then entered into by the two princes.

It had been previously decided that the Duke of Lorraine should have the control of the person of René until he had attained his fifteenth year; that on that same day the parties should be betrothed, and that on the following day the marriage ceremony should take place.†

At the time that the articles of this marriage were published in Lorraine, and when the nobles were joyfully taking their oaths, another assassination occurred which struck consternation throughout France. This was the murder of John "Sans Peur," Duke of Burgundy, in open day, on the bridge of Montereau, on the 10th of September, 1419.

It might have been apprehended that Philip, the

1419.
Villeneuve Bargemont.

---

* This agreement states,—

1stly. That on the day of Pentecost, 1419, the Count of Guise should return from his journey into Anjou, the object of which would be to obtain the consent of his mother.

2ndly. That he should repair to Bar, where the Duke of Lorraine would meet him, to arrange the conditions of the marriage.

3rdly. That they should then fix the period when René should be conducted to Nanci, and cease to reside with his uncle, that he might be entirely under the *surveillance* of his future father-in-law.

† Villeneuve Bargemont ; Dom Calmet ; Biographie Universelle.

next heir to the Burgundian States, would seek to revenge his father's death on all the members of the Angevine family; but happily this was not the case, for although he vowed eternal enmity against the Dauphin (who was suspected to have commanded the criminal act), he had not the injustice to involve others indiscriminately. He did not, therefore, offer any opposition to the alliance which the Duke of Lorraine was about to make with the brother-in-law of one, whom he regarded as his father's assassin, but received with favour the ambassadors sent by that prince to condole with him on his misfortune.*

Profiting by this unexpected kindness, and fearing that other difficulties might arise, the Cardinal of Bar immediately passed an act to confirm the adoption of René, and his resignation to him of the duchy of Bar and the Marquisate of Pont-à-Mousson,† conditionally on his taking the name and arms of Bar.‡ This act was passed at St. Mihiel, on the 13th of August, 1419, and the treaty of marriage, agreed upon the preceding year, was then also ratified.§

The dower of Isabella was fixed at 5,000 livres annually, or 4,000 only in the event of Duke Charles having a male heir to succeed him in Lorraine. This

* Villeneuve Bargemont.

† The Marquisate of Pont-à-Mousson appears to have comprehended St. Mihiel, Briey, Longwy, Marville, Saucy, Stenay, Longuyon, Foug, Pierrefort, Condé-sur-Moselle, and l'Avantgarde.

‡ In the shield of the complete arms of Bar, René was allowed to carry a small escutcheon with the arms of Anjou.

§ The historian of Lorraine informs us that King Henry V. of England having demanded the hand of Catherine, the daughter of Charles VI., for himself, hearing that the Duke of Burgundy was reconciled to the French king, feared that this would re-unite the forces of France, and oblige him to abandon his conquests in that kingdom. He, therefore, applied to the Duke of Lorraine, and asked his daughter Isabella in marriage for his brother the Duke of Bedford, hoping by this alliance to unite Duke Charles in his interests, and place France between two fires. It is, however, surprising that Henry V. was ignorant that the Duke of Lorraine had already contracted his daughter to René of Anjou, in March, 1418.

princess had, besides, the sum of 40,000 livres, ready money.

All the States of Barrois had been convoked upon this occasion. The sister of the Cardinal, Bonne of Bar, was also present. She was the wife of Valeran of Luxembourg. The Count of Ligny was also there, besides Jean of Sarrebruche, Bishop of Verdun, and the three abbots of St. Mihiel, La Chalade, and Lisle en Barrois. The same day the Cardinal and the Duke of Lorraine mutually engaged to appoint René and Isabella as their heirs; and they obliged all their vassals to take oath to acknowledge them as their legitimate sovereigns after their death.[*] When these arrangements were confirmed on both sides, Yolande of Arragon, called by the chroniclers "La belle Reinne de Sicile," conducted her son to his uncle, to whom she had already sent Mansard de Sue, bailiff of Vitry, to signify her willingness to take the name and the arms of Bar. The Cardinal then prepared to conduct his young nephew to Nanci, there to entrust him to the care of the Duke of Lorraine, when an unforeseen obstacle occasioned a delay equally fruitless and unexpected.

Arnould, Duke of Berg, the husband of Mary of Bar, a sister of the Cardinal, had entertained secret pretensions to the duchy of Bar, and had even been eager to make it known immediately after the battle of Agincourt; but repulsed by the energetic measures of Duke Edward, he had continued at peace until René became the declared heir to this duchy, when, aroused by the feeling that this adoption would annihilate for ever his own claims, his disappointed ambition stimulated him to a new enterprise. Assembling his troops he advanced with rapid strides, and attacked the forces of the Cardinal; but no sooner did that

* Dom Calmet; Villeneuve Bargemont; Godard Faultrier.

prelate appear, with René, in arms against him,
than he was defeated in a pitched battle, and taken
prisoner.[*]

Rejoicing in their success, the Cardinal and his
nephew then proceeded to the capital of Lorraine,
where the nobles of the two duchies came, to ratify
solemnly the promises and conditions stipulated in
the contract of St. Mihiel. So great was the satisfaction universally expressed on witnessing the cordial
affection which existed between the betrothed, that
Duke Charles could no longer defer the marriage,
notwithstanding the youth of the affianced, René being
only twelve years and nine months old, and his consort
still a child.

Isabella, who was born in 1410, has been described
as being at the time of her nuptials, tall in person,
and possessing regular and uncommonly beautiful
features. To a mind above her age she united
strength of character; and the gentle piety of her
mother, Margaret of Bavaria, seemed to have been
transmitted to her as a precious inheritance.

René was equally remarkable among the young
lords of Lorraine. He was distinguished by an open
physiognomy, and large eyes "à fleur de tête;" he
was fair and fresh coloured, and his amiable manners
attracted the attentions of the ladies, and had already
rendered him dear to his young betrothed.[†]

Henri de Ville, Bishop of Toul, a worthy prelate
and a relative of the Duke of Lorraine, was chosen to
officiate as priest at this marriage, which was celebrated on the 14th [‡] of October, 1420, in the Castle of
Nanci, with the greatest pomp which could be displayed; and as one author tells us, amidst a joy which

1420.
Moreri.

[*] Villeneuve Bargemont.
[†] Villeneuve Bargemont; Godard Faultrier.
[‡] The 14th of October in the MS. prayer book of King René.

seemed to approach delirium. The same rejoicings prevailed throughout Barrois upon this union, formed under such happy auspices; and it was generally regarded as the means of annihilating former animosities and divisions, and of restoring that happiness which had long been banished from every heart.[*]

Few events rendered the early years of René's wedded life remarkable. During this period of happiness, his leisure was devoted to his studies; indeed after their marriage the young bride and bridegroom continued both in their own way to pursue their education, which they completed under the active *surveillance* of Margaret of Bavaria, Charles of Lorraine, and the Cardinal of Bar, three notable characters of that age; of whom the two former were so peculiar as to claim especial notice.

Margaret of Bavaria, the mother of Isabella, was the daughter of the Emperor Rupert, and one of the most virtuous princesses of her time. She lived in such complete retirement at her palace at Nanci that she was almost a stranger to the pleasures of her court, and occupied herself in works of benevolence and in founding pious establishments. Her life has been written in Latin by her confessor, Adolphus de Cirque, a Chartreux. He says, " she lived an austere life, chastising herself with fasting and wearing sackcloth," and he relates of her, that, " having found a little book entitled " La Rosaire Evangelique," containing the life of Our Saviour and of the Holy Virgin, this princess was so deeply touched by it that it was continually in her hands. The Almighty, by this means, poured so much blessing on her soul, that she became a model of every virtue. He bestowed upon her also some miraculous gifts, and even granted her several

---

[*] Moreri; Bodin; Monfaucon; Dom Calmet; Biographie Universelle; Villeneuve Bargemont; Monstrelet; Sismondi; Godard Faultrier.

victories in her husband's favour. Of these, not only
the people of Lorraine, but also foreigners and the
Duke's enemies, bore witness. Upon one occasion the
Duchess, while the combat lasted, caused public prayers
to be offered in the city, and ordered a solemn procession, at which she assisted barefooted, and with tears
implored the succour of heaven for her husband's
cause. After the battle of Champigneules, the vanquished prince acknowledged that the victory was not
owing so much to the valour of Duke Charles, as to
the Duchess Margaret, who had appeared at the head
of the army with a brilliancy that their eyes could not
endure. This occurred a second time under other circumstances; and the enemy, who were put to flight,
afterwards declared that they had been terrified, and
unable to support the presence of this princess whom
they had beheld at the head of the army of Lorraine."
When asked by her confessor if she had been present
at the battle, the Duchess replied, " That it would not
have become either her sex, or her condition; but that
she had addressed her prayers to Jesus Christ, implor-
ing the protection of her subjects." Her prayers were
always—" Lord, thy will be done and not mine; "
and she never asked of God either the death or captivity of her enemies.

We shall be less surprised at the influence which
this extraordinary woman held over the minds of the
people, when we contemplate her exceeding piety.
Such was the self-control she had obtained that her
humility, patience, temperance, disinterestedness, and
charity were unequalled. She visited the hospitals
with her ladies, and personally waited on the sick,
and dressed their wounds. By her means several
sick persons were restored to health; and when this
became publicly known, the afflicted ones were
brought from afar to the gates of her palace, that

as she passed them on her way to church, she might bestow upon them her blessing. Many of these were cured; but the Duchess declared that she could do nothing for those who remained in their sins, or wanted faith, or who placed greater confidence in the art of medicine than in the goodness of God.

The Duchess took great care of her servants; nor would she allow her daughters to remain in idleness, but set them herself an example of useful occupation. On fast days and Sundays she gave them instruction in the scriptures, conducted them to church and to the Lord's table. Her mornings were all spent in devotion, her afternoons in the care of her household and attendance on the poor. She confessed herself daily, took the holy sacrament every feast day and Sunday, and submitted her body to a severe scourging when the Duke, her husband, was absent. Such was the austere life of Margaret of Bavaria.

The Duke of Lorraine, on the contrary, was not very devout. He did not attribute the advantages he obtained to his wife's merits, and still less to his own; but to the prayers of the good people who prayed for him. The Duchess, however, was somewhat afflicted at the temporal prosperities enjoyed by Lorraine, fearing that God might reward her during her life for the little good she did, and deprive her in eternity of that bliss which was her only ambition.

Charles of Lorraine had no taste for solitude, and his capital became, during his reign, the centre of the most brilliant fêtes. The Duke was one of the most polished and intellectual princes of his time, although naturally of a warlike disposition and educated in the battle-field. That portion of his time which was not employed in war, or in the gratification of his passions, he devoted to literature. He was particularly fond of history, and it was said of him that he never passed a single day without reading some chapters of Livy or of Cæsar's Commentaries, his favourite authors, which he took with him on all his expeditions. Often, in speaking of himself, he would say that, "in comparison with Cæsar, he seemed to be only an apprentice in the art of war."

It may be inferred that this prince did not fail to encourage his pupil René in the love of study, and from the period of his first visit to his court also may have originated the taste and talents of René for music, a science in which Duke Charles delighted. He was always surrounded by the most eminent musicians of the day, and evinced his own love for music by playing skilfully on several instruments.* We are informed that René was engaged alternately at the courts of Lorraine and Bar in the cultivation of music and painting, the study of the ancient languages, legislation, and feudal customs; and he thus acquired, during the short intervals of peace, an education superior to the age in which he lived.

While occupied by such agreeable studies the life of René must have been tranquil and happy; but it was only a brief period. As early as the 10th of November, in 1420, this prince was at once awakened to the anxiety of protecting his states from a powerful competitor, to repulse whom it might even be required to unite with others in some military expeditions.

The Duke of Lorraine had, upon his daughter's marriage, taken on himself the care of the estates of René, as well as the charge of the person of his son-in-law; and he was occupied in November of 1420, in obtaining the recognition of Isabella as his successor,

1420.

* Dom Calmet; Villeneuve Bargemont.

in case he should die without male issue. To this he had been compelled by the conduct of his own nephew, Antoine de Vaudemont, who, from motives of interest, had not participated in the general satisfaction upon the marriage of René and Isabella. He had long enjoyed the hope of reigning in Lorraine after his uncle's decease, but the union which had just taken place had destroyed his illusions, and he could with difficulty restrain his feelings of resentment on beholding himself superseded by an Angevine prince. The age of René precluding explanation, De Vaudemont stifled his resentment at the offence and injustice, as he considered it; yet his apparent composure gave occasion for serious apprehension. This prince, who had been born in the midst of political storms, had aspired to personal distinction; and priding himself on his illustrious ancestry, he thirsted to add glory to his race. He was a devoted subject, a faithful friend, and a respectful relative. His noble character, and especially his frankness, added to his military talents, had secured him some powerful allies. As an enemy he was the more to be feared, as it was well known that justice and good faith only could make him draw his sword; but, when indeed he did so, his haughtiness led him on to extremes, even beyond the bounds of prudence, for he did not estimate the chances of war, nor the misfortunes and oppressions which might drive a people to despair. Such was the character of a prince, who, unable to endure even the shadow of an injustice, had so unexpectedly found in the youthful René a powerful rival, against whom he only awaited the opportunity of revenging himself.

Antoine de Vaudemont insisted that the Salic law being still in force in his family, Lorraine, a fief male, ought not, under any pretence, to revert to a female, or

to leave his family by marriage. Finding, however, that
he could not prevail upon his uncle to revoke his will
in favour of Isabella, this prince declared that upon the
death of Charles of Lorraine he would prove his rights,
and obtain with his sword that inheritance of which he
considered himself so unjustly deprived. These menaces
made it necessary for the Duke of Lorraine to call upon
the nobles of his States to swear to perform the conditions of his will; and he also caused his daughter to
be crowned as his immediate heiress.*

1424.
Dc fa
Calmet.

On the 5th of February, 1424 (according to the
chronicle of Lorraine), Isabella, Duchess of Bar, made
her first entrance at Pont-à-Mousson, where many
gentlemen, knights, and esquires awaited her, and
celebrated her arrival there by jousts and grand
fêtes.† On the 1st of August of the same year
Isabella gave birth to her eldest son, John, afterwards
Duke of Calabria. This event was commemorated
with rejoicings in Lorraine. Her eldest daughter,
Yolande, was not born until two years later, in 1426,
with a twin-brother called Nicolas, Duke of Bar, who
died young.‡

The second daughter of René and Isabella, the
renowned Margaret of Anjou, was born on the 23rd of
March, 1429, at Pont-à-Mousson, which was then one
of the finest castles of Lorraine and had formed a part
of her mother's dower.

1429.
Dom
Calmet.

The infant Margaret was baptized, under the great
crucifix in the Cathedral of Toul, by the bishop of that
diocese. Her sponsors were her uncle Louis III., King
of Naples, and Margaret, Duchess of Lorraine, her
maternal grandmother.§

* Moreri; Dom Calmet; Bodin; Biographie Universelle; Godard Faul-
trier; Barante.
† Dom Calmet.
‡ Moreri; Bodin.
§ Moreri; Dict. Historique des Femmes Célèbres.

René's faithful nurse, Theophaine la Magine (who, by this time, had doubtless advanced in experience as well as in age,) was appointed[*] to watch over the first years of this favoured child, who inherited the excellence and talents of her father; to these, as she grew up, she added the beauty and grace of her mother, afterwards appearing as a bright star in the horizon, destined to shine conspicuous with transcendent lustre.

At a very early age Margaret of Anjou gave proofs of those virtues which win the affections, and of such great abilities as seldom fail to command the notice of the world. In her case they led to the splendours of a throne, where she became immersed in difficulties and afflictions.

In the military expeditions which René undertook with the Duke of Lorraine and the Cardinal of Bar, he was very successful. He effectually checked the aggressions of the Count de Vaudemont, and in all his enterprises exhibited great activity, ardour, and bravery. It was during the sojourn of this prince on the borders of the Meuse that he improved himself in the profession of arms, while engaged in repelling the rebellious vassals; until, fatigued with such petty warfare, he sought to enlarge his sphere, and was induced to join the forces of Charles VII.

It was just at that remarkable era when Joan of Arc[†] had miraculously effected the deliverance of Orleans,

---

[*] Dom Calmet; Moreri; Baker.

[†] René had already seen the heroic shepherdess of Vaucouleurs, on her first appearance in the presence of Duke Charles, at Nanci. She had there spoken of her high mission, and in reply was reminded of her unfitness for war; in order to inspire the Duke and his court with confidence she requested to have a horse brought to her, when, springing upon this high battle-horse without the use of the stirrups, she seized, with a martial air, a lance which was handed to her, and executed in the court of the castle several courses and evolutions as well as the best-trained man-at-arms.

René of Anjou was blockading the city of Metz which the Duke of Lorraine had besieged. Had that prince been influenced by policy or prudence, he would have remained neutral in those contests which desolated France; but his affection for King Charles, his brother-in-law, and his predilection for the French, irresistibly impelled him, with all the enthusiasm of a youthful breast, to join the royal standard on the plains of Champagne, where his brothers, Louis III., Duke of Anjou, and Charles, Count of Maine, had already appeared. Nor could the solicitations of the Cardinal of Bar, or of the Duke of Lorraine, deter him from his purpose. The experience of these princes led them to fear the results of the union of the English with the Burgundians against themselves, should they declare war against them; but René, unmoved by their arguments, left the siege of Metz almost by stealth, and his conduct was soon justified by the success of the cause he embraced.

1429.
Mezerai.

It was on the 16th of July, 1429, the eve of the same day on which King Charles was consecrated in the church of St. Denis, that René joined him, bringing with him the Damoisel de Commercy and other lords; and he afterwards accompanied that monarch in his brilliant career of triumphs and conquests, serving him with devotedness and fidelity.*

René ventured, although but twenty-one years of age, to second the advice of Joan of Arc, the Duke of Alençon, Dunois and others, contrary to the counsel of the powerful La Tremouille. He soon became united with all the great generals of France, Potou, La Hire, the Duke of Bourbon, and still more intimately with Arnaud de Barbazan, called " le chevalier sans reproche," and it was with this general that he appeared before Paris. They seized together on

* Biographie Universelle; Villeneuve Bargemont; Godard Faultrier.

Pont-sur-Seine, Chantilly, Pont Saint Maxence, and Choisy, and finally they entered with Charles VII. at St. Denis. Then detaching himself from the royal army, René distinguished himself particularly at the head of his troops, by the taking of the fortress of Chappes, in Champagne, near Troyes, where, with 3,000 men, he defied 8,000 English and Burgundians united,* and triumphed over them in spite of the efforts of their skilful chief, Antoine de Toulongeon. Also at the village of La Croisette, near Chalons-sur-Marne, René gained a victory over the English.†

When this prince was rejoicing in his good fortune, and becoming daily more illustrious by the success he obtained in the cause of the neglected and despised " King of Bourges," as King Charles was styled, he was compelled to quit the field of action somewhat hastily, being summoned to attend the death-bed of his warm-hearted and generous relative, the Cardinal of Bar. With deep and unfeigned regret, René paid his last tribute of respect and honour to the memory of his uncle, who died in 1430, and then, repairing to Bar, he attended his funeral obsequies.

1430.
Biographie Universelle.

This loss was almost immediately after succeeded by that of the Duke of Lorraine ; and scarcely had René taken possession of the territories of his uncle, when he was called upon to assume the reigns of government over the dukedom of Lorraine. Charles, the second Duke of Lorraine, expired on the 23rd of January, 1430,‡ and was interred in St. George's Church at Nanci. He left a will, made in 1425, abrogating his former testament, and prescribing the manner in which his son-in-law should govern in Lorraine, in the event

1430.

* Monstrelet says the number was only 4,000.
† Biographie Universelle ; Barante ; Godard Faultrier ; Monstrelet.
‡ Some place the death of Duke Charles in 1431.

of the decease of his wife Isabella.* René of Anjou thus became an independent prince, and was solemnly acknowledged by the nobles and clergy of the two States.

René made his entrance into Nanci with Isabella, both mounted on magnificent chargers, amidst the blessings of the multitude, and the olden cry of " Noel! Noel! " The clergy and the most distinguished of the nobility attended them, according to ancient usage ; and near an antique stone cross, erected at the gate of St. Nicholas, the Duke and Duchess dismounted, previous to their entry into the city. They gave their horses to the Chapter of St. George, who preceded them, bearing the cross and the *cuissard* of the holy knight. The *Veni Creator* was then chanted by the people.

René and Isabella were thence conducted in procession to the ducal church ; they knelt before the high altar, and the Dean presented to them a half-expanded missal. " Most high and honourable seigneurs," continued the aged ecclesiastic, " we beg of you to take upon yourselves to swear that you will conform to the duties which your predecessors of glorious memory have been accustomed to respect, in compliance with ancient usage, on their entry into the duchy of Lorraine, and the city of Nanci." " Willingly," replied René and Isabella, and laying their hands on the sacred volume, they swore by their hopes of paradise, faithfully to maintain the rights of Lorraine. The Duchess Margaret, who was dressed in mourning, was delighted to see her daughter thus honoured.†

The history of the Middle Ages offers nothing more

* Dom Calmet's Hist. of Lorraine ; Biographie Universelle ; Godard Faultrier.

† Chronicle of Lorraine.

solemn than these acts of religion, in which the people, the clergy, and nobility summoned a prince on his accession to the crown to protect their franchises, their liberties and privileges. This admixture of loyalty and rudeness, of submission and independence always prevailed in these free customs of Lorraine.

The earliest acts of René developed a maturity of wisdom rarely discovered in a prince of two-and-twenty, the age at which he had succeeded to his inheritance of Bar and Lorraine. The people of these countries, who had so lately been rejoicing in their reunion through the marriage of René and Isabella, were destined to experience the vanity of their hopes and expectations, and to feel no less than their Duke and Duchess, the cruel vicissitudes of war, for Lorraine was again plunged into an abyss of evils after the death of Duke Charles. On the occasion of this visit of René, he concluded with the city of Metz a peace which was happy and lasting. He called to the presidency of his council, the virtuous Henri de Ville, Bishop of Toul; assembled about him men the most distinguished for their merits and learning, and renounced fêtes and pleasures to devote himself to the administration of the duchy. A law against blasphemers, a statute which granted an indemnity to men at arms whose horses had been killed in his service, and other letters patent in which he consigned to certain cities and abbeys his protection and a confirmation of their privileges, have been preserved as pledges of his faith and constant solicitude.

This epoch of the life of René was no doubt the happiest of his career. Blessed by his subjects, at peace with his neighbours, he had not yet felt the gales of adversity, and no reverse had tarnished the *éclat* of his arms. It is pleasing to dwell on the

tender solicitude he felt for his people, his brilliant
valour, and his sincere piety; and also on the virtues
of the good Isabella, whom heaven had rewarded by
granting her four beautiful children, bright ornaments
of the Court of Lorraine.

René visited successively all the towns of his duchy,
and received, in his progress through them, the most
affecting proofs of devotion and love. For the first
time the strife of arms was not heard in Lorraine, and
but for the ambition of the Count de Vaudemont,
nothing had occurred to disturb the general tranquillity
and happiness.*

An oath had been taken by the Count de Vaudemont to maintain with his sword his right to the
Duchy of Lorraine, and he pretended that the fief was
male, and could not pass to René by the right of a
woman. This prince had been educated in the camp,
had served in eight pitched battles, and was inured to
war; he therefore despised the youth and inexperience
of René, and when required to do homage to the
young Duke, on taking possession of Lorraine, he posi-
tively refused. The fortress of Vaudemont was immediately besieged by René, but the garrison being
assured of assistance, defended it for three months
with great valour. This was but the commencement
of a grievous war. No two leaders could be more
opposed to each other in their views and interests.
The Count de Vaudemont had always belonged to the
Burgundian party, while René, a son of Louis II. of
Anjou, one of the greatest enemies the House of
Burgundy had ever had, had not only joined the
French army, but had made deplorable war upon
the Burgundians, assisted by Arnaud de Barbazan,
First Chamberlain to the King of France, by whom
he had been distinguished as " le chevalier sans

* Dom Calmet ; Barante ; Biographie Universelle ; Godard Faultrier.

reproche " and permitted to assume the *Fleurs-de-lys* for his arms.

To recompense René for the services he had rendered him, King Charles at this time sent him some reinforcements led on by his friend Barbazan. René was also joined by the Bishop of Metz, the Counts of Linanges and Salu, the Lord of Heidelburg, the Sire of Sarrebruche, the Sire of Châtelet and others, with whom he united a considerable army. On the other side was the Marshal de Toulongeon, who, taking part with the Count de Vaudemont, rendered him no little assistance by raising for him an army in Burgundy and Picardy; and, as a further means of promoting his cause, he circulated a report that the object of René, after the defeat of the Count de Vaudemont, was the conquest of all Burgundy. A tax of 50,000 francs was accorded by the States of Burgundy, and Duke Philip also taking part with the Count de Vaudemont, supplied him with a large body of troops, headed by Antoine de Toulongeon, who, having been defeated before the fortress of Chappes by René and Barbazan, eagerly thirsted for revenge.[*] This army, amounting to 1,000 or 1,200[†] men, all experienced in war, advanced towards Vaudemont, and in order to provoke René to fight, commenced by ravaging his territories.

This prince, much affected by witnessing the misfortunes to which his people were thus exposed, became impatient to terminate the contest by a decided battle, and quitting the blockade of Vaudemont, advanced to meet his adversaries on the plain, where they had strongly entrenched themselves. The Burgundians, however, were not sufficiently numerous to

[*] Bodin ; Barante ; Monfaucon ; Sismondi ; Monstrelet ; Mezerai ; Biographie Universelle ; Godard Faultrier.

[†] Monstrelet says 4,000.

sected it; and provisions failing them, the Marshal advised a retreat into Burgundy, much to the chagrin of the Count de Vaudemont. They had already begun their march, when they were overtaken by René, and challenged to fight. The Lord of Toulongeon replied that he was prepared for battle, and such was the gallant bearing of this party that Barbazan, perceiving it, would have prevented the engagement, advising delay, and representing that the want of provisions would soon compel the Burgundians to retreat, but he was not listened to, so urgent were the younger knights for the attack.

1431.
Bodin.
The two armies met, on the 2nd of July, 1431, on the plains of Bulgneville, near Neufchâteau, and in this battle, called "La journèe des Barons" on account of the number of lords present, the Count de Vaudemont gained the advantage by making a sudden attack with his artillery, and the Duke of Lorraine was defeated. His general, Barbazan, was killed, and René himself wounded, and taken prisoner along with two hundred of his followers. The total loss of the vanquished was estimated at 3,000 men.* The engagement lasted but an hour; some even say, but a quarter of an hour. René had fought in this battle like a lion, and was not overcome until blinded by the blood which flowed from a wound on the left brow, the mark of which he carried to the grave.

The Marshal de Toulongeon conveyed his prisoner with all speed into Burgundy, where, at first, René was confined in the château "de Talent," near Dijon, but afterwards removed to that city, and im-

---

* Bodin; Moreri; Dom Calmet; Monfaucon; Barante; Sismondi; Mezerai; Monstrelet; Baudier; Biographie Universelle; Godard Faultrier.

prisoned in a tower of the palace of the Dukes of
Burgundy.*

Isabella meanwhile, with her children and her
widowed mother, Margaret of Bavaria, had remained at
Nanci, to await the issue of the battle of Bulgneville,
which ended so fatally for the interests of the Duke of
Lorraine. The first news of this disaster was conveyed
to these princesses by some of the affrighted fugitives
from the battle. They told the unhappy wife of the
capture of her lord. "Alas!" exclaimed Isabella,
clasping her child, the little Margaret,† to her bosom,
"Alas! where is René? He is taken, he is slain!"
"Madam," they replied, "be not thus abandoned to
grief; the Duke is well, though disabled, and a prisoner
of the Burgundians." But the Duchess appeared inconsolable. The news of René's defeat was speedily
confirmed, and when Isabella was assured that her
husband's life had been spared, she became more composed, and prepared, with the assistance of her mother,
to take such steps as the exigency of the state
demanded.

These courageous princesses, far from being overcome by this terrible shock or by the trouble and
consternation which ensued, were only animated to
greater exertions. They soon displayed the utmost
firmness and presence of mind. They immediately
convoked the Council, and Isabella appeared in the
midst, dressed in a long mourning veil, and leading her
four little children. As she entered the hall, she exclaimed, "Alas! I know not if my husband be dead
or taken?" "Madam," replied the lords who were
present, "be not discomforted; Monsieur the Duke has
indeed been taken by the Burgundians, but fear not, he
will be ransomed. By the grace of God, we will see

1431.
Villeneuve
Bargemont.

* Moreri; Biographie Universelle; Monstrelet; Godard Faultrier.
† Then only two years old.

the end of this war. The Count Antoine would have the
duchy, but it is well defended. We will not cease to
make war with him, and in a short time your husband
will be released." At these words the good Duchess
was a little consoled. She commanded, by the advice
of her council, a general levy in Lorraine and Barrois.
In a few days a numerous army was assembled, well
furnished, and to these were added the remnant of the
army which had escaped from Bulgneville ; and these
were conducted by the valiant knights before Vezelise,
having repulsed the attacks of the Count de Vaudemont. On the sixth day of the siege this unfortunate
town was taken and sacked to the utmost. They also
took the fortress of Toullo, and guarded Nanci from
a *coup-de-main.* Deputies were sent to most of
the towns to exhort the people to maintain their
fidelity to René, and to refuse obedience to any
orders which might emanate from the Count de
Vaudemont.

To this prince, their kinsman yet their most bitter
enemy, the unhappy Isabella and her mother even
ventured to address themselves in person. They obtained an interview with him at Vezelise, when with all
the pathos and energy inspired by misfortune, they
represented to him the evils attendant on a civil war
in Lorraine, and so affecting were their supplications
that they obtained from the Count a truce for three
months, from the 1st of August to the 1st of November,
and which afterwards was prolonged to the 25th of
January following.*

While Isabella was thus engaged in courageously
defending her rights to her paternal inheritance and
preserving her duchy from invasion and civil war,
René, from the solitude of his prison, was vainly ad-
dressing to Duke Philip numerous messages. This

---

* Villeneuve Bargemont ; Godard Faultrier.

prince, however, at a distance from his capital, refused
to listen to any treaty respecting the freedom of his
illustrious captive.   Hard and austere as the Duke
must then have appeared towards his prisoner, yet
Philip of Burgundy was not insensible to feelings of
compassion, or unable to appreciate merit.   When he
came, some time after, to Dijon, to preside at the
Chapter of the Order of the Golden Fleece, and to
bestow the collars of this Order on his victorious
generals, Vergy, Toulongeon and others, who had been
triumphant at the battle of Bulgneville, he remembered Duke René, and when passing the Tour de
Bar, he stopped, and commanding the guards to
admit him, he then hastily entered the prison, and
evinced his great sympathy towards his captive whom
he subsequently often revisited, showing great satisfaction in his society.

The Council of Lorraine regarded with the deepest
sympathy their Duchess, in her afflicted and desolate
condition, being left with four young children—two
boys and two girls—described as the most beautiful
ever seen.

The intercessions of the unfortunate Isabella with
her hostile kinsman, the Count de Vaudemont, although
somewhat availing for her country, were altogether
useless in procuring the liberation of her husband.
René had become the prisoner of the Duke of Burgundy, who consigned him to a tedious incarceration
in his own dominions.   The first days of René's captivity passed in the fortress " de Talent; " these were
days of sorrow; but he expected to be transferred to
Dijon, and hoped for the change, as promising him a
less rigorous confinement.   Orders were, however,
received by the Marshal de Toulongeon to convey his
illustrious prisoner to Bracon-sur-Salins.   At this
place the governor of the castle, Antoine de Bracon

surnamed Simard, was entrusted with the care of
René; and the dungeon being in a ruinous condition,
this prince was placed, for a time, in the Saulnerie or
Salt-mine. At the expiration of four months, a con-
tagion breaking out near this spot, René was, by
orders of the Council of Burgundy, conducted to Dijon.
The Council was, indeed, too much interested in the
preservation of the life of René to risk it by such a
distemper, but its members were also influenced by
other motives in the removal of their captive.

Several attempts had been made to rescue this
prince, and another being discovered in November of
1431. this year, 1431, it caused so much alarm to the
Bishop of Langres, and to the Council of Burgundy
over whom he presided, as to occasion them to write,
during the night, to the bailiff of Châlons, to whom, at
that time, was entrusted the chief *surveillance* of their
prisoners. This new enterprise was undertaken by
Robert de Baudricourt, who assembled in the little
town of Gondricourt a body of soldiers devoted to the
Duke of Lorraine, and equally resolved with their
leader to procure his freedom, even at the risk of their
lives. The dispositions had been made with the
greatest secrecy; and a German taken prisoner at
Bulgneville, who had been just set free, contrived to
acquaint René, while he was being conveyed from the
Salt-mine to the château de Bracon, of the plan concerted for his deliverance: but the Duke's removal to
the château de Rochefort, near the town of Dôle,
completely defeated this project.

In this new abode René was only permitted a few
days of repose, when he was conducted to Dijon, and
such severe measures were there resorted to for
his security, that he became convinced he must renounce every hope of escape. The most delicate
attentions were, notwithstanding, paid to him, in order

to make his captivity less painful. The melancholy situation of the youthful prisoner was also mitigated by the presence of the Bishop of Metz, of Erard de Châtelet, of the brave Rodemark, of the faithful Vitallis and others, who had all been taken prisoners, like himself, by the Burgundians. René was incapable of selfishness, and he hastened to guarantee a part of the ransom required of his companions in misfortune, and having thus assisted in procuring their return to Lorraine, he remained himself a solitary captive in the Tour de Bar, at Dijon, which ever after retained this name from its illustrious inmate.*

One of the first cares of René, after the battle of Bulgneville, was to found, at the chapter-house of Notre Dame de Vancouleurs, a perpetual mass for the soul of Barbazan his general, and for all those who had been slain in that engagement. Not confining himself to this act of piety, this religious prince, shortly after his arrival at Dijon, had a chapel erected on the right of the choir of the palace church, under the invocation of Notre Dame and his patron St. René. Amidst these sacred occupations and duties, how many sorrowful thoughts and protracted regrets must have assailed him! In the solitude of his prison, René found leisure to reflect on the early disappointment of all his prospects of glory and of happiness. A single battle had deprived him of the flower of his army, of liberty, and, perhaps, even of his states; had separated him from all he held dear, and had banished for ever his projects for the welfare of Lorraine. He felt but too sensibly—from the excessive precautions taken for the security of his person—the great importance which Philip, Duke of Burgundy, attached to his prisoner, and he contemplated the calamitous influence which his imprisonment would have over his future life.

* Villeneuve Bargemont.

Thus he gradually fell into a sombre melancholy, which was much augmented by the recollection of his wife and four helpless children; and although treated with all the regard due to his misfortunes, rank, and personal merits, a deep grief took possession of his heart. Nothing seemed to alleviate his sorrow, and even the very distractions offered him became importunate. The most absolute solitude could alone soothe him.

It was at this mournful epoch of his life that René, in order to escape from the *ennui* which consumed him and from his melancholy reflections, had recourse to the fine arts, which he had constantly cultivated. He applied himself with great assiduity to the study of painting, music, and poetry, and these, which had already delighted him in his youth, proved his consolation under misfortune, and afterwards became the solace of his old age. The first fruits of his talents for painting René consecrated with affecting piety to the decoration of his newly constructed chapel in the palace church, in which he placed the arms of Bar. In the same manner, that which he had ordained the foundation of, in the church of the Carthusian friars of Dijon, was ornamented by his own hand. He afterwards painted his own portrait on a window of the Duke's chapel. Two years later there were placed there the emblazoned arms of nineteen knights of the Toison d'or, who had been present at the Chapter held in 1433. Thus the portrait of the Duke of Lorraine was found surrounded by the escutcheons of the greater part of the generals who had borne arms against him at Bulgneville.

Nor was it only in the company of the muses that René solaced his captivity: he employed himself in more serious studies, and if his genius was aroused, his judgment also became matured amidst the reflections which his solitude awakened. He learnt the value of the study of history, which forestalls the lessons of experience, and he engaged earnestly in the difficult science of administration, and in the art of war in which he had already received so severe a lesson; in short, he learnt how to profit in the school of adversity. The rich library of Philip was situated at no great distance from the prison of René, and it may be presumed that this illustrious captive was permitted to explore its literary treasures, and that this fortunate resource proved conducive to his resignation, while it also prompted him to the useful occupation of that time which he had so much at his own disposal.*

The Duchess Isabella, meanwhile, with her mother, Margaret of Bavaria, continued indefatigable in their endeavours to obtain the release of René. When they found their hopes of carrying him off were disappointed by his removal to Dijon, they applied themselves to their relative, the Emperor Sigismond, and also despatched an embassy to the Duke of Burgundy, to demand the liberation of the Duke of Lorraine at whatever price. Erard de Châtelet (himself but just ransomed out of the hands of the Sire de Vergy), was employed by the two princesses in this embassy; and, as they neglected nothing to secure the success of their attempt, they previously concluded with the Seigneur de Vergy (who, at this time, had great power at the court of Philip) a treaty, the articles of which had been drawn up by the Council of Dijon.

The success of Erard de Châtelet's embassy was unfortunately annulled by one of those rare fatalities which occasionally set aside the wisest combinations and arrangements of human foresight. The benevolent protection of Sigismond, which had been exerted in favour of René from the very origin of the pretensions of the Count de Vaudemont, now rendered null this

* Moreri; Villeneuve Bargemont.

embassy. The Duke of Burgundy having learnt that the Emperor had recognized his prisoner as Duke of Lorraine, haughtily opposed the right he arrogated to himself, and protested that he alone had the power of disposing of the fate of René.*

This reply, so discouraging to the two princesses, caused Margaret of Bavaria to endeavour to procure, by a personal application, the mediation of King Charles VII. She set out accompanied by Henri de Ville, Bishop of Toul, and Conrad Bayer, Bishop of Metz. At Lyons she found the Count of Genoa, the brother-in-law of the Duke of Burgundy and his father, the Duke of Savoy, whom she sought to interest in the release of René. She then proceeded to rejoin the King of France, who was at that time traversing a part of Dauphiné.

Isabella of Lorraine also presented herself before King Charles, being unable to restrain her impatience to learn his resolves. Several ladies and gentlemen of her court attended Isabella on this journey, and to this visit has been attributed the origin of the passion of King Charles for the fair and amiable Agnes Sorel, who accompanied her benefactress on this occasion. The beautiful Agnes, placed in the flower of her age near the person of Isabella of Lorraine, had received in her palace and under her eye the most finished education, and the example of every virtue; but the attractions of her mind and person became the unfortunate snare which led to a brilliant celebrity, and the "Damoiselle de Fromenteau," deceived by bad counsels, had the weakness to sacrifice her reputation to the dangerous pride of passing for the mistress of her king. It was her gaiety, pleasing manners, and agreeable conversation which fascinated this monarch as much as her beauty. Of this last it was said, that it

* Villeneuve Bargemont.

exceeded the beauty of any other woman in France, and she was distinguished as "la belle des belles." When she had attained the rank of declared favourite, Agnes made use of the influence which the superiority of her character had given her, to awaken noble sentiments in the breast of King Charles who was naturally inclined to indolence.* She was charitable to the poor, and liberal in her donations for the repair of churches and the relief of distress. It was at this time, when Queen Isabella, full of anxiety and deep interest in the result of her mission, came to plead on behalf of her beloved husband, that she sought to avail herself of the ascendency which the beauty, elegant figure, and intellectual conversation of Agnes Sorel were obtaining over the King. Isabella engaged the fair Agnes to espouse her cause, and to use her influence with Charles VII. to obtain his assistance in procuring the release of her husband. It must be observed here, that it was not only the King who was pleased with the merits of the fair Agnes, but his Queen also; and Mary of Anjou, little fearing for her own future happiness, at this period entreated that Isabella of Lorraine would permit her favourite to enter her service. But the beauty of the amiable Mary had not yet fixed the heart of her husband, and the time soon arrived, when, detained at Loches by a royal order, her days were passed in sadness; and amidst the joyful exultation of the triumph of King Charles, the tears of his consort flowed in her cheerless retreat, not far from the castle of Agnes Sorel. When King Charles visited Anjou, the most brilliant fêtes were given for this lady, at Saumur, whilst the English ravaged the country and carried mourning and desolation throughout the provinces of Maine and Anjou.†

* Villeneuve Bargemont ; Hallam ; Monstrelet ; Chalon.
† Bodin ; Monstrelet.

A short time previous to the arrival of the Duchess of Lorraine at the court of France, René, who probably was ignorant of this step, had sent instructions in full to his Seneschal, Charles of Haussonville, and others, to appear in his name in the presence of the Duke of Burgundy who was then in Flanders, to sustain his interests against the Count de Vaudemont. In the interval, however, Philip had left Lille, and after traversing some of his provinces, came to Dijon on the 16th of February, 1432, with his nephews, the Counts of Rethel and Nevers.[*]

1432.
Villeneuve
Bargemont.

We are told that upon entering this city, so great was the impatience of the Duke of Burgundy to behold René, that, without taking any repose, he proceeded immediately to the Tour de Bar. Thus it was that in the narrow compass of a prison, these two princes, both descendants of King John, for the first time beheld each other; the one being at the height of his power, called the "Great Duke of the West" and the "equal of kings," and the other appearing in the lowest depth of misfortune, as his captive. These princes were only disunited by the dissensions of their families, while their brilliant tastes and excellent qualities were such as to ensure their mutual esteem.

They both experienced much gratification at this meeting, and Philip especially embraced René tenderly. He dismissed all their attendants, and enjoyed a long and affectionate interview with his prisoner.

When about to separate, René agreeably surprised the Duke, his cousin, by presenting him with his own portrait, which he had copied on glass, and also that of John "Sans Peur," whose features he had rendered with fidelity. These proofs of the talent of René were, by the orders of Philip, placed in one of the Gothic windows of the church of the Carthusian friars founded

* Villeneuve Bargemont.

by his ancestor, Philip "le Hardi;" and for a long time they were objects of great interest to travellers, though now lost to France.

The Duke of Burgundy's visit to Dijon had no relation to René, although he was so eager to behold him. The design of the Duke in this journey was to preside, with the utmost pomp which was customary in those days, over a Chapter of the Order of the Golden Fleece instituted in January, 1430, on the occasion of the second marriage of Philip. It is probable that Isabella of Portugal was there with her husband, and also that René sought permission to assist in a ceremony so analogous to his tastes. Philip saw his prisoner several times, he frequently invited him to his banquets, and as he became more and more acquainted with the amiable disposition of René and the gentleness and grace of his manners, he felt all the early prejudices, which had been instilled into him against this prince, vanish away.* Nor did he confine himself to these outward marks of interest. He appointed, on the 1st of April, the meetings for the consideration of the conditions which should be exacted for his release, and to fix the epoch of his liberation. It would even appear that from the 1st of March, 1432, René regarded himself as free.† In the first session the Chancellor of the Duke of Burgundy read through the articles of this provisionary treaty, and at the second meeting they were accepted. "René therein makes mention at length of the obligations under which he was to the affectionate prayers of his mother-in-law and of the princes of the blood; he acknowledges the kindness and courtesy of the Duke of Burgundy; submits, as a guarantee of his word, to give as hostages his two young sons, John and Louis of Anjou; he moreover

1432.
Villeneuve
Bargemont;
Monstrelet.

* Villeneuve Bargemont.
† Heures Manuscrites du roi René.

concedes to the Duke Philip the castles of Clermont in Argonne, Châtillon, Bourmont, and Charmes; and consents to pay the Burgundian troops that were to form their garrisons." For greater security, on the 16th of the same month, thirty gentlemen of Lorraine, who were devoted to their Duke and the greater part of whom had been present at Bulgneville, undertook, upon oath, that "that prince should return within the Tour de Bar on the 1st of May, 1433," but if he failed, they were to surrender themselves prisoners at Dijon one month after the expiration of the term assigned. Besides these clauses of the treaty, there was a pecuniary ransom not yet stipulated, and upon which were exacted in advance, 20,000 saluts d'or, as well as 18,000 florins claimed by the Marshal de Toulongeon as the ransom of the Sire de Rodemach. René subscribed without hesitation to all these conditions, in order to get free, and that he might return to Lorraine, once more preside over the government of his states, and by his presence afford some remedy for the accumulated evils which overwhelmed his people. There was yet, however, one condition more added to these numerous exactions, and this was still more painfully extorted from him.

The imperious Count de Vaudemont had again taken up arms, and at the head of 7,000 men threatened to possess himself by force of the duchy with which they refused to invest him. When he heard of the negotiations entered into at Dijon he again proclaimed his rights, and took active measures with the approval of Philip, only consenting to remain at peace in expectation of a final decision, conditionally, that René should bestow the hand of his eldest daughter Yolande upon his own son, Ferri of Lorraine.

At first René rejected this demand, and his repugnance was only too just; but motives of general policy prevailed, and he submitted this point to his council. It was afterwards referred by René and Antoine to the arbitration of the Duke of Burgundy to determine the conditions of this marriage, and it was finally settled that Yolande should receive 18,000 florins of the Rhine as her dower, the half of which sum should be appropriated to the purchase of a domain for the betrothed. It was agreed that the parties should be affianced on the 24th of June of the same year, and that afterwards the princess Yolande should be conducted to Neufchâtel, and confided to the care of Count Antoine de Vaudemont until the day of the marriage. This treaty was signed by the two princes who were reconciled to each other, and all the articles were duly observed, to the great joy of the people.

In a letter addressed about this time by René to the Regency of Lorraine, in which he required them to send his two sons to him, we find stated the considerations which induced him to submit himself to these rigorous exactions. " The misfortunes and divisions caused in my states by my detention, make it a law for me," says he, " to employ as soon as possible all the means in my power to put a speedy end to them."

The return of René was indeed imperatively demanded by the grief of his beloved wife and mother, as well as by the miserable condition of Lorraine. John of Fenestranges, Grand Marshal of Lorraine, Gerard of Haraucourt, Seneschal, James of Haraucourt, Bailiff of Nanci, Philip of Lenoncourt, and others, conducted John and Louis of Anjou to Langres and thence to Dijon, where they arrived on the 28th of April, previous to their father's liberation. René finally left his prison on the 1st of May, 1432,* and about the same period Yolande, his eldest daughter, was

1432

* Moreri ; Monfaucon ; Biographie Universelle ; Sismondi ; Monstrelet ; Mezerai ; Baudier ; Villeneuve Bargemont ; Godard Faultrier.

separated from her mother, and departed to the
Countess de Vaudemont.*

1432.
Monstrelet. It was at this time that René entered into a treaty
with two princes, with whom he had been for some
time at war. These were two brothers, the Counts of
St. Pol and of Ligny; the latter had conquered Guise,
a city which had formed part of the inheritance of the
Duke of Bar, and which René had ceded to his mother,
Queen Yolande, in 1424, when her guardianship ended.
For the security of this place René freely gave up the
Castle of Bohein, in the presence of many of his
nobility, by his orders assembled. Upon this occasion
the proposals were made for the marriage of Margaret,
René's younger daughter, with the Count of St. Pol's
second son, Peter of Luxembourg;† but this was deferred until another meeting.‡

Margaret of Anjou, the fourth child of René and
Isabella, was at this period scarcely three years of
age, and just commencing her education, at Nanci,
under the eye of her illustrious mother. By this tender
parent she was carefully instructed, and gave early
promise of the talents and beauty which afterwards so
much distinguished her.

1433.
Monstrelet. The Duke of Burgundy, in 1433, held the feast
of the Golden Fleece, at Dijon; and shortly after,
being invited by Amé, eighth Duke of Savoy, to be
present at the marriage of his son, the Count of Genoa,
about to be united to the daughter of the King of
Cyprus, at Chambery, the Duke repaired thither with
an escort of two hundred knights and esquires. René
of Anjou was also there. He was received with the
greatest respect by the Duke of Savoy, and was placed
at the nuptial banquet next the bride. There were

---

* Villeneuve Bargemont; Biographie Universelle; Monstrelet.
† The equerry of the Count of St. Pol had taken René prisoner.
‡ Monstrelet; Villeneuve Bargemont.

also present, the uncle of the bride, the Cardinal of
Cyprus, the Count of Nevers, and the heir of Cleves.
On the day of the arrival of the Duke of Burgundy,
the wedding took place, and it was followed by a
plentiful feast, and a succession of diversions. At this
court was seen a luxury quite regal, and the most
exquisite politeness.

It was here that René beheld for the first and last
time, Margaret, the daughter of the Duke of Savoy,
who, at this time, was preparing to rejoin her husband,
Louis III., Duke of Anjou. This princess, resplendent
in beauty, youth, and grace, was the ornament of the
wedding feast.

After these fêtes, Margaret of Savoy immediately
set out for Italy, with a numerous suite. Philip and
Amé also departed; they only separated at Chalons,
where, by an act of the 26th of February, the Duke
of Burgundy completed his marks of generosity towards
his prisoner, by prolonging the period of his freedom,
and allowing his two sons to go and meet him at
Nanci.*

It was in the interval of this journey to the Court of
Savoy that Charles VII., his Queen Mary, Charles of
Anjou, and the Duke of Bourbon, not satisfied with
the treaty of Brussels, had made overtures to the
Regency of Lorraine, to act directly, and even without
the authority of René, with the Emperor Sigismond.
This monarch appeared in fact to be the only arbiter
whose right of decision regarding the sovereignty of
Lorraine could not be disputed. The Bishops of Metz
and Verdun undertook earnestly to commence this
delicate negotiation, and supported by the French
ambassadors, they had all the success they could
anticipate; consequently, René and the Count de
Vaudemont were summoned to Basle, where the

* Monstrelet ; Villeneuve Bargemont.

Emperor was staying, in order that in his presence they should maintain their respective pretensions. One thing, however, had not been considered, viz., that René, who was only free on his parole, could not absent himself without the consent of the Duke of Burgundy, and that it became necessary to inform this prince of all that passed. The Duke was hurt that René should have thus acted without his knowledge, and at a moment when he was himself showing so much generosity towards his captive. At first, he haughtily refused to permit René to depart from Nanci; but, on reflection, he consented; requiring, however, that in their father's absence, his two sons, John and Louis of Anjou, should be conducted to the Tour de Bar. This order was immediately executed, and René quitted Lorraine, followed by some gentlemen, who all arrived at Basle at the same time as the Count de Vaudemont, on the 23rd of April, 1434.[*]

1434.
Villeneuve
Bargemont.

The relationship of the Emperor Sigismond to René,[†] as much as the apparent justice of his cause, inclined him to favour his young relative. Thus, in his reception of the two illustrious competitors with the greatest marks of regard, he yet could not help exhibiting peculiar goodwill towards René. His court and Council participated in this feeling, which became so manifested, that it could not escape the observation of the Count de Vaudemont. This prince fearing, and not without reason, that this prejudice would influence the decision of the tribunal of the empire, caused an act to be committed to paper, in Latin, declaring his opposition to any judgment unless the title produced by his rival should be first communicated to him; and so anxious was he that this writing should be delivered safely into the hands of Sigismond, that he accom-

---

[*] Biographie Universelle; Godard Faultrier; Villeneuve Bargemont.
[†] He was the son of a sister of Louis I. of Anjou.

panied the lawyers and advocates who were to present it. He entered with them into the cabinet of this monarch, and after it had been read, began to discuss it himself; but he was interrupted by Sigismond immediately, who told him he perfectly understood his reasons, and that he would confer with his Council about the matter. This abrupt manifestation of the Emperor's will did not prevent one of the Count's advocates beginning a long harangue, in which, going back to the origin of Lorraine, he sought to prove that the duchy being a fief male, was not transferable by marriage; and in support of his arguments, he brought so many quotations foreign to the case, that the Emperor at last offended, withdrew, leaving the Bishop of Passaw, the Count of Œtingen, and Chicala, his Aulic Counsellor, to listen to the conclusion of the discourse.*

The next day, the 24th of April, the Duke, with his principal officers, went in state to the cathedral of Notre Dame at Basle, where a mass of people awaited his arrival, expecting that the investiture of Lorraine must be irrevocably fixed. Each person was seated according to his rank. When Sigismond was about to ascend the magnificent throne which had been prepared for him in the choir, the Count de Vaudemont advanced to him, and solicited and obtained from him permission to plead his cause in public. His advocate then commenced his harangue, which, as he entered into minute details and repeated facts already well known, was of great length; but he was, notwithstanding, heard in profound silence. He had scarcely finished when the Emperor made a sign to his Aulic Counsellor to pronounce judgment. Chicala then, with a loud voice, said, " that the Emperor being well instructed on this important proceeding, and of the respective titles of

* Villeneuve Bargemont.

the august pretendants, and having reflected on it maturely, as well as the princes and lords who composed his Council, gave, by provision or grant, the Duchy of Lorraine to René of Anjou; yet without prejudice to the future rights of the Count de Vaudemont."

Sigismond then motioned to the young prince to draw near, received his oath of fidelity, and recognised him as Duke of Lorraine, according to all the formula in use from time immemorial. This prompt and unlooked-for decision much disconcerted the Count de Vaudemont, who instantly quitted the assembly, earnestly protesting against the validity of this judgment, and with his mind intent on disturbing anew the tranquillity of his fortunate rival, he departed from Basle.[*]

René, meanwhile, full of joy and gratitude, and desiring to profit by a second prolongation of his liberty granted to him by the Duke of Burgundy, dated the 1st of May, bade adieu to Sigismond.

The universal joy upon his arrival at Nanci, convinced this prince how much his presence was desired by the people of Lorraine, and how perfectly they comprehended his attachment to them. In their congratulations of one another they seemed to forget their past sufferings, and even sought to erase their remembrance from the minds of those individuals who had endured the most. Deeply affected by these sentiments, René in his turn sought to give proof of his own satisfaction, and ordered preparations to be made for a general fête, to be held at Pont-à-Mousson, on the 11th of the same month. All the lords of the neighbouring States were invited to join it, with a guarantee that they should return to their houses in

* Moreri; Barante; Monfaucon; Villeneuve Bargemont; Baudier; Godard Faultrier; Mezerai; Biographie Universelle.

safety. This precaution was indispensable in those times, when even the highways were not free from peril.

At the tournaments, balls, and other amusements that succeeded, René and Isabella presided, which afforded general satisfaction. The greatest order and harmony prevailed, interrupted only by one event, which happened at the close of these diversions and might have led to serious results.*

Robert de Sarrebruche, not having been invited to this fête, probably on account of his bad conduct at Bulgneville,† regarded this neglect as a deadly affront, and to revenge himself, concealed himself with some soldiers in a thick wood through which the knights of Metz would have to pass, and taking them by surprise, dispersed some and captured eighteen of them, whom he brought to Commercy.

This audacity was resented by René, who assembled several noblemen of Lorraine and a large body of troops, and marched upon Commercy, which the Damoisel resolved to defend to the utmost; but he was unable to repel the efforts of René, and was only preserved from the just punishment of his temerity by the mediation of the Constable of Richemont, to whom René was under some obligations.

These princes resolved to raise the siege of Commercy, and decided that Robert de Sarrebruche should go to Bar, whither they were themselves about to proceed. At this place the Damoisel, throwing himself at the feet of René and the Constable, acknowledged his repentance, and promised upon oath never again to take up arms against the Duke of Lorraine, on pain of forfeiture of a large sum of money. After this,

---

* Villeneuve Bargemont.

† He was one of the knights whose imprudent counsel in favour of the attack caused the defeat of René.

Robert de Sarrebruche was set free, but soon afterwards an accidental circumstance rekindled his anger, and he threatened René haughtily. The Constable, enraged at this conduct, caused him to be arrested, and compelled him to subscribe to the conditions which had been exacted from him. At this time also, some other quarrels with the neighbouring lords engaged the attention of René.*

It would appear that the Duke of Lorraine, although bound to return to his prison at the expiration of a year, viz., on the 1st of May, 1433, continued to enjoy his liberty for two entire years, without any desire being manifested on the part of the Duke of Burgundy to terminate it. Had he not, indeed, felt the fullest confidence in the honour of René, he had his two sons for hostages, who were answerable for him; in short, everything seemed to lead to the belief that this prince would continue still to exercise the same generosity towards his prisoner.

The solemn judgment, however, pronounced by the Emperor Sigismond, at Basle, had made the Count de Vaudemont more than ever the enemy of René, and it was with the utmost vexation that he beheld the strong attachment of the people of Lorraine to their Duke. He perceived that his own cause would be ruined, if his rival remained at liberty, and in the exercise of the sovereign power; he therefore renewed his entreaties with the Duke of Burgundy, that his rights should be recognised, and complained that they had taken away from him a prisoner who belonged to him only, as the chief of the victorious army at Bulgneville. He even retraced, in a long memoir, the circumstances of that eventful day; and in conclusion, supplicated the Duke of Burgundy to leave him master of the fate of René, or, at least, to oblige him to return to his

* Monstrelet ; Villeneuve Bargemont.

prison. These reiterated solicitations at last prevailed with Philip, who, finding some of the Count's reasons unanswerable, sent one of his heralds-at-arms to the gate of René's palace, to enjoin him " to return without delay to the Tour de Bar," agreeably to the act of the 6th of April, 1432.*

The rejoicings of his family and subjects upon the decision of the Emperor Sigismond were scarcely over, when Philip's abrupt command was received by René to return to his prison.

The severe mandate struck with dismay the Council of Lorraine, who, in unison with the unhappy Isabella, vainly endeavoured to alter the mind of Philip, or to delay the accomplishment of the cruel sentence. Equally useless were their attempts to picture to this Duke the misfortunes which would inevitably be renewed in their country, which had but just been spared so many miseries—the will of Philip was irrevocable.

The people of Lorraine would have fought for the freedom of René, but it was to no purpose that they urged this noble-minded prince to allow them to do so; his word had been pledged, and he said, " he preferred to submit to the lot which awaited him, rather than endure the dishonour of breaking his word." His sense of honour prevailed over natural affection. Unappalled by a gloomy futurity, he tore himself from the tender embraces of his family, and while hastening to obey this cruel sentence and resume his chains, he seemed to have adopted the saying attributed to his great grandfather, John, King of France—"Que si la foi et la vérité étoient bannies de tout le reste du monde, néanmoins elles devroient se retrouver dans la bouche des rois." Thus did this prince gain the esteem even

* Monfaucon ; Moreri ; Mezerai ; Biographie Universelle ; Baudier ; Godard Faultrier ; Villeneuve Bargemont.

of his enemies.* This action of René was the more
noble, because at this time he was supported by his
relative, Charles VII., by a multitude of his former
companions in arms, and especially by subjects who
were devoted to him, and thus he was able, had he
desired it, to oppose open force to the commands of
Philip. This admirable trait of character has, however, been blamed by some authors, who, unable to
appreciate his greatness of soul, have beheld in it only
a deficiency of courage and weakness of mind.†

René was conveyed again to his prison at Dijon, but
a formidable league having been formed to liberate
him, it was no longer deemed prudent to let him
remain in the Tour de Bar, and they hastened to
conduct him to the château de Rochefort.

The lords of Burgundy, hearing that Charles VII.
sought to get him removed from the town, came to
him, and said, " Sir, you have dwelt here long enough ;
you must come with us." The Duke replied, " Alas !
where do you want to take me to ? " To which they
answered, " Never mind, we will take you to a good
place ; we shall make good cheer, and we will live
with you." They then conveyed him to Bracon.‡

Again we behold this prince in confinement at the
finest period of his life, and separated from all he held
most dear in the world, and this also when he had
scarcely learnt his power of doing good ; he had besides, at this time, lost every prospect of obtaining his
freedom.

What sources of reflection must have been presented to him in the caprices of fortune to which he
had already been subject ; and who, more than this
prince, had reason to dwell with sadness on the chain
of events which often composes man's destiny, when,

* Sismondi ; Biographie Universelle.
† Villeneuve Bargemont.   ‡ Chronique de Lorraine.

amidst the gloom of his prison, a kingdom was presented to him in perspective, yet in receiving its crown he was destined to lament the loss of a brother he tenderly loved!

It was during his imprisonment at Bracon that René was visited by the Baron of Montelar, a gentleman of Provence, who was charged to announce to him the death of his brother, Louis III., Duke of Anjou, whose rights and possessions now became the inheritance of the Duke of Lorraine. He was also informed by this baron of the favourable intentions of Queen Joanna towards him, and of the devotion of the people of Provence.

René truly mourned the loss of his brother, which, together with the sad tidings of another bereavement quickly succeeding, much augmented the gloom of his captivity.

Vidal de Cabanis, another gentleman of Provence, arrived at Bracon on the 15th of March, 1435; he came to inform his master of the death of Queen Joanna II. on the 2nd of February, and of her adoption of René, and confirmation of the disposition which his brother had made to him of all his rights to the kingdom of Naples, Sicily, and Jerusalem.* After having beheld the last moments of the Queen of Naples, the only offspring of the House of Duraz-Anjou, Vidal had set off in haste in order to instruct René in all the details which might interest him, and above all to depict to him the affection of the Neapolitans for his family—a just and touching homage to the memory of his father, as well as to that of the unhappy Louis III. This testimony of devotion on the part of Vidal de Cabanis much affected René, who embraced his faithful messenger with kindness

1435.
Villeneuve
Bargemont.

* Moreri; Bodin; Monfaucon; Gaufridi; Sismondi; Godard Faultrier; Monstrelet; Biographie Universelle; Villeneuve Bargemont.

M 2

and called him his loyal servant. He shed tears afresh for the loss of his brother, lamented the death of Queen Joanna, and endeavoured to understand thoroughly, by means of his faithful ambassador, the actual condition of the kingdom of Naples.

. It was difficult for René to calculate on the part which the Court of Rome would take at this juncture between Charles VII., who favoured René, and Alphonso V., the competitor of René. The Pope himself had even been nourishing, in secret, pretensions to the kingdom of Naples. The support of this pontiff could not therefore be relied upon.

With much more certainty did René estimate the friendship of the Duke of Milan; he thought he could naturally rely upon his support, since he was doubly allied to him on account of Valentine, Duchess of Orleans, and Margaret of Savoy, whose eldest sister he had married. It was, nevertheless, highly important that he should not be forestalled in the good opinion of Philip Visconti, and also equally necessary that René should show himself in person in Italy, in order not to give time for the zeal of the Neapolitans to abate. René could now see clearly how much his loss of liberty would cost him, but he had no hope of softening the Duke of Burgundy, and the only means he could adopt for the preservation of Naples was to dismiss his consort Isabella very promptly to Provence, and even to Naples, with the unlimited powers of Lieutenant-General. The ambassador himself undertook to go to the Duchess and apprise her of it; he then quitted the fort Bracon, and René became from this time more than ever a prey to anxiety of mind.[*]

The elevation to the throne of Naples, so unlooked for, yet so flattering to the heart of René, had no influence in procuring his liberation from prison. The

* Villeneuve Bargemont.

Duke of Burgundy was even more urgent than ever, and watchful for the security of his captive. René, perceiving at length that his severity was unabated, dismissed Queen Isabella into Italy, as he had arranged with the faithful Vidal de Cabanis, hoping by this means to preserve in his interests the Pope and the Duke of Milan, to arouse the zeal of the Angevine party, and to overthrow the intrigues of Alphonso, King of Arragon, who still laid claim to the throne of Naples in right of his former election.[*]

Queen Isabella at this time mourned the loss of her respected mother, Margaret of Bavaria, who had died on the 27th of August in the previous year, at Nanci. After the death of Duke Charles, the widowed Margaret had built an hospital at Einville-aux-jurs (which had been part of her dower), and there she had resided, in the constant exercise of charity, distributing alms liberally to the poor, and serving them with her own hands. Thus had she passed her time to the end of her pious life.[†]

The virtues of the noble Isabella appear to have been called forth by adversity, justly entitled "the school of heroes." We have now to follow the consort of René in a career in which she displayed a bold and enterprising spirit, and such superior talents as rendered her justly deserving to be ranked among the number of the most illustrious princesses of the fifteenth century. To great political abilities, Isabella, at the age of five and twenty, united a persuasive eloquence, and an exterior affable and imposing. These, added to her natural vivacity and ardour, rendered her capable of engaging in a great enterprise, of conquering its ob-

---

[*] Dom Calmet. Monfaucon; Bodin; Villeneuve Bargemont; Mezerai, Biographie Universelle; Godard Faultrier.

[†] Margaret of Bavaria was interred in the church of St. George, Nanci, by the side of the Duke of Lorraine, her husband.

stacles, braving its perils, and bringing to her allegiance
all such Neapolitans as were still undecided, or opposed
to her interests.*

This princess had one great incentive to exertion,
one only object in view, in this vast enterprise; but
this was dear to her heart, long and earnestly desired
— the liberation of her husband from captivity —
this it was which nerved her to more than feminine attempts. She despaired of softening the Duke
of Burgundy, and her grief at her husband's misfortunes determined her on sustaining his rights, in the
hope, however remote, that by fulfilling the wishes of
the Provençaux and the Neapolitans, she might hasten
the time, or obtain the means, to set her husband free.
With these views, Isabella committed the care of her
government of Lorraine and of Bar to the Bishops of
Metz and Verdun, and prepared for her expedition,
while a crowd of lords sued for the honour of accompanying her. Two of her children were at this time
absent from her : John, Duke of Calabria,† the eldest,
shared the captivity of his father at Bracon, but whether through the favour or severity of the Duke of Burgundy is not known ; while Yolande, the eldest daughter
of Isabella, had become the pledge of peace with
the Count de Vaudemont, and had gone to reside
with his Countess. Louis, Marquis of Pont-à-Mousson, the second son of Isabella, and Margaret of
Anjou, her youngest daughter, only remained with
her, to share the dangers or participate in the honours
of their mother's enterprise.‡ With these beloved
children, this courageous princess set out for Naples.
In her way thither she first visited Provence, and
was received with transports of joy by the people of

---

* Villeneuve Bargemont.
† This title was inherited by the eldest son of the King of Naples.
‡ Biographie Universelle ; Bodin.

Aix. She there convoked a General Assembly of the States, and took oath always to maintain the privileges of the capital and of all Provence. In return she received the homage and oaths of fidelity of that corporation, and of those of the principal cities of the country. The Provençaux had been recently visited by a pestilence, as well as by a long and disastrous war; but during the short visit of Isabella, her prudence, firmness, and the amenity of her manners so gained upon the hearts of the people, that in spite of their misfortunes they evinced the utmost eagerness to supply their new sovereign with men, money, and vessels.

With these supplies the Queen of Naples (for thus henceforth she must be styled) resolved to embark at Marseilles. Upon entering this town, another cordial welcome not a little affected the princess, to whom these public rejoicings manifested the interest they felt for her cause.*

Isabella's first care had been to make herself acquainted with the parties which divided Naples. Her next precaution, before she set sail for the shores of Italy, was to ascertain the dispositions of her allies, and to this end she dismissed the Archbishop of Aix, Amino Nicolai, on an embassy to the Duke of Milan. The venerable prelate was accompanied by three deputies, who had been devoted to Louis III. These, viz., Vidal de Cabanis, Louis de Bouliers, Viscount de Reillanne, and Charles de Castillon, were to bring back the reply of Philip Visconti to Isabella, who, upon receiving it, was to be prepared to set sail for Naples.

It is interesting to behold how Queen Isabella, even at a time when her mind was occupied by these political measures of so much importance in the commencement of her new career,—it is interesting, we

* Biographie Universelle.

say, to regard the tender wife, ever mindful of the smallest things which could divert the melancholy or alleviate the sufferings of her unfortunate husband. Thus having herself admired the picturesque aspect of the castle of Tarascon, (which had been finished by Louis II. of Anjou in the year 1400,) Isabella employed a skilful painter to take a view of it, and then sent the artist with his work to exhibit it to René, at Bracon.

Symptoms of a violent pestilence at Aix had driven the Queen to take refuge in the village of Tarascon, a place separated from Languedoc by the Rhone, and here the appearance of Isabella and her children excited the most lively joy; indeed, wherever they went, the same welcome was manifested. " The people of Tarascon admired the young Prince and Princess as if they had been two angels who had descended from heaven. In the streets, which were decorated with festoons, garlands, and flowers, there were bonfires blazing, songs and public rejoicings; chants of music in the churches, and everywhere continual benedictions."*

Queen Isabella was too impatient to show herself at Naples to wait very long for the return of her ambassadors, and finding they did not appear, she no longer thought it prudent to delay her departure. She gave orders to William de Baux, Lord of Maillane and St. Vallier, to visit in her absence all the posts and fortifications on the coasts of Provence which might require to be defended against the incursions of the Catalomians. On quitting the Provençaux, Queen Isabella expressed in the most lively manner her grief at parting from them, and at leaving her husband and her son in captivity; indeed, so affecting was her farewell, that her new subjects voted by acclamation a sum of 25,000 florins for the ransom of the Duke of Calabria.†

* Chronique de Lorraine.   † Villeneuve Bargemont.

The fleet of Queen Isabella consisted of five galleys, armed and equipped at Marseilles, which cast anchor in sight of Frejus about the beginning of October. The Queen took on board the Bishop of that city, Jean Bernaud, who was ambassador of Charles VII. at the Council of Basle, and had been distinguished for his virtues and extensive information. While in full sail for the coast of Frejus, the Queen's deputies from Milan, bringing the most satisfactory despatches, disembarked at Marseilles, and set out again immediately for Naples. After a fortunate passage, Isabella appeared at Gaêta, and was received with the respect due to her as sovereign.

Being informed that in this place many of the partisans of Alphonso had taken refuge, and guided by some treacherous or imprudent counsels, the Queen displaced Ottolini Zoppo, whom the Duke of Milan had made Governor of Gaêta. This act of authority, the consequence of which Isabella did not foresee, afterwards proved highly prejudicial to her interests. She quitted Gaêta, however, in full confidence, and proceeded to disembark at Naples.*

* Villeneuve Bargemont.

CHAPTER II.

" Why, then I do but dream on sov'reignty,
" Like one that stands upon a promontory,
" And spies a far-off shore where he would tread,
" Wishing his foot were equal with his eye,
" And chides the sea that sunders him from thence,
" Saying, he'll lade it dry, to have his way."

SHAKESPEARE.—*Henry VI.*

IT was somewhat extraordinary that the two competitors for the crown of Naples, after the death of Queen Joanna, were both prisoners at the same time: René of Anjou being detained in the Tour de Bar by the Duke of Burgundy, and Alphonso of Arragon still a prisoner of Philip Galiezzo, Duke of Milan. When these princes recovered their liberty, the war was resumed with great vigour; meanwhile, it was only through the energy and courage of Isabella of Lorraine that the Angevine cause was sustained in Naples.

The consort of René of Anjou arrived in the Neapolitan capital on the 18th of October, 1435, a few months after the death of Joanna II., and found the people strongly predisposed in her favour, not merely

1435.

from the choice of their late queen, but more especially from their attachment to Louis III., who, by his great condescension, had won all their hearts.

Queen Isabella was conducted, with her son Louis and her daughter Margaret, to the Capuan castle, the ancient residence of the Angevine princes. In their way thither, they traversed the city under a magnificent canopy of velvet, embroidered with gold; and they were met by a deputation, headed by the Count de Nola, of sixteen lords, nominated by the late queen, who all paid their compliments to their new sovereign, and gave her a most gracious reception.

These lords immediately took their oaths of fealty and obedience to the Angevine queen, and their example was followed by a crowd of barons, while deputations of the various classes of the people pressed forward to welcome her, and proclaim her the Queen; in short, the Neapolitans bestowed the crown on Isabella of Lorraine amidst transports of universal joy.

This excellent princess was far from exulting in the high position to which she had, so suddenly, been advanced; she was but too well aware that with the regal diadem come many responsibilities; and to her, the anticipation of trials and difficulties, which to struggle against and overcome would require the utmost resources of her genius.*

The kingdom of Naples, once so flourishing, was at this time without troops, finances, or even an influential chief. The Neapolitan generals had too often changed sides from caprice or interest; and finally had arrogated to themselves independent authority. Therefore had not Queen Isabella possessed a strong mind,

* Villeneuve Bargemont; Denina; Sismondi; l'Abbé Millot; Hallam; Godard Faultrier.

she would have been discouraged by the aspect of
affairs; for she had but a small number of generals of
approved fidelity, and she was, as yet, only acknowledged in the capital; but her firmness, moderation,
goodness, and prudence, soon placed her at the head
of a powerful army, and strengthened the devotedness
of the nobles and old partisans of the House of
Anjou, who already idolized their heroic queen.
Certain it is, that had not fortune, in favouring
Alphonso, created continually unforeseen misfortunes
for René, the conduct of his courageous and enlightened consort would have confirmed for ever the
crown of Naples to the Duke of Anjou and his posterity, and this testimony has been given by all impar-
tial historians.   The result, however, was unfortunate;
and Queen Isabella sustained, with a noble and
undaunted spirit, only an unequal contest with
Alphonso during three years, at the expiration of
which time she was rejoined by the King, her
husband.*

The claims of the House of Anjou, which Isabella
was so nobly representing, were founded on the adoption of Queen Joanna I.; who, to punish the ingratitude of her cousin, Charles III., had disinherited
the branch of Duraz. No descendant of Charles of
Anjou now remained, but the line of Duraz was not
extinct.

Alphonso, King of Arragon, on the contrary, based
his rights upon the choice of Joanna II.; for although
his adoption by this princess had been revoked, it was
pretended that it was a reciprocal treaty, and that to
be annulled the consent of both parties was required.
The Spanish king had besides a claim to the Neapolitan throne, anterior to that of the Angevine princes,
transmitted by Constance, the daughter of Manfred, to

* Villeneuve Bargemont.

the line of Arragon; and in Sicily, Alphonso already reigned as the nearest heir of the Normans by whom this kingdom was founded.*

With no less right than either of these competitors, Eugène IV. had claimed the crown of this kingdom, which had been enfeoffed to the three Houses of Hauteville, Hohenstauffen, and Anjou; conditionally, that it should return to the Church on the extinction of the legitimate line in these Houses. This happened at the time of Queen Joanna's death, when Eugène IV. immediately announced his rights, but he found it impossible to make this important conquest. Being driven, at length, from the Papal dominions, Eugène resided at Florence, and, while there, he interdicted the two rivals fighting, at the same time forbidding the people to obey them; and he nominated as Governor, in his own name, Giovanni Witteleschi, Patriarch of Alexandria, who, no less a soldier than an ecclesiastic, was able to maintain with the sword the rights of the Pope, his master.

It had been the design of Alphonso to anticipate the arrival of the French in Italy, and he speedily organized a large body of Spanish soldiers from Sicily, with which he entered the kingdom of Naples, and was there joined by Giovanni Marzano, Duke of Suessa, and other nobles, with their followers. With these he besieged Gaêta, one of the richest and finest ports on the Mediterranean. The inhabitants had, upon the death of Queen Joanna, invited the Genoese to keep a garrison there, until the legitimate heir to the Neapolitan throne should be acknowledged; and François Spinola had been appointed Commander by

* The illegitimacy of Manfred, however, rendered these claims invalid, as they also became by the number of females who had passed from House to House, as well as by a prescription of an hundred and seventy-five years.—*Sismondi ; Denina.*

the Genoese, with Ottolini Zoppo to support him, who was secretary to the Duke of Milan. Thus was the town ably defended, the garrison established, being composed of 300 Genoese soldiers, besides some Milanese troops, who repulsed Alphonso most effectually. This prince also found, that although he was acknowledged as sovereign by many of the Neapolitans, a strong party still remained in favour of King René, which induced the Spanish prince to seek the assistance of Pope Eugène. This pontiff constantly refused him, saying, " that if his claims were as incontestable as he represented, he could commence by laying down his arms, and ceasing to make war."

This answer irritated Alphonso, who immediately sought to show an ardent zeal for the Council of Basle, and wrote to the Pope to engage him to obey its decrees. He then advanced to Rome, and had nearly made himself master of the city, when Witelleschi appeared, and defeated his project.[*]

The engagement which decided, for the time being, this struggle for power, and in which Alphonso was taken prisoner, occurred on the 5th of August, 1435. In the following October, Queen Isabella arrived at Naples, to the support of the Angevine cause. Most effectually could Pope Eugène have advanced the interests of this Queen, but all his endeavours were rendered useless by the peculiar dangers of his own position, being threatened by the thunders of the Council of Basle, and his own authority contested. Thus, finding his tiara insecure, his conduct became variable, and he finally consulted only his own personal interests.

The removal of the Governor of Gaêta by Queen Isabella, served as an excuse for the Arragonese

1435. Sismondi.

* Eccles. Hist.; Sismondi; Villeneuve Bargemont.

faction to raise discontent, suspicion, and division; and after the departure of the Queen, the agents of Alphonso became audacious, and invited Don Pedro, the brother of Alphonso, to land with his troops and take possession of Gaêta, which they did without opposition, and made known their success to Alphonso.*

This prince, meanwhile, had been seeking to prejudice the Duke of Milan, whose prisoner he was, against Isabella. Visconti was a weak, though an affable and generous prince, and when Alphonso had discovered his character, he set to work to aggravate the affront which had been offered by the Queen in the removal of the Governor of Gaêta. When possessed of this place, Alphonso became more bold in his arguments against the Angevines, and exerted himself to prove to the Duke of Milan, that his real interests forbade him to support René. "If he is once acknowledged sovereign of the kingdom, you will soon see," said he, "this prince leagued against you with the ambitious Charles VII. The Alps will be an insufficient barrier to protect you. All Italy will become the object of his efforts, and the Milanese will, doubtless, be the first invaded. You are not ignorant that the Court of France has already discussed whether, even during your lifetime, she should not assert the rights on this principality, transmitted by Valentine of Milan. Remember that the ties of blood are but a vain phantom, that vanishes before interest or ambition; and forget not, that the Duke Galeas, your father (whose sister had espoused the brother of Charles VI.), feared nothing so much as the French. Does Philip then believe he has less cause to dread them?" This representation, made by a prince so eloquent as Alphonso, made so great an

* Sismondi ; Villeneuve Bargemont.

impression on Philip Visconti, that, adopting without reserve the views of his captive, he gave him his liberty without ransom at the end of the month of October, and previous to their separation, a treaty of alliance was signed between them. The Duke of Milan did not even consult the Genoese on this step, so much was he fascinated by his royal prisoner.*

Alphonso of Arragon, having thus obtained his freedom, hastily quitted Milan. After a short stay in Spain, he went to Gaêta, and arrived there on the 2nd of February, 1436. His presence revived the zeal of his partisans, and attracted to his cause many who had hitherto been undecided. Deputies came also from several neighbouring cities to him, and hoisted his standard; in short, from this time he had every reason to hope for success.

1436.
Sismondi.

One error had, however, been committed by Alphonso in concluding his treaty with Philip Visconti, viz., in considering Eugène IV. as one of their enemies. This was impolitic,—and the Pontiff, already disposed to favour René, now decided on recognising him as King of Naples, and sent to Isabella, who needed troops, the same Witteleschi who had been employed previously to take possession of the kingdom in the name of the Church. In April of this year, the Patriarch of Alexandria arrived in the Neapolitan territories, with 4,000 foot soldiers and 5,000 horse, to render assistance to the Angevine queen. They succeeded in taking by assault several fortresses, and encountered Jean des Ursins, Prince of Tarentum, the Arragonese chief, whom they routed, and thus suddenly arrested the efforts of Alphonso.†

This salutary diversion enabled Isabella to drive

---

* Villeneuve Bargemont; Sismondi.
† Sismondi; Villeneuve Bargemont.

away from their strongholds some seditious captains, who, until that time, had contrived to maintain themselves there. The Queen also dismissed the brave Michael Attendolo, with the young prince Louis, her son, to subdue Calabria. Thus, by her activity and wisdom, Queen Isabella speedily prevailed on the people to announce themselves in her favour, and she received the homage of the principal towns in the kingdom. These first successes, and the alliance with Eugène IV.—which Isabella sought to confirm — were celebrated at Naples by demonstrations of the most lively joy. Brilliant tournaments were, for several days, held in honour of the Queen, and jousts, balls, and all the varied amusements customary in that age.* Isabella showed but little satisfaction at these multiplied fêtes, for her mind was pre-occupied by the condition of René, and of Lorraine.

While striving with all her means, as well as with all her heart, for the prompt deliverance of her husband, she supplicated Eugène IV., whose benevolence was never failing, to interest himself in procuring the freedom of René immediately, seeing how much needed as his presence as chief, in order to preserve the union and discipline of the army engaged in his cause. This tender solicitude prevailed with the sovereign pontiff, who attempted to move the generosity of the Duke of Burgundy by representing the extraordinary example of disinterestedness of the Duke of Milan, and by his earnest prayers that the Duke of Anjou might be promptly restored to his family and subjects. This wish had, indeed, become general throughout France as well as Italy, and its expression became more energetic.

In the preceding year, while Queen Isabella was traversing Provence, a meeting had taken place at

---

* Villeneuve Bargemont ; Bodin ; Godard Faultrier.

Nanci, on the 19th of September, at which were present the Bishops of Metz and Verdun, and the ancient knights; and these engaged, at all sacrifices, to obtain the release of René, and to support him in the conquest of his kingdom. Again, in November of that year, the nobles of Barrois and Lorraine assembled, naving taken the resolution to employ their persons and property for the deliverance of their duke.

These affecting details reached even the prison of the unfortunate René, who then thought of making an appeal to the devotedness and generosity of all his subjects. This excited a fresh burst of affection and loyalty, and in reply to his noble confidence, each one taxed himself to the utmost, being willing to contribute, according to his ability, for the ransom of his sovereign. The Regency received from all parts similar offerings and proposals; and one knight in particular, whose name ought to have been recorded in history, not content with expending a sum of 18,000 saluts d'or,* engaged, without reserve, all the fiefs and domains he possessed.

These unquestionable testimonies of affection were made known to the Duke of Burgundy at the same time as the supplications of the Pope, but that prince had become still more inexorable towards René. He even wished to conceal from his captive the constant proofs of affection and loyalty so eagerly evinced for him by his friends and subjects. It appears that all communications, from his people or from Queen Isabella, to the unhappy prisoner were intercepted by the Duke of Burgundy; so that, the more earnest the desire manifested to break his fetters, the closer were they actually drawn, and the more remote appeared the day of his liberation.†

---

* The salut valued 25 sols.—Villeneuve Bargemont.
† Villeneuve Bargemont.

From this time René was subjected to a discipline more rigid than before, kept in severe restraint, and no longer permitted the indulgence of communicating with any of his family. It was during this solitary confinement in the castle of Bracon, where René, yet in the flower of his age, was languishing in hopeless captivity, being secluded from intercourse with mankind, and receiving no intelligence of those he loved and no succours from his numerous allies, that "believing himself forgotten by everybody," says Duhaillan, and seeking to express a mute but eloquent grief, he painted, very appropriately, round the walls of the chamber where he was immured, and on the glasses, *des oublies d'or*, or wafers of gold, as emblematical of the isolation into which he was plunged. These "*oublies** or cornets (little horns) of gold," were painted by him with great taste, and disposed at unequal spaces, signifying, by this delicate invention, that his people had consigned him to oblivion. These paintings are still to be seen in the chateau, and are proofs of the skill of René, and of his exquisite taste in the art.† In addition to these, as we are told, René painted several other subjects on the thick walls of his prison, and scarcely knowing how to dissipate the *ennui* which consumed him, he traced there also a great number of sentences, or moral reflections suggested to him by his melancholy situation.‡

---

* " On appelle *oublie* une espèce de pâtisserie légère d'une forme spéciale. Dans la phrase sur le roi René, cette expression forme un jeu de mots. Le bon roi donnait au mot *oublie* le sens du latin *oblivium*. L'étymologie véritable d'*oublie* ne se prête guères, il est vrai, à la pensée du bon roi : oublie (petit gâteau) vient de *oblitus*, offert ; mais afin de donner un corps à l'expression de sa pensée, René d'Anjou a joué sur les deux sens si différens des mots *oublie*, gâteau ; et *oubli*, oblivium. Ce jeu de mots est intraduisible en Anglais. Le calembourg était fort en honneur du temps de René, et les blasons en sont pleins."

† Chronique de Provence ; Biographie Universelle ; Dom Calmet ; Nostradamus.

‡ Villeneuve Bargemont.

At length the period arrived when this prince was
destined to receive the reward of his fortitude and
resignation.   The Duke of Burgundy, moved by so
many petitions, appeared to be appeased, and on the
1436.
Villeneuve
Bargemont. 11th of April, 1436, sent his Chancellor, Rolin, and
Jean de Fribourg, Governor of Burgundy, to acquaint
his captive with the conditions of his release.   These
demands of Philip were so exorbitant, that, when
submitted to the Council of Lorraine, they decreed it
right to reject them.   René, being informed of their
resolve, wrote to the Regency that they had merited
his esteem, in refusing to sanction a dishonourable
treaty; that he would never have signed it himself; and
that he would prefer to remain all his life a prisoner,
rather than purchase his liberty on conditions so bur-
densome to his people.   "If I die," he added, "in this
cruel captivity, he who detains me gains by it only the
shame of having thus reated a prince who would not
otherwise be his prisoner.   For the rest I place my
confidence in heaven, and in my just rights."

After so many disappointments, René happily found
that virtue never loses its empire over a generous heart.
The noble spirit with which he had protested against
an act which he thought injurious to his States, dis-
armed Philip, and perhaps made more impression on
his mind than the persuasions of the Pope, of the
Council of Basle, of Charles VII., and of all the princes
of the blood, who had all now united to make a last
attempt for the liberation of the Angevine prince.   To
effect their object, these combined powers, in concur-
rence with the Council of Lorraine, carried forward
their negotiations with the Duke of Burgundy, and
their efforts were ultimately crowned with success;
the treaty being ratified and the royal prisoner set free.

There is much obscurity and contradiction in the
writings of this period, some authors asserting that

René quitted Bracon for the Tour de Bar, and that
he was afterwards conducted to Lille, where Philip
held his court, and where he received the Chancellor,
the Duke of Bourbon, and others, and finally concluded
the treaty. Other historians have, with more truth,
fixed these meetings at Dijon, where Philip was residing on the 4th of November, 1436, and from whence
he repaired to Arras; leaving René, guarded by thirty
gens d'armes, at the château de Talent.

While at Dijon the Duke of Burgundy had shown
great favour towards his young cousin; he had
evinced great joy at again beholding him, had often
admitted him to his table with the Chancellor, Rolin,
and in their discourses the principal points of his release were determined. At these interviews Rolin
conceived so favourable an opinion of René, that upon
his master's departure he offered him his support.

The treaty commenced at Dijon in November, 1436,
was terminated at Brussels on the 28th of January,
1437. The ransom of René of Anjou was fixed at
200,000 golden florins (upwards of 83,000*l.*) and
the cession of several places; amongst these were
the manors of Cassell and of La Motte-aux-Bois,
which had been formerly added to the Duchy of Bar
as the dower of a princess of Flanders. René engaged
to pay 100,000 crowns in the month of May, 1437,
and the same sum at Dijon the following year; and
the remaining 200,000 whenever he might be in complete possession of the kingdom of Sicily. For security René gave the seal of twenty lords of Lorraine
and of Bar, ten of Anjou and Maine, and ten of Provence, and all these lords agreed to become prisoners
in the forts of Besançon, Dijon, or Salins, should René
forfeit his engagement.

There were other articles of the treaty, which they
urged should be mollified, but it was in vain. Philip

further insisted—First, that René should observe a
neutrality between the French, the Burgundians, and
the English.　Secondly, that in order to establish
peace between these powers, René's second daughter,
Margaret of Anjou, should espouse King Henry VI.
of England, without prejudice to the marriage before
agreed upon between her sister Yolande and Ferri of
Vaudemont.*　Thirdly, the Duke of Burgundy required, that, should the sons of René die without male
issue, the inheritance of Lorraine should devolve on
Yolande, or her heirs, and that this princess should also
receive, at her nuptials, a dower, consisting of a large
sum of money.

Such were the terms upon which René could alone
hope to obtain his freedom ; but while the arbiters
of the two parties were discussing the amendments in
this treaty, at Brussels, the captive prince was transferred anew to the fort Bracon, his son, the Duke of
Calabria, being a prisoner, on parole, in the Tour de Bar.

The modifications which René hoped to obtain were
prevented by the artifice of the Count de Vaudemont,
who contrived, by means of one of his friends, to
counteract the generous efforts of the Chancellor,
Rolin, and to neutralize his exertions in favour of the
Angevine prince.†　Thus René was compelled to subscribe to these hard conditions.　He made concessions
of every kind, and after promising a large sum of
money, the cession of several cities, the mortgage of
the Duchy of Bar, and even of his own person—after
consenting to the marriage of his daughter Yolande,
then nine years of age, to Ferri, the eldest son of his
enemy the Count de Vaudemont, by which union Lorraine would be restored to the male heir of that family—

* The Pope had granted a dispensation of kindred, for this marriage, on
the 3rd of April, 1435.
† Villeneuve Bargemont.

after all these engagements, the unfortunate René was liberated.*

The news which René had received from Italy is said to have hastened his termination of this treaty, and after having given his full consent to the conditions, the Duke of Burgundy at first only set him free on his parole, on the 11th of February, 1436; but, if he profited by this authority for some months, René must still have been in apprehension of captivity, since we find that the Duke of Bourbon, the Marshal de la Fayette, Christopher of Harcourt, the Constable of Richemont, and the Count de Vendôme, arrived at Rheims, on the 18th of October, to unite with Renaud of Chartres to obtain the release of René from the fort Bracon. They came to Salins early in November, and on the 7th of that month the Chancellor, Rolin, in their presence, drew up and caused to be signed the act for René's liberation. Finally, this prince departed from his prison of Bracon on the 25th of November, 1436. It being impossible that the enormous sum demanded by Philip could be raised immediately, a number of lords of Lorraine, each having four knights, again offered themselves as hostages, to be confined in one of the towers of Besançon, for one month beyond the expiration of the term granted him.

The position of René was so sensibly felt, that, notwithstanding the embarrassed state of his finances, he received from King Charles VII., 20,000 florins; from the Bishop of Verdun, 8,000; from the Prince of Orange, 15,000; and a number of persons of less note also contributed to the first payment of his ransom.

After a rigorous captivity of five years' duration, the joy of René on quitting the mountains of Jura may

1436.
Godard
Faultrier.

* Biographie Universelle; Monstrelet; Bodin; Sismondi; Monfaucon; Barante; Villeneuve Bargemont; Baudier; Godard Faultrier; Mezerai.

well be imagined; yet even this was not altogether unalloyed, for he had left his son, the young Duke of Calabria, still detained as a hostage in the Tour de Bar. René was accompanied at his departure by the Chancellor, Rolin, as far as Pont-à-Mousson, the princes of France having returned to Charles VII. They afterwards all repaired to the Duke of Burgundy, at Lille, on the 25th of December, in order to ratify this important treaty. René also went to Lille, after a short stay at Pont-à-Mousson, and was present, as well as the Count of Vaudemont, at the Burgundian court upon this occasion. René happily profited by this meeting; for Philip, on the 1st of January, receiving the compliments of the season from René, generously cancelled part of his debt, as a gift, amounting to 200,000 saluts d'or.

Philip then conducted René and the French princes from Lille to the city of Arras, into which he made his entry with the utmost display of pomp and magnificence, surrounded by these princes, and the chief of the nobility of Burgundy, and several of the clergy, one of whom, the Bishop of Liege, had two hundred horses in his suite. Fêtes and rejoicings followed, commemorative of the peace just concluded; and while thus engaged, Philip sought, by various means, to make René forget the melancholy days of his imprisonment; and he gave him a new mark of his generosity, calculated to affect him much. He offered him for his son, the young Duke of Calabria, the hand of Mary of Bourbon, his niece, the daughter of Charles, Duke of Bourbon, a proposal joyfully accepted by René, after which Philip further remitted him 100,000 saluts d'or.*

The first use which René made of his freedom was

---

* Monfaucon; Villeneuve Bargemont.

to go and return thanks to the States of Bar and Lorraine, for their exertions to procure his release. The chief nobility of these duchies met him at Pont-à-Mousson, where he arrived on the 28th of February, 1437. He consulted with them on the necessities of his States, on the subject of his ransom, and other matters. During the course of these deliberations René went to Dijon, and brought back from thence his son, the Duke of Calabria. To those individuals whose devotedness and fidelity had been so eminently displayed towards him, René next proceeded to express, not only in words, but by various acts still in his power, the gratitude of his heart. Amongst these were Erard de Châtelet, Henri de Bar, the Sire de Rodemark, and others, to whom he made gifts of money or property; and to the people of Salins, who had shown so much interest for him, he granted the privilege of passing through his States without being subject to any of the tolls which were established there. The noble liberality of René extended even to his enemies. To the Damoisel de Commercy, (who, ever faithless to his engagements, had been taken with arms in his hands by the Regency, in August, 1436,) this prince gave liberty without ransom. In addition to these benefits, René made provision for the poor, and sought to render stable and uniform the administration of Lorraine. Nor was this prince wanting in his just tribute of gratitude to Charles VII. Leaving all the magnificent fêtes, prepared in Lorraine and at Metz, to celebrate his return, René quitted Nanci, attended by his chief knights, and repaired to Tours, where the King of France was then residing.[*]

Soon afterwards René proceeded to Angers. Here

1437.

---

[*] Villeneuve Bargemont; Biographie Universelle; Godard Faultrier.

he again received fresh testimonies of the affection and zeal of his people. It was during his stay in this province that René concluded the marriage of his son John, the Duke of Calabria, with Mary, the daughter of the Duke of Bourbon. This union was celebrated in April, 1437, at the city of Angers.* The Duke of Calabria, at this time but twelve years of age, had already shown much aptitude for study, and it was easy to foresee that he would one day be distinguished for his talents and virtues. His education had been first superintended by Henri de Ville, but this prelate died while his pupil was detained in Burgundy. Those whom René selected to succeed him in this office were Jean Mauget, Nicholas of Haraucourt, Jean de Laland, and others, all of them distinguished for their talents and virtues, and especially Palamede de Forbin, who had been attached to the young Duke of Calabria even from his infancy. To the castle of Tucé, near Saumur, René next repaired, and there he passed a few days with his mother, Queen Yolande, now advanced in years. He then visited the other towns of Anjou, and received the oaths of fidelity of his people; after which he departed for Provence, being unable to yield to the wishes of the Angevins for his prolonged stay in their province, the state of his affairs at Naples requiring his presence. †

After the first successes of Witteleschi, Queen Isabella had flattered herself that she had found a loyal and courageous defender; but no sooner had this general become initiated in the secret of the state, than he abandoned her cause, and by this perfidy the Queen lost those advantages she had with such great difficulty obtained. It was only in Naples that Isabella could hope for support, and she therefore redoubled her in-

* Some writers date this event in 1434.
† Monfaucon ; Monstrelet ; Villeneuve Bargemont ; Godard Faultrier.

stances for the presence and assistance of the King, her husband.*

René had resolved to go to Provence without again visiting Lorraine, where he had made provision for the care of his States. He had committed the government into the hands of the Bishops of Metz and Verdun, and Erard du Châtelet; but it would seem that this gave offence to Antoine de Vaudemont, who doubtless had expected to see his son, Ferri, appointed to the Regency during the absence of his new relative, and that he should himself have unlimited power over this country. His former resentment revived at the want of confidence, as he called it, on the part of René; and instead of promoting peace, he sought only to excite civil dissensions. Such was the condition of affairs when René of Anjou was preparing for his expedition to the kingdom of Naples.

In Provence, René experienced an enthusiastic reception. He entered Arles on the 7th of December, and reached the city of Aix on the 13th of the same month. He soon gained the affections of his new subjects, and they evinced their interest and zeal by supplies of men and money. When he had, with paternal care, provided for the necessities of this country by wise laws and regulations, he went to Marseilles. At this place he received the congratulations of the ambassadors of Pope Eugène, and of the Doge of Genoa, upon his release from captivity; and during his stay at this port, the Genoese sent him a fleet, with which he sailed to Genoa. His arrival was celebrated by a number of fêtes, and René, while thus detained, formed strong ties of friendship with Thomas di Fregosa, one of the most distinguished doges of that republic. At length, with the additional reinforcements given to him at this

1437.
Villeneuve
Bargemont;
Godard
Faultrier.

* Villeneuve Bargemont ; Godard Faultrier.

prejudicial to René's cause, the people interpreting that he had but little hope of preserving the kingdom. The populace too often exhibit a natural disposition to regard things in the worst point of view, in short, to look to the dark side; wherefore reputation, in warlike matters, contributes infinitely to success.

René had so secured to himself the love of the people of Naples, that they were willing to undergo many privations and dangers for his sake, especially when they beheld him so willingly participate in their sufferings.

The hopes of the besieged rested on Count Sforza, who had been earnestly solicited by René to come to his aid.   This general was still at the head of a flourishing army, and he set out in January, 1442, to defend or reconquer the fiefs he had inherited in the kingdom of Naples.   In this expedition, however, he was so unsuccessful that before the expiration of the year, he no longer possessed a single fief of all those which his father had acquired with so much labour and such numerous victories.   In the details of this war it would appear that the conduct of the Pope, which was in contempt of a sworn peace, occasioned the defeat of Sforza, and thus deprived René of his last hope of the conquest of the kingdom of Naples.* Alphonso had obtained possession of Capria, Gaëta, Aversa, and Acerre.   A fresh treason soon gave him the command of the capital.

After he had provided for the safety of his family, the courage of René seemed to be aroused. He gave his orders with energy, and going with activity from place to place in the town, he divided with his people the small store of provisions which remained to them. These were, however, insufficient for their necessities, and hunger pressed hard upon them; at last, one

1442.

* Daniel ; Mariana.

poor widow was refused bread. In her despair, this woman ran to the conduit-maker, Annello, who was a partisan of Alphonso, and told him of a subterranean passage, by which the Spanish troops could enter the town. This news was conveyed by Annello to Alphonso, who despatched some of his generals with 250 soldiers, under the guidance of Annello. These Arragonese invested the capital by night. Their guide enabled them to introduce themselves with lighted torches, at midnight, through the same aqueduct which, nine centuries before, had enabled Belisarius to obtain possession of the city. When René was informed that his enemies had penetrated into the town, he ran in great haste to the combat, but the darkness increased the confusion. The walls were scaled, and a desperate fight ensued. René fought bravely, for he still had hopes; but the gates were forced in, and the Arragonese columns, one after another, rushed into the city. Thus was Naples taken by Alphonso, while the Angevine prince, in the midst of a thousand dangers, had only time to escape, sword in hand and with his horse covered with blood and foam, to the Château-Neuf. This was his only retreat on the fatal night of the 3rd of June, 1442.*

1442.
Godard
Faultrier;
Mariana;
Daniel.

After this catastrophe, the faithful Genoese offered their vessels to René, who, having no longer any resource, availed himself of this means to make a hasty retreat into France.

Two days after his defeat, René embarked. He sailed first to Porto Pisano, and from thence went to Florence to complain to Pope Eugène IV. of his want of faith. This pontiff, to console him, gave him the investiture of the kingdom which he had just been compelled to abandon. In the vain contest for this kingdom René had experienced the treacherous and

* Bodin; Godard Faultrier; Mariana; Daniel.

selfish desertion of his numerous allies. After the capture of Aversa all the very powerful and wealthy family of Caldora went over to Alphonso, and the army of Sforza, sent to his aid by the Duke of Milan, was beaten near Troya, in Apulia. Thus Alphonso gained the ascendancy, and René was compelled to yield the field to his adversary, who founded the line of Arragonese kings in Naples upon claims more splendid than just.*

About the same period that the Spanish monarch was engaged in the capture of Naples, a league had been formed by Pope Eugène, the Venetians, Florentines, and Genoese, to drive out the Arragonese from all Italy; but this enterprise failed, owing to the want of unity amongst their forces; and after the departure of René, the conqueror became possessed of the whole of the kingdom. Alphonso made a triumphal entry into Naples; and being earnestly desirous of a reconciliation with Pope Eugène, he prevailed on him to acknowledge him the following year as king, and also his son Ferdinand as his successor.†

From Florence René repaired to Genoa, where he experienced a friendly reception from the Doge, Fregosa. He then proceeded to Marseilles, and after an absence of four years and a half, arrived there at the end of the year 1442.‡

1442.

The general testimony of historians is, that René of Anjou, although so unfortunate in the issue of his enterprise in Italy, "had perfectly fulfilled all the duties of a valiant soldier and a skilful general." At this period even he felt that he could not, and ought not, to renounce all hope; and he, therefore, sent into

* Bodin; Mariana; Hallam; Godard Faultrier; Daniel; Sismondi; Eccles. Hist.
† Mariana; l'Abbé Millot.
‡ Daniel; Godard Faultrier: Eccles. Hist.

Italy, Vidal de Cabanis and Charles de Chatillon, in order that they should send him such intelligence as might be favourable to his future interests.

Many troubles had arisen in Lorraine during René's expedition into Italy; the prince did not, therefore, prolong his stay in Provence. Being, however, desirous of visiting the principal cities, he went to Tarascon at the commencement of February, 1443. At this place René received William Haraucourt, Bishop of Verdun, Pierre de Beaufremont, Seigneur Charny, and Antoine de Gaudei, the secretary of the Duke of Burgundy, who had been sent by this prince to negotiate the marriage of his nephew, Charles, Count of Nevers, with the second daughter of René, Margaret of Anjou.

1443.
Villeneuve
Bargemont;
Don
Calmet.

This princess had nearly attained her fourteenth year, and already gave indications of those personal charms and mental qualifications for which she was afterwards so much distinguished; and these, doubtless, had great influence in fixing the choice of her new suitor. The Count of Nevers had been affianced to Jane of Bar, daughter of Robert of Bar, Count of Marche, and afterwards had been on the point of marrying the Duchess of Austria, but finally he decided in favour of Margaret of Anjou.

Both René and his consort, Queen Isabella (who had arrived at Tarascon), eagerly accepted these proposals, and the contract of marriage was signed on the 4th of February, 1443.

René agreed to give with his daughter the sum of 50,000 livres as her dowry, and the Duke of Burgundy guaranteed to settle upon her a jointure of 40,000 livres; but René, on his side, wished that in consideration of this alliance the Duke would forego the 80,600 ecus d'or, which he owed him, and for which he held, as security, the cities of Neufchâteau, Preny, and Longuy. The Duke, at length, consented to remit that sum, and the interests, in consideration of a reasonable indemnity, and upon this, René, as an equivalent, gave up Clermont, Varennes, and Vienne, in Argonne. There was one clause, however, inserted, which gave infinite displeasure to the Count de Vaudemont. It declared that the children of Margaret should be heirs of Sicily, Provence, and Bar, to the exclusion of the children of Yolande, her eldest sister, who was affianced to Ferri de Vaudemont, the son of Antoine; yet with a reservation, that, if Yolande should marry a second time, the male children of that alliance should exclude the descendants of Margaret from the paternal succession, in reservation of the duchy of Bar, to which they were legally entitled. King René could not possibly have marked in a more decisive manner the displeasure he felt against the House of Vaudemont. This arrangement was bitterly complained of by both father and son, and the former carried his complaints to King Charles, the arbiter and guarantee of the late treaty which had fixed the pretensions of the two houses. Charles VII. then demanded reparation of René, and even threatened to take up arms should he oppose the treaty of 1441. Antoine still claimed René as his prisoner, and King Charles referred the affair to the Parliament, the proper judge of the Duke of Burgundy; but he reserved to himself that which related to the said treaty. Thus was the marriage of the Count of Nevers deferred, and ultimately its accomplishment prevented, for while these questions were agitated, another, and a more irresistible offer was made for the hand of the Princess Margaret.*

1443.
Villeneuve
Bargemont.

The rest of this year, 1443, was passed by René either at Aix or Marseilles, where he devoted himself to the administration, and especially to the most

* Dom Calmet ; Villeneuve Bargemont.

effectual means to prevent the landing of the Arragonese forces. While at Marseilles, René received
intelligence of the death of his mother, Yolande of
Arragon, Queen Dowager of Sicily. She died on the
14th of December, 1443, at the Castle of Saumur,* and
was interred in the Cathedral of St. Maurice, at Angers.
The life of this princess had been distinguished by a
multitude of acts of piety and benevolence, and the
Provençaux, who had been acquainted with her
virtues and estimable qualities, sincerely united in the
just regrets of their sovereign.†

At the time of the departure of René for Naples, the
Count de Vaudemont had felt offended, for two reasons :
first, because he did not form one of the Regency
Council, and next, at the reports circulated of the King's
repugnance to grant his daughter Yolande to his son,
Ferri. Being apprehensive lest this princess should be
taken away from him, or, perhaps, embittered against
René's ministers, he collected his troops, encouraged the
incursions of the rebels, and even took great numbers
of them into pay, and enticed to his party Robert de
Sarrebruche, who was ever ready to break his oaths.‡
Thus hostilities commenced, and Antoine and the
Regency were alternately conquerors at this period,
which was signalized by pillage, conflagration, and
murderous combats. Charles VII. at length resolved
to put an end to these excesses, and summoned the
parties to appear before him ; at first, they apparently
submitted to the conditions this monarch imposed, but
the war again broke out with increased fury.

At this period Louis of Anjou, having been appointed   1443,
Lieutenant-General, entered Lorraine. He found the

---

* The castle of Saumur had been granted to Queen Yolande, as part of
her dowry, in order that she might pass there the remainder of her days.
† Bodin ; Godard Faultrier.
‡ Villeneuve Bargemont.

country devastated by bloodshed and civil contention, and he was compelled at once to take decisive measures. Although only twelve years of age, he defended with vigour the town of Bar, caused the siege to be raised, and compelled Robert de Sarrebruche to capitulate in the citadel of Commercy; but while the laurels of victory were thus gathering on his youthful brow, death' suddenly deprived the country of this hero of noble promise.

1444.   Louis, Marquis of Pont-à-Mousson, expired, after a short illness, in 1444,* and had not the happiness of again beholding his father, who was preparing to come to Lorraine, to endeavour by his presence to terminate the troubles of his people. René, however, subsequently abandoned this intention, either through the grief he felt on his son's death, or from his anxiety to defend his province of Anjou from the attacks of the English, who had been making great progress in Maine.

Louis de Beauvau having been dismissed with unlimited powers into Lorraine, René set out for Poitiers, to rejoin the King of France, while Queen Isabella departed for Nanci.

King Charles VII. and René afterwards proceeded together to the city of Tours, where they arrived at the same time as Charles of Orleans, who had just reappeared at the French court, after many years of captivity in England. It was here that this prince, so renowned for his mental accomplishments and poetic talents, for the first time beheld René, and they contracted an intimate friendship, the constancy of which shed many charms on their subsequent lives. René also found himself in the presence of all his old companions in arms, and he again resigned himself to his taste for

---

* Louis died, it is believed, in January, 1444, but the precise date is not recorded. He was interred in the church of St. Antoine, Pont-à-Mousson.

fêtes, which had only been interrupted, or laid aside, whilst he engaged in his warlike expeditions. The whole court rejoiced at his coming, for he was known to be a prince who loved pleasure, and brought in his train men of wit and amusement. *

The presence of René at Tours was of great service to King Charles, who, upon the occasion of the treaty of peace with England, about to be concluded, specially charged this prince with the care of directing this important affair.

René first obtained a truce for eight months, and he then discussed with consummate skill their reciprocal interests, thus striking at the root of the negotiation, and by his firmness and clear perception, contrived to terminate the disagreements which might have occasioned a new war. Many were the conferences held with a view to establish a permanent peace, but so many difficulties arose that it was found to be impracticable, and only a truce was agreed upon, the terms of which were dated the 21st of May, 1444.

1444.
Monstrelet.

During the course of this negotiation, in the month of April, a proposal was made on the part of England, which apparently altered the position of René, and ought to have consoled him for his late misfortunes. This was a treaty of marriage, proposed by the Duke of Suffolk, between his master, King Henry VI., and Margaret of Anjou, the second daughter of King René.†

The satisfaction of René may readily be imagined, for such a measure could not have been anticipated, since the King of England was, at this time, considered as all but betrothed to the daughter of the Count of Armagnac, and this new offer seemed also to remove every prospect of a fresh dissension between the two

* Godard Faultrier ; Villeneuve Bargemont.
† Villeneuve Bargemont ; Godard Faultrier ; Monstrelet.

kingdoms, and placed the daughter of René in a rank the most flattering to the ambition of a father.

The only dowry exacted by King Henry was the cession of the rights, transmitted to René by Yolande of Arragon, on the kingdom of Minorca. He renounced the rest of her succession, and he restored the town of Le Mans to Charles of Anjou, and to René all his possessions which had been taken from him by the English.*

By this marriage, which was willingly agreed to by all parties, and soon after concluded, the House of Anjou-Plantagenet was, after the lapse of several centuries, united, on the throne of England, to the Second House of Anjou-Sicily.†

* Villeneuve Bargemont.   † Godard Faultrier.

CHAPTER III.

KING HENRY.—" Was ever king that joy'd an earthly throne
    " And could command no more content than I !
    " No sooner was I crept out of my cradle,
    " But I was made king, at nine months old ;
    " Was ever subject long'd to be a king,
    " As I do long and wish to be a subject ! "
               SHAKESPEARE.—*Henry VI.*

King Henry V.—His death and will—The characters of Bedford and Gloucester — Quarrels of Gloucester and Beaufort — Losses in France —
Death of the Duke of Bedford—Contests in the Cabinet—The influence
of Cardinal Beaufort—Education and character of Henry VI.

PREVIOUS to the attempt to delineate the character,
and narrate the eventful career of Margaret of
Anjou, it will be advisable to take a slight survey of
the English court; that stage whereon she was destined to act so conspicuous a part, and where her
conduct, it has been said, involved the happiness of
almost all her adherents, leading to contentions, civil
warfare, and to the misery of herself and family. That
these unhappy results emanated from the misrule of
the Lancastrian queen may, however, be disproved by
patient inquiry into the facts of history, even amidst
the confusion of the records of turbulent times, rendered almost contradictory through the party spirit of
historians.

It will be found, that, far from being the cause of so
much misery, Margaret was herself misguided and
unhappy; the victim of the intrigues of designing
men, already at variance in their country, to which she
came as a stranger, yet where her high talents, and the
noble qualities of her mind and heart, alone enabled

her, subsequently, to maintain her position as sovereign.
Neither did she succumb to her adverse fortunes, until
she had proved, to the utmost, her heroism and devotion to her husband and his country.

1422.
Eccles.
Hist.

Henry V., the conqueror of Agincourt and one of
the greatest heroes of his age, held, for a brief period,
the sceptre of England with an able and vigorous
hand; for he had gained renown by other than military
skill, and had evinced the greatest endowments and
good qualities.   In the prime of life, however, and
in the midst of his victories in France, he was seized
with sudden illness, which caused his death; and he
left his crown to an infant son, nine months old.

It was the destiny of this little prince, Henry VI.,
to lose all the foreign conquests of his warlike sire,
who, as if apprehending misfortunes, had taken many
wise precautions for the futurity of his infant son.

On his death-bed Henry V. conjured his nobility
assembled around him to remain united, in order to
preserve the interests of his son, whose education he
intrusted to the care of the Earl of Warwick, and
appointed his brother, the Duke of Bedford, Regent of
France, and his youngest brother, the Duke of Gloucester, Regent of England, during his son's minority.
He recommended them also to cultivate the friendship of the Duke of Burgundy, and to offer him the
Regency of France.   His advice also was, that they
should retain their prisoners of war until his son
should be able to judge of their disposal himself, and
on no account should they make peace with the
French, unless by the surrender of Normandy they
could obtain an equivalent for their losses.*   Such
were the commands of the dying monarch, who was
so much beloved, respected, and admired.   How prudent were these injunctions, but how soon disregarded

---

* Holinshed; Baker; Sandford; Howel; Rymer's Fœdera.

by his relatives and subjects! Private passions and
individual prejudices too often arise to overthrow the
wisest plans of human foresight.

Shortly after the remains of Henry V. were consigned, with the utmost pomp, to their last earthly
resting-place, a division took place in the English
Cabinet. Objections were raised to the Regency of the
Duke of Gloucester, whose uncle, Beaufort, Bishop of
Winchester, directing a search into precedents, declared the claims of Gloucester were unconstitutional.
The Council, however, wished to conciliate the Duke,
who strongly urged his right from his relationship
to the crown, and his brother's will appointing him to
that office, more especially from the absence of the
Duke of Bedford in France, but in vain; he was made
" Protector " of England in the absence of Bedford,
and thus advanced to a dignity which commanded
respect but conferred no real authority.

1422.
Lingard;
Hume.

All real power was vested in the Council of Regency,
at the head of which was the Bishop of Winchester.
This ambitious and grasping prelate appears to have
commenced from this time an incessant rivalry, and a
great contest for power, with his nephew, the Duke of
Gloucester, who naturally felt depreciated and continued to struggle against his adversary. Thus, during
the infancy of Henry VI., the influence of these two
powerful individuals alternately swayed the Council of
England, rendering her measures ineffective or abortive,
and eventually, most disastrous.

The nation had appeared to acquiesce in the arrangement for the Protectorate. Gloucester, however, from
this period ceased to regard his uncle as a friendly
kinsman, but rather as one who consulted his own
private interests at the expense of his relatives and his
country.

In France, the Duke of Bedford, who was an accomplished and able prince, sustained the interests of his nephew, prosecuting the war with vigour, supported by many skilful generals. Numerous towns and castles were taken, and finally, a decisive victory gained at Verneuil.[*]

These rapid successes of the English soon reduced King Charles VII., (who had just acceded to the throne,) to the most desperate condition. He could not maintain his troops, or the splendours of his court, and at last found himself unable to procure even the necessaries of life for himself and the few who remained attached to his person.

Suddenly a new phase was presented in the drama, and strange and unexpected events occurred to revive the spirits of Charles. These were the mission of Joan of Arc, and the recall of the Duke of Bedford to England.[†]

It was to interpose and accommodate in the dissensions of Gloucester with his uncle Beaufort, that the Regent was compelled to abandon the scene of action in France, where he had been so prosperous.

The Duke of Bedford was no less prudent in council than valiant in the field. Endowed with superior genius, and the perfect master of his own passions, he found little difficulty in adjusting the differences of his kinsmen. His brother, Humphrey, Duke of Gloucester, was possessed of eminent virtues and talents, to which he added such extensive information in science and literature as would have placed him on an equality with the Duke of Bedford, had not his inordinate ambition and violent passions caused him to commit errors which gave his enemies the

---

[*] Holinshed; Sandford; Baker; Rymer's Fœdera; Howel; Barante.

[†] Holinshed; Rymer's Fœdera; Barante; Mezerai; Anquetil; Milles's Catalogue.

advantage. He was also censured for his haughty demeanour, yet he was the universal favourite of the people, and when deprived of power in the Cabinet he took part with the ancient nobility, in whose neglect and discontent he, in some degree, shared. The members of the Council were ever watchful to prevent this duke's assumption of authority, and as they knew he could not displace them, they were not afraid of offending him. In time, a confederacy was formed against him, headed by the Bishop of Winchester.

The exertions of Gloucester to reform the Church, and thus to humble his opponents, involved him in many quarrels with them, in which they gained the advantage through the hasty temper of the Duke.

The Duke of Gloucester had also imprudently married the Countess of Hainault, and in the attempt to secure her inheritance he had employed some troops sent to the Regent for the war in France; he had, likewise, involved himself in a personal quarrel with the Duke of Burgundy, whose alliance and friendship were much required in the prosecution of the French war. In all these matters, in which the interests and welfare of the country were involved, the Duke of Bedford was compelled to mediate. At first his remonstrances, and those of the Council, were ineffectual, so incensed was Gloucester by his dispute with his uncle, the Bishop, which had indeed risen to a great and dangerous height.[*]

1425.
Holinshed.

Early in the contest for supremacy between Gloucester and Winchester, the people of London had taken part with the former, who was their favourite, but this interference had been resented by the latter, who caused many persons to be accused of treason

* Rapin ; Carte ; Baker ; Holinshed ; Sharon Turner ; Fabian ; Barante ; Life of Chicheley ; Pol. Vergil ; Ecoles. Hist.

and thrown into prison. This gave rise to murmurs and complaints against the arbitrary measures of the Bishop, who, to suppress the spirit of rebellion, garrisoned the Tower, and ordered Sir Richard Wideville " to admit no one more powerful than himself."

This step, which exhibited the great power of the clergy at this time, excited the highest displeasure in the Duke of Gloucester, who, on returning from abroad to take up his residence in the Tower, was refused admittance. His first impulse was to resent this affront by closing the city gates against the Bishop of Winchester, and he next applied to the Lord Mayor for an escort of five hundred men, to conduct him in safety to the King at Eltham. The Bishop, finding the city gates closed, attempted to force his entrance, and then barricaded the road with his numerous retinue, to prevent the egress of the Duke. In this hostile position, the effusion of blood seemed inevitable; but a temporary pacification was, with great difficulty, effected, through the mediation of the Archbishop of Canterbury and the Duke of Coimbra, a prince of Portugal, who were obliged to ride eight times in one day between the offended parties. The complaints of the two parties were finally referred to the arbitration of the Duke of Bedford.

To such a height had the differences of these distinguished adversaries attained, that the general peace and welfare of the capital was in imminent danger; the shops were closed, all traffic obstructed, and the citizens were obliged to keep watch and ward to prevent the evil consequences which the hostile appearance of the partisans in this quarrel hourly threatened.

The Regent was thus compelled, by a hasty summons from the Bishop of Winchester, to abandon his important conquests in France, in order to adjust these petty dissensions at home, at a time when, after the victory of Verneuil, the forces of King Charles might have been effectually crushed.*

The Duke of Bedford could not approve of the hasty and passionate conduct of his brother; neither was he satisfied with the interference of the citizens of London, towards whom he evinced his displeasure. He gave orders for a meeting of peers at St. Alban's, and also for a Parliament at Leicester, whither the members were commanded to repair unarmed; but such was the animosity of the two parties that there was great difficulty in enforcing these orders.

The Duke of Gloucester came forward in Parliament with a personal accusation against his opponent, comprised in six articles, four of which related to personal grievances; and in one of these the Bishop was accused of attempting the life of the Duke on his way from London, by placing armed men on the road to assault him. Of the other two accusations, the first charged that prelate with having garrisoned the Tower, with intent to get the young King into his power; in the last it was intimated that the late King had accused the Bishop of an attempt on his life, and of having instigated him to dethrone the King, his father. Of these last charges the Duke of Bedford readily acquitted his uncle; for the favour with which Beaufort had always been distinguished by Henry V. was sufficient testimony of his innocence. Finally, the eight lords, who had been chosen as arbitrators on this occasion, succeeded in persuading the Bishop of Winchester to make an apology to the Duke, and thus effected a reconciliation.

The differences also of the lords who had taken part with these powerful adversaries were, in their turn, adjusted, and peace and unanimity restored. This

* Sandford; Barante; Rymer's Fœdera; Baker; Anquetil.

CHAPTER IV.

" Speak ! hast thou seen her? will she be my Queen ?
" Quick, tell me ev'ry circumstance, each word,
" Each look, each gesture ; didst thou mark them, Suffolk ? "
                              SHAKESPEARE.—*Henry VI.*

" Did not the Heavens her coming in withstand,
" As though affrighted when she came to land ?
" The earth did quake her coming to abide,
" The goodly Thames did twice keep back his tide ;
" Paul's shook with tempests, and that mounting spire,
" With light'ning sent from heaven was set on fire ;
" Our stately buildings to the ground were blown.
" Her pride by these prodigious signs was shown
" More fearful visions on the English earth,
" Than ever were at any death, or birth."—DRAYTON.

Propositions of marriage for King Henry—He is affianced to the daughter of the Earl of Armagnac—This earl is taken prisoner—Negotiation for peace with France, and a proposal for the hand of Margaret of Anjou—The Earl of Suffolk, his family, and pretensions—His embassy to Tours—Policy of the English ministers—Margaret of Anjou and her accomplishments—A truce signed—The marriage proposed and determined upon—No dower required—Suffolk returns to England, and obtains the sanction of Parliament—Suffolk's eulogium of Margaret of Anjou—Nuptials by proxy—Margaret comes to England—Her illness—The marriage—Progress to London—The coronation—The King confides in the Queen, who unites in the party of Cardinal Beaufort.

IT was easy to perceive that the lady, whosoever she might be, who should become Queen of England, would decide the balance of power between the contending parties in the Cabinet, and consequently each became desirous of selecting their king's consort from a family likely to be favourable to his own peculiar interests.

The first matrimonial alliance proposed, was by

the Duke of Gloucester. In the terms of the treaty for peace with France, in 1439, instructions were given to propose the marriage of King Henry VI. with one of the daughters of Charles VII. This conference, however, was broken up, and this lady became afterwards the wife of the son of the Duke of Burgundy.

The continuance of the wars between the two kingdoms at length excited the commiseration of all Christendom. The Pope had exhorted the two monarchs to put an end to the effusion of blood, and several conferences had taken place between the Cardinal of Winchester and the Duchess of Burgundy, the result of which was the appointment of a meeting to treat about a peace, the Dukes of Brittany and Orleans being the mediators.*

The Duke of Gloucester next proposed the union of his young monarch with the daughter of the Earl of Armagnac, and finding that the rich provinces of Gas-cony and Auvergne would be this lady's portion, he thought the marriage would prove acceptable to the people. It was also expected that this alliance would serve as a protection to Guienne. The Count of Armagnac, who had taken possession of the inheritance of the Countess of Cominges for which the King of France was also a competitor, justly fearing the power of that monarch, had earnestly sought to ally himself with England, in order to maintain himself in his new acquisitions. He proffered the hand of his daughter to King Henry VI., with a handsome dower, adding to a large sum of money the full possession of all his towns and castles in the province of Aquitaine, which had formerly belonged to England.†

---

* Rymer's Fœdera ; Rapin ; Sharon Turner.

† Baker ; Sandford ; Hall ; Beckington ; Rymer's Fœdera ; Rapin ; Monstrelet ; Barante ; Hume ; Henry ; Sharon Turner ; Lingard.

The ambassadors from the Count of Armagnac were graciously received by King Henry, who, on their return, dismissed Sir Edward Hall, Sir Robert Roos and Thomas de Beckington,* the King's secretary, to complete the contract.

This marriage had been warmly advocated by the Duke of Gloucester, but it was no less dreaded by the Cardinal and his party, who liked not to receive a princess so much in favour with their opponent; and it appears not improbable that they gave some hints respecting the intended match to King Charles, as the event, which so speedily followed, seemed to show. In the month of May, 1442, the ambassadors of Henry VI. set out with his instructions for the conclusion of this marriage. Early in the following month, the King of France, who was much displeased at the combination forming against him, despatched the Dauphin with a powerful army to invade Guienne, and this enterprise was so successful, that within eight days the whole country had rebelled against King Henry. Treachery as well as force seems to have been employed to undermine the influence of England, a report having been spread that no relief was to be expected from this country. The appearance of the ambassadors, and the perusal of King Henry's letter restored the confidence of the people, succours being promised them, which they earnestly desired, but the extraordinary negligence of the English in the fulfilment of these promises can with difficulty be explained. The ambassadors appealed strongly to the King; they wrote also to Lord Cromwell, the treasurer, and their messengers were accompanied by the Archbishop of Bourdeaux, who was deputed by the inhabitants to represent their situation. Despatches were again sent, on the 17th of

---

* Thomas Beckington, of Beckington, Somersetshire, Bishop of Bath and Wells. A great benefactor to the Church of Wells.

'October, to the King, the Duke of Gloucester, and the Cardinal of Winchester. The letter to His Majesty described the state of Guienne, the successes of King Charles, and the non-arrival of succours from England. The ambassadors assured the King that if only a few men had been sent, the French monarch would in all probability have been made prisoner, and the country might have been preserved.

It was the general opinion that this marriage was strenuously opposed by the Earl of Suffolk; and one of the subsequent charges against this nobleman was the breach of this contract. He was charged with having acquainted the King of France with the proposed marriage the moment it was agitated, and with having thus caused the invasion of Guienne, in the month of June.* From this period, until the close of that year, the rapid successes of the French, and the surprising negligence of the English in not sending succours to that province, caused a change in the sentiments of the Count of Armagnac; and if the conduct of the Count, which had excited the suspicions of the English ambassadors, did not finally dispose King Henry to break off this alliance, the result was inevitable, from the seizure of the dominions and person of the Count, who, with his two daughters and youngest son, were taken prisoners by King Charles.

Thus was the marriage of the King of England deferred, or rather set aside; for this nation did not scruple to put an affront on a prince who was unfortunate and unable to revenge himself; and while the princes of Christendom united their endeavours to establish peace between the two kingdoms, another union, more agreeable to King Henry though not

* Monstrelet, on Hall's authority, says that this was done by the Cardinal of Winchester, from hatred of Gloucester.

more fortunate for the English nation, was decided
upon.[*]

The Cardinal of Winchester, on his part, had also
selected a bride for his sovereign. His choice had not
been determined with less political foresight than that
of his rival; and great secrecy appears to have been
observed before this important decision was divulged
to the public. It was two years after the negotiation
with the Count of Armagnác, that the Cardinal, (ever
anxious to procure peace, while in his eagerness to
frustrate the measures of his opponents he seemed
even to disregard the public good,) dismissed an embassy to negotiate with France, and to adjust the
terms of a peace, to which the late severe losses had
inclined the people to agree.[†]

1444.
Holinshed,

After the death of the Duke of Bedford, the Cardinal
had introduced into the Council William de la Pole,
Earl of Suffolk, who had so far succeeded in ingratiating
himself into the royal favour that the King became
attached to him, and blindly followed his suggestions.
From this time it would appear that the Cardinal made
this earl instrumental in his own ambitious projects,
employing him to gain the King's consent to the new
alliance he proposed, and to receive all his instructions
for the completion of this marriage.

The Earl of Suffolk did not inherit the great talents
which had distinguished some of his ancestors. His
grandfather, Michael de la Pole, was born of mean
parents, but his eminent abilities enabled him speedily
to obtain great wealth, and also the notice of
Edward III., who took him into the number of his
privy council. He became Chancellor of England, and

* Baker ; Hall ; Holinshed ; Lond. Chron.; Sandford ; Carte ; Fabian ;
Monstrelet ; Beckington's Journal ; Villaret ; Mezerai ; Rapin ; Sharo n
Turner ; Barante.

† Carte ; Rapin ; Lingard ; Barante ; Villaret.

in 1385, Richard II. created him Earl of Suffolk; but with the decline of the authority of this monarch, the influence of Michael de la Pole decreased also, and he died an exile from his native land. His son, Michael, lost his life at the siege of Harfleur, and the earldom was bestowed by Henry V. on the third son of this nobleman; but he was slain at the battle of Agincourt, in 1415. Thus, his brother William succeeded to the titles and estates, to which he added the ample dower of his wife, Alice, the granddaughter of Geoffrey Chaucer, the poet.[*] The Earl, although not endowed with more than ordinary abilities, was courageous and ambitious. He expected to advance himself and his party to the highest estimation with his sovereign, but this attempt was not unaccompanied with danger; supported, however, by the favour of the Cardinal, he was well received at court, and successful in obtaining the young King's sanction for him to procure for his consort the lovely princess Margaret, the daughter of René of Anjou.[†]

The learning and surpassing charms of the poor but unrivalled daughter of King René had been reported to the young sovereign of England, "who was anxious to enter into the endearing restraints of the most holy Sacrament of marriage;" and he resolved, if possible, to obtain her hand. For this purpose a secret negotiation with her father was commenced; and the King obtained a portrait of the youthful Margaret, which made him more than ever desirous to conclude the contract.

King Henry, though feeble and destitute of those

---

[*] Alice Chaucer had been already twice married; having first espoused Sir John Philips, Knt. Her second husband was Thos. Montecute, Earl of Salisbury, who, at his death, left her great riches.—*Stow; Milles's Catalogue; Lyson's Mag. Brit.; Allen's York; Monstrelet; Biograph. Brittanica.*

[†] Rapin; Barante.

commanding talents which shone conspicuously in
his father and his grandfather, was still peculiarly
susceptible of the influence of learning and great
talents. It was for these—possessed by Margaret of
Anjou in so eminent a degree—that she was selected
by Cardinal Beaufort for the consort of his sovereign.
He had the discernment, doubtless, to perceive how
singularly fitted was this princess to guide the well-
meaning, but weak and irresolute Henry, who seemed
formed by nature as well as by education, to be
governed implicitly.

When on the point of engaging in this embassy, the
Earl of Suffolk showed a little reluctance, whether
feigned or real, and professed himself unequal to the
undertaking. He was not ignorant of the risk he
incurred; and however ambitious of advancing himself
with his sovereign and the nation, he confessed his
incapacity, and presenting a petition to the King,
modestly begged to be released from this undertaking;
or, if denied this favour, entreating to be secured from
any after penalty, should he fail in the object of his
embassy. He also showed great caution in receiving
his instructions. It is probable that he might justly
fear the resentment of the Duke of Gloucester, who
would be sure to oppose this measure; or, it might be,
that he was conscious that he should incur the penalty
of an Act passed in the reign of Henry V. against any
one who should conclude peace with the King of
France without the consent of the three estates in both
realms.

To remove these objections an instrument was signed
by the King and his Parliament, which granted pardon
beforehand to the Earl (who in this instrument is called
" grand seneschal of his household, and ambassador ")
for any error of judgment which he might commit in
his double capacity, provided he arranged the nego-

tiation for the peace and the marriage to the utmost of his abilities.* Thus provided, the Earl of Suffolk set out, about the beginning of Lent, 1444, for the city of Tours, where this important negotiation was commenced. He was accompanied by Dr. Adam Moulins, Keeper of the King's privy seal and Dean of Salisbury, Sir Robert Roos † (the former colleague of Beckington), Richard Andrews ‡ (Doctor of Laws), the King's secretary, Sir Thomas Hoo, Knight, and John Wenlock, Esqr..§

1444.
Holinshed;
Rymer's
Fœdera;
Sismondi;
Speed;
Rapin;
Mezerai;
AnquetiL

These distinguished individuals were met in the city of Tours, where King Charles held his court, by many foreign ambassadors and persons of illustrious birth, amongst whom the Angevine princes held a distinguished place. Thither repaired, on the part of King Charles, the Duke of Orleans, Louis of Bourbon, the Earl of Vendôme, Grand Master of the King's Household, Pierre de Brezé (steward of Poitou), and Bertram de Beauvau, Lord of Persigné, who had all been appointed by this monarch to adjust the terms of the peace with England. The ambassadors from Spain, Denmark, and Hungary appeared as mediators between the two kings.

It was a large assembly, and great sums were expended, and there was much display in apparel at these

* See Appendix, p. 415.

† It is probable that it was for Sir Robert's services on this occasion the offices of Chamberlain and Customer of the town of Berwick were granted to him for life, by Henry VI., in 1445.

‡ Richard Andrews was a Fellow of New College, and Warden of All Souls' College. This last he resigned in 1442 for a more conspicuous station. Besides ecclesiastical preferments of great value, he filled the honourable office of Secretary to King Henry, and took, in that capacity, a part in the treaties of this reign. He was especially distinguished by his attendance on Margaret of Anjou in France, and on her progress to England for her coronation.—*Life of Chicheley.*

§ Stow; Carte; Speed; Holinshed; Rymer's Fœdera; Paston Letters; Allen's York; Eccles. Hist.; Beckington's Journal; Life of Chicheley; Daniel; Barante; Monstrelet; Baudier; Godfrey's Charles VII.; Rapin; Hume; Lingard; Sharon Turner; Davies's Chron.

was dismissed to France to supply his place, and while serving as Lieutenant-general, died in that country. His son Henry evinced great enterprise and courage, and when scarcely nineteen years of age, offered his services for the defence of Normandy, which so pleased the King that he created him Premier Earl of England, and as a mark of distinction, permitted him, and his heirs afterwards, to wear a gold coronet upon his head in his own presence, as well as elsewhere. He also gave him a seat in Parliament. He granted him also the reversion, after the death of the Duke of Gloucester, of the islands of Guernsey, Jersey, Sark, Herm, and Alderney, for the yearly rent of a rose, to be paid at the feast of St. John the Baptist. Besides these, he conferred upon his favourite the government of Calais, the castle of Bristol, and many other grants. At last, as the utmost extent of his prerogative, he made him King of the Isle of Wight. This Duke, who, from his extreme youth was called in the public documents of that period, "the Child Warwick," received so many favours from King Henry, that it excited the envy of the Duke of Buckingham, and as much was to be apprehended at this time from the feuds of the nobility, in order to prevent any ill consequences from the differences of these two noblemen, it was declared by Act of Parliament, " for the appeasing of the strife betwixt them for pre-eminence, that from the 2nd of December next ensuing, they should take precedence of each other alternately, one that year and the other the next, as long as they should live together." Further, it was enacted that the survivor should, during his lifetime, have the precedence of the other's heir. By the death of Warwick in the following year, the main point was determined, and the Duke of Buckingham then obtained a grant immediately to himself and his heirs, "above all dukes whatsoever, whether of England or of France, excepting those of the blood royal." This unpardonable pride in Buckingham was united to a baser avarice, and from an old record we learn of his imprisonment of two gentlemen, whom he thus obliged to sign away their right to an inheritance, which the Duke divided with a younger brother of the family.*

Henry VI., whose attachment to the Duke of Warwick, his great favourite, had induced him to create him "King of the Isle of Wight,"† in the year 1445, crowned him with his own hands. This was the highest honour he could bestow to express his affection for this young nobleman, and to show his respect for his father's memory, and remembrance of his services. It proved the last favour the Duke could receive, since he was taken off in the flower of youth, on the 11th of June, 1445, at twenty-two years of age; and was buried at Tewkesbury.‡

How much contrasted were the characters of the Dukes of Warwick and Buckingham, and how deeply the former must have been regretted by the youthful monarch.

King Henry, after having conferred the distinctions on his chief nobility, dismissed the Marquis of Suffolk to the Continent to espouse, and bring over, the Princess Margaret. In this embassy the Marquis was

---

* Dugdale ; Biograph. Britannica.

† This island was possessed by Humphrey, Duke of Gloucester, who held it until his death, when it fell into the King's hands.

‡ The Duke left an only daughter, but two years old, who became Countess of Warwick. This young lady was afterwards committed to the care of Queen Margaret, consort of Henry VI., and then intrusted to William de la Pole, Marquis of Suffolk, at whose manor of Newelme, in Oxfordshire, she died on the 3rd of January, 1449, having not quite attained her sixth year. She was buried in the Abbey of Reading, near the remains of her great grandmother, Constance Lady Despenser, daughter of Edmund Langley, Duke of York. After her death, Ann, the sister of the late Duke, became his sole heir, and her husband, Richard Neville, Earl of Salisbury, took, in her right, the title of Earl of Warwick.—*Biograph. Brit.; Stow; Dugdale's Antiq.; Milles's Catalogue; Barante; Baker; Masters's Corp. Chr., Cam.; Selden; Monstrelet; Paston Letters.*

princess had exhibited so much skill and prudence in
the peace of Arras, that she was ever after intrusted
with the affairs of Burgundy, and engaged in all
matters of treaty. She appeared brilliantly attended
by the chief nobles and ladies of Burgundy; and, as
the representative of her house, she submitted to the
King the grievances of the Duke, her husband.

Her success was not, however, proportionate to her
exertions, and on this occasion she was compelled to
make some concessions. A definitive treaty was concluded between René of Anjou and this princess, the
King of France being arbiter of the differences of the
Dukes of Anjou and Burgundy; and thus were terminated the discussions, that had been so incessantly
revived, on the subject of the entire payment of the
ransom of that prince. The Duke of Burgundy was
obliged to restore to René the two cities of Neu-
château in Lorraine, and Clermont in Argonne, of
which he had obtained possession, and to acquit him
of the sum he had engaged to pay for his ransom,
conditionally, that he should settle on the Duke and
his heirs the town and castlewick of Cassel in Flanders.* René had received these by gift from his late
uncle, the Cardinal of Bar.

The news of the truce and of the alliance with
England was received universally with the utmost
joy. The oppressed inhabitants of certain portions of
France and Normandy were even so sanguine as to
imagine that their misfortunes were at an end; while
those who had been confined for so long a time within
the fortified towns rejoiced in again returning to the
country to cultivate their neglected lands, and the
tradesmen to resume their long forsaken business.
The intercourse between the two nations was again
conducted on more advantageous terms to both par-

* Barante; Biog. Universelle; Monstrelet; Daniel; Godfrey; Monfaucon.

ties, and their commodities were exchanged to their mutual satisfaction.

The festivities attendant on the departure of the young queen to her husband further strengthened and confirmed the kindly feeling which had been revived between the two countries ; and when Queen Margaret herself appeared with her splendid cavalcade of English nobility on their way to England, led on by the Marquis of Suffolk, they were welcomed with heart-felt rejoicings and demonstrations of universal joy.

King René and Queen Isabella accompanied their daughter as far as Bar-le-Duc, where they bade her farewell, with " floods of tears" and many prayers to God for her welfare. Her brother, the Duke of Calabria, and the Duke of Alençon, then attended her as far as St. Denis. How tenderly must Margaret have been beloved, and how worthy was she of such love, that so much grief and regret was evinced on her leaving an impoverished father to share in all the honours of a throne!

The young queen proceeded to the land of her husband, conducted by the Marquis of Suffolk, with suitable magnificence, first to Paris, in which city she was well received, and thence she was afterwards conveyed through the province of Normandy.*

Many and curious are the details of the expenses of the Lady Queen Margaret's tedious progress. These interesting and amusing accounts, by John Breknoke and John Everdon, of the outlay for the Queen's escort and attendants—" the chief nobles, barons, ladies, damsels, knights, scuttifs, and other officers, besides servants, sailors, running footmen, horses, &c."—are well and minutely described; and besides, we gather from these statements some facts of this journey which unavoidably fall in with these honest

* Godfrey's Hist. of France.

previously to her appearance in public before her new subjects. Accordingly "John Pole, a valet, was sent from Southampton to London with three horses, by command of the Marquis of Suffolk, to fetch Margaret Chamberlayne, tyre maker, to be conducted into the presence of our lady, the Queen, touching various business of the said lady, the Queen, and for going and returning, the said Margaret Chamberlayne was paid there by gift of the Queen, on the 15th of April, 20s."

From the mention made by the royal bridegroom in a letter written in his usual quaint style to his Chancellor, we discover that the malady which had so very unexpectedly detained his beloved consort was no other than the small-pox. This alarming disease caused great anxiety to the King, who, after having so long waited for his expected bride, was not a little heartstricken at this sudden affliction on the beloved object of his affections. Leaving the Queen to the care of her attendants and others in the hospital, "God's House," for a time, "the King stayed at Southwyke, passing his careful moments, as well as he could, amidst the charming pastures and forests of Southbere and Porchester." We are told that King Henry could not keep the feast of St. George at Windsor Castle, on account of "this sickness of his most dear and best beloved wife, the Queen." How long this anxious period lasted we are not exactly informed; but when the Queen recovered, happily without any detriment to her uncommon beauty, she rejoined the King at Southwyke, where he had waited, still watching with deep interest until she became convalescent. Finding then that she was still unable to bear the fatigues of travelling, he caused his marriage to be performed, with all the necessary ceremony.°

° In the year 1133 King Henry I. had founded in the church of St.

On Thursday, the 22nd of April, 1445, Kemp, Archbishop of York, united the royal pair in the Priory Church of Southwyke, near Porchester, in Hampshire.[°] The venerable Bishop of Salisbury, Master Aiscough, gave them the blessing, saying, "This marriage, the people believe, will be pleasing "to God and to the realm, because that peace and "abundant crops came to us with it. And I pray "the Heavenly King that he will so protect them with "his own right hand that their love may never be dis- "solved, and that they may receive such blessing as "the Psalmist speaks of; 'Thy wife shall be as a "fruitful vine by the sides of thy house: thy children "like olive plants round about thy table. Behold, "that thus shall the man be blessed that feareth the "Lord.'" (*Psal.* cxxviii.)

The learned prelate made a discourse at some length on the dignity of marriage, and in praise of that sacrament. In conclusion, he said, "I desire that my lord "may abide in that sacred alliance on which he has "now entered, and may in faith possess these good "things of marriage which have been assigned to it by "St. Augustine—'*faith*, that he may not break his con- "jugal vow—*offspring*, which may both be lovingly "brought up and religiously educated—and a *sacra- "mental vow*, that the wedlock may never be dissolved: "for these are the great things of marriage.' Oh! "may this wedding be, as was in old time the wedding "of Tobias and Sarah, of which it is said, that 'they "celebrated their marriage feast in the fear of the

1445.
Holinshed;
Biondi;
Sandford;
Carte;
Stow;
Henry;
Villaret.

Mary's at Porchester a priory of canons of the order of St. Austin, which seems to have been not long after removed to Southwyke, where it continued until the dissolution.—*Dugdale; Speed; Tanner's Notitie Monastica.*

[°] Holinshed; Hall; Fabian; Carte; Howell; Eng. Chron., Camd. Soc.; Baker; Speed; Sandford; Toplis; Pol. Vergil; Stow; Rymer's Fœdera; Beckington; Kennet; Sharon Turner; Henry; Warner's Hampshire.

"Lord.' (*Tobias* ix.) 'Oh! may it be the cause of
"peace among the people, even as peace was given
"unto the Jews on the marriage of Esther.' (*Esther*
"ix. 18.) 'Oh! may it be so high and holy an
"ordering, that, at the last, those words may be
"worthily verified in the case of the married pair;
"' Blessed are they which are called unto the marriage
"supper of the Lamb.'" (*Rev.* xix.)°

When the marriage ceremony was concluded, Queen
Margaret received as a bridal gift, from one of her
attendants, a lion,—a very unsuitable present for a
lady's pet; but it was graciously received, and conveyed, at the King's expense, to the Tower of London,†
Where this noble *compagnon de voyage* came from we
are not informed; but his keep, and travelling expenses,
with a separate carriage, were included in the outlay of
the King's servants, the sum of 3*l.* 6*s.* 4*d.* being paid
to John Fouke of Peryn, galleyman, who took charge
of the lion.

This strange gift would seem to have been made
from one acquainted with the courage and fortitude
of the Queen, and given in compliment to those high
personal qualities which became afterwards so prominent in the eventful and stormy circumstances of her
reign. Had the King himself been able to wield the
sceptre, how different would have been Queen Margaret's course; but the whole career of Henry VI.
showed him to be a good and pious man, but totally
unequal to rule a divided realm like that of England.
He loved the Queen with an ardour to which his
heart and pure mind required him to set no bounds;
and they might have been happy in their marriage had
not the personal friends of the Queen been unfortu-

* Capgrave's Illust. Henries; English Chron. Camd. Soc.; Davies's
Chron.

† Robert Mansfield was the keeper of the menagerie in this reign, and
had a good salary for his office.

nately regarded as the enemies of the people. The King, and also the Queen, saw the evils of war and the desirableness of peace, and they laboured incessantly to this end; but the people were not cured of their *penchant* for war, and preferred the uncertain spoils of victory to the more certain gains of trade and industry.

As soon as the Queen could travel, (about the beginning of May,) she commenced her progress to the capital, which she entered on the 18th of May, 1445. In her journey to the metropolis she received every possible demonstration of respect and admiration, and even of enthusiasm.

1445.
Holinshed;
Rapin.

All ranks of her new subjects eagerly came forward to welcome the arrival of a princess, of whose personal and mental accomplishments they had heard so much; and her youth, beauty, and elegance converted even her enemies into admirers, making them forget their prejudices against her, on account of her relationship to the royal family of France, and the poverty of her father which had obliged King Henry to receive his bride without a dower. All those who had most opposed this marriage now became eager to evince their respect to their charming sovereign. The Duke of Gloucester, especially, hastened at this time to prove to his new mistress that principle alone had actuated him in his late opposition, and he sought, by his marked attentions to the Queen, to show her that he also shared in the general admiration of her personal charms. At the head of five hundred of his retainers, handsomely arrayed in his livery and badge, he met her at Blackheath, and conducted her to his palace, named "Placentia," at Greenwich, where she was invited to refresh herself; the Duke taking this opportunity to ingratiate himself into her favour.[*]

* Holinshed; Hall; Fabian; Carte; Stow; London Chron.; Kennet; Speed; Henry; Lingard; Baudier; Sharon Turner.

The chief nobility rivalled each other in the splendour of their equipages and their tokens of respect, bringing their retainers and servants in liveries, and exhibiting all the pomp and splendour possible. They wore in their caps and bonnets, in compliment to the Queen, the humble Marguerite, or daisy, which seemed even more surprisingly to have started into notice and esteem than the beautiful queen herself;[*] and, as the poet writes,—

     "Of either sex, who doth not now delight
     "To wear the daisy for Queen Marguerite!"[†]

This little flower, chosen by the Queen, was, indeed, a true emblem of her conjugal fidelity; for amidst the misfortunes and rude tempests of her after life, her constancy to her husband, and his fortunes, remained unshaken.[‡]

The authorities and livery companies of the city also came out to meet Queen Margaret, as well as many of inferior rank. These were dressed in blue gowns and red hoods, with sleeves embroidered, each of them with some device, expressive of their art or trade, by which they might be known. By this equestrian procession the new Queen and her escort were conducted through Southwark to the city, and lodged in the bishop's palace, near St. Paul's.[§]

Upon her entrance into the capital, the Queen was greeted by many splendid shows and goodly pageants, agreeable to the taste of the age. Southwark and the city of London were "beautified," as Stow relates, "with pageants of divers histories, and other shows of welcome; marvellous, costly, and sumptuous." There were represented gods and goddesses,

---

[*] This little flower also shone conspicuous upon the royal plate.
[†] Drayton.   [‡] Holinshed; Stow.
[§] Holinshed; Stow; Fabian; Carte; London Chron.; Baudier; Kennet; Chron. of London Bridge.

angels, and ancient worthies. The cardinal virtues, personified, were seen issuing forth from artificial woods and temples, constructed of pasteboard and other flimsy materials, and were made to recite the praises of Queen Margaret, while they scattered flowers and garlands at her feet. On her approach to London Bridge she was greeted by the most splendid of the famous pageants prepared for her by her admiring subjects. The first pageant, erected at the foot of London Bridge, was an allegorical representation of Peace and Plenty. The motto was,—

"Ingredimini et replete terram."
"Enter ye, and replenish the earth."

Then were the following lines addressed to the Queen:—

" Most Christian Princesse, by influence of grace,
" Daughter of Jerusalem, our plesaunce
" And joie, welcome as ever Princess was,
" With hert entire, and hool affiaunce ;
" Cawser of welthe, joye, and abundaunce,
" Youre citee, your people, your subjects all,
" With hert, with worde, with dede, your highness to avaunce,
" Welcome! welcome! welcome! unto you call."

These verses were from the pen of Lydgate; he was the universal muse of his age, and so easy of access, that he was consulted on all occasions. He was the poet of the world, as well as of the monastery to which he belonged. His talents were resorted to, with equal success, whether a mask for the King was intended, or a May-game for the aldermen and sheriffs. Lydgate was also the champion of the fair sex, and wrote a panegyric, not on their personal charms or accomplishments, but giving a recital of their inflexible chastity and religious fortitude, by which he ennobled their character, and gave a better demonstration of his own respect and esteem.

Upon the bridge another pageant was placed. It represented Noah's ark, bearing the words,

" Jam non ultra irascar super terram ; "
" Henceforth there shall no more be a curse upon the earth." *

The verses recited before it were :—

" So trusteth your people, with assuraunce,
" Throwghe your grace, and high benignitie,
" 'Twixt the realmes two, England and France,
" Pees shall approche, rest and unity ;
" Mars set asyde with all his cruelty,
" Which too longe hathe trowbled the realmes twayne,
" Bydynge your comforte, in this adversité,
" Most Christian Princesse, our Lady Soverayne.

" Right as whilom, by God's myght and grace,
" Noe this arke dyd forge and ordayne,
" Wherin he and his might escape, and passe
" The flood of vengeaunce caused by trespasse ;
" Conveyed about as God list him to gyne, [gye]
" By meane of mercy found a restinge place
" After the flud upon this Armonie.

" Unto the Dove that browght the braunche of peas,
" Resemblinge your simpleness, columbyne,
" Token and sygne that the flood shuld cesse,
" Conduct by grace and power devyne ;
" Source of comfort 'gynneth faire to shine
" By your presence, whereto we synge and seyne
" Welcome of joye right extendet lyne,
" Moste Christian Princesse, our Lady Soverayne."

At Leadenhall was " Madam Grace, Chancellor de Dieu," and again verses were recited. At St. Margaret's Inn, Cornhill, other verses were given. At the Great Conduit, in Cheapside, another recitation was made, and " the five wise and five foolish virgins " were represented. Lastly, at the Cross in the Cheape, " the heavenly Jerusalem ;" and at Paul's Gate, " the funeral, resurrection, and judgment ;" both these last having, like the preceding pageants, appropriate verses from the pen of Lydgate.†

* Gen. viii. 21.

† Stow ; Fabian ; Londiniana ; Harl. MS. ; Chron. Lond. Bridge ; Speed ; Sharon Turner ; Warton's Eng. Poetry.

Amidst these demonstrations of joy, and of welcome, was the admiring Queen conducted in royal state into the metropolis, previous to her coronation; everything calculated to afford her pleasure having been provided at considerable expense.

Margaret, who was at that time little more than fifteen years of age, must have been highly gratified with her reception in England. After her splendid progress through the city, she was conducted to the Tower, where she reposed during one day. Then followed the ceremony of coronation, which took place on Sunday (being the first Sunday after Trinity), the 30th of May, 1445. The Queen rode to Westminster Abbey, where the solemn rites of her coronation were performed by John Stafford, Archbishop of Canterbury, and were attended with even more than the accustomed magnificence, for Parliament was then sitting, having met on the 25th day of February, previous to the arrival of the Queen.

1445.
Holinshed;
Biondi;
Rapin;
Speed;
Carte;
Lingard;
Sismondi;
Henry.

The coronation feasts were splendid.* No expense was spared, and various royal gifts were bestowed, and many valuable crown jewels redeemed, in order to be presented to the beautiful queen at "the tyme of ye solempnytie of her coronation." Amongst these were the "Ilkyngton coler," a costly gift; also a "pectoral," adorned with gems, for which King Henry had just paid a sum equal to £15,000.†

A tournament was held for three days, in proof of the universal joy of the nation. The feasting being held within the sanctuary, and the jousts in the courtyard before the Abbey, and in the royal presence. The people departed, as the contemporary chroniclers have declared, "well satisfied."‡

* To the chief butler alone was given 1,000*l.*
† See Appendix, p. 419.
‡ Holinshed; Biondi; Fabian; Carte; Eng. Chron. Camd. Soc.; Hall; Sandford; W. of Worcester; Baker; Chron. of Brute; bib. Harl.; Stow;

Such was the commencement of the career of Queen Margaret,—such the favourable reception of the fair sovereign from whom so much was expected! The disappointment of the people, however, began early to be manifested, and sad and bitter must have been the reflections of Margaret, at a subsequent period, upon those events which, after such a gracious reception, had deprived her of the love of her people.

This marriage has been universally esteemed most unfortunate for King Henry, for his Queen, and for the English nation.[*] Those historians, however, who call Queen Margaret "proud and vindictive,"[†] and who attribute all the evils of this disastrous reign to her wilful passions, must surely be blinded by prejudice, and forgetful of that impartiality which ought ever to be the distinguishing characteristic of an historian.

We are also more especially guided to liberality in our judgment of this queen, when we reflect on the general high esteem with which she was regarded by her own nation, and by the French king; and when we consider the united praises, by all historians, of her early character and conduct. One author informs us —"her talents and noble qualities had been so much celebrated, that it was reasonable to expect, that when she should mount the throne, they would break out, and shine with still superior lustre." Another says, " she was a princess who, to the beauties of her body, added all the perfections of the mind." A third says, " she was endowed with an excellent understanding, sagacity, and prudence, very reasonable and considerate, and diligent in all her designs, &c."[‡] Again, we are told that " in personal beauty she was superior to most women, in mental capacity equal to most men;"

Toplis; Baudier; Rapin; Sismondi; Lond. Chron.; Lingard; Sharon Turner; Beckington; Cont. Hist. Croyland.

* Holinshed; Hall; Speed; Rapin; Stow.

† Biondi; Villaret.   ‡ Hume; Baudier; Female Worthies.

and another writer says of this queen, that "she was a beautiful woman, and of a genius and capacity superior to most women; and also of a bold and masculine spirit."[*]

It should also be remembered that at the age of fifteen, when, notwithstanding her aspiring temper, she could not have acquired much experience, she was at once introduced to a court where two violent and turbulent factions prevailed; to a nation prepared, by the example of their governors, for mutiny and complaints; and to a weak king, who, far from being able to govern others, had scarcely a will of his own.

Of the duties of Margaret's newly-acquired dignity, perhaps this last, the guidance of her husband, was not the least difficult to accomplish. As her husband and sovereign she owed to him respect and obedience; but even these the easy temper and feeble frame of King Henry disposed him to yield up, while the natural goodness of his heart claimed only the love and good-will of his consort, his servants, and his subjects. Meanwhile his consort was called upon to rule, almost without a helm or guide; yet we are not informed of any open violation of duty on the part of the youthful queen, but on the contrary, she even preserved the affections of her husband entire, and remained faithful to his fortunes throughout life.

King Henry, who had been easily gained by the praises bestowed on the Princess Margaret before he beheld her, was even more readily captivated by her charms when united to her. Won by her address, he resigned the reins of government to her more able hands; and Margaret, quickly perceiving the incapacity of her husband, seized the opportunity of appropriating to herself an authority, which, probably, she had been desirous of obtaining.[†] Her lively and ambitious

---

[*] Lingard; Toplis.   [†] Baker; Henry.

which should have only attached to her ministers.[*]
Some writers affirm that these ministers had preconcerted the ruin of the Duke whatever it might cost
them, and that to further these views they had selected Margaret of Anjou for their Queen.[†] Added to
the number of the Duke's adversaries, there were
other powerful individuals, who, prepared for mischief
and violence, were envious of Gloucester. Of these
especially was conspicuous the Duke of Buckingham,
who entertained a private pique against him for
having promoted the advancement of Henry, Earl of
Warwick, to the precedence of every duke, thus
wounding the pride of many of the nobility of England. Buckingham's pompous array of titles, and his
lineal descent from the same race as the rival kings of
York and Lancaster, made him unwilling to forgive
any infringement of his aristocratic dignity; thus he
stood foremost in the confederacy to humble the power
of Gloucester, for having once presumed to be greater
than himself. The Marquis of Suffolk, who owed his
elevation to the Cardinal, lost no opportunity to insi-
nuate to his master, that the Cardinal was, of all his
subjects, the most to be confided in; thus daily sinking
the credit of Gloucester, whose counsels were always
opposed to those of Beaufort. Another who was devoted to the Cardinal, the Archbishop of York, was
also instrumental in confirming the suspicions of the
King. In short, they so contrived by their united
efforts, that Henry daily gave his uncle some new
mortification, which the haughty and impetuous spirit
of Gloucester could not brook without complaints or
threats against the authors of these affronts. His
resentment, however, only hastened his ruin.[‡] The

* Holinshed; Pol. Vergil; Hall; Barante; Rapin; Speed; Henry;
Hume.
† Villaret; Henry; Hume.
‡ Pol. Vergil; Speed; Rymer's Fœdera; Rapin.

frequent attacks of his enemies, added to the disgrace
and captivity of his wife, were motives quite sufficient
for his retiring from court; some assert, however, that
the Duke's great power had excited the jealousy of the
Queen, who was ambitious to reign alone.   Certain it
is, that Queen Margaret's first step was to sanction the
endeavours of the Duke's enemies to exclude him from
the Council-chamber, and from all share in the government.   In this attempt the Cardinal of Winchester and
the Archbishop of York were the most active.   Some
persons were suborned to bring false accusations against
the Duke concerning his conduct during the Protectorate; the chief of which were, that he had put to
death several individuals upon his own authority, and
that he had aggravated the sentence passed on
others.

Such, however, was the rigorous administration of
justice by this virtuous prince, that it had solely called
forth the enmity of those who feared the just punishment of their crimes, and who hated him for his plain-
ness in declaring their offences.*

The Duke of Gloucester had ever spoken in the
Council-chamber with the freedom to which his birth,
rank, and services entitled him; but this only excited
the rage of his enemies, who oppressed him and coun-
teracted his influence.   He had no longer any weight
in the Cabinet.   The Duke's power was, however, considerable in the kingdom, owing to his popularity with
the people, who believed he was zealous for the interests and honour of his country; and from his high
rank and extensive domains, and also being the presumptive heir to the throne.†

When the Duke of Gloucester appeared before the
Council to reply to the charges preferred against him,

1446.
Rapin;
Holinshed.

* Holinshed; Hall; Baker; Pol. Vergil.
† Barante; Villaret.

so ably did he prove his innocence, and so clear and convincing was the evidence he gave, that even his enemies, who were his judges, were compelled to acquit him, and to desist from their projects. The citizens of London raised great commotions in consequence of this attack upon the character of the " Good Duke," and the praises of the public favourite were re-echoed throughout the streets of the metropolis, and curses denounced upon his enemies.* From this time Gloucester was rising in the public estimation, and the increase of his popularity still augmented the wrath and jealousy of his political antagonists, who, it is said, became convinced that nothing short of the ruin of the Duke would enable them to establish their own power. They feared, and with reason, that in the event of Gloucester one day mounting the throne, he would inflict a just punishment on them for the crimes he had so often endeavoured to expose. The death of Gloucester was consequently resolved upon, and the ministers were not slow in effecting their wicked purpose. They did not resort to the common course of justice in their iniquitous proceedings, for they had already found it impracticable, and open assassination was too hazardous an attempt.

These crafty ministers devised a new and certain means to get rid of their rival, and by which they were at the same time enabled to conceal the authors of the crime.† It has been asserted that this means for effecting the destruction of the Duke was invented by Queen Margaret, or at least received her sanction, and that the ministers would scarcely have ventured of themselves to attempt the life of the presumptive heir to the throne. It is added that the Queen's accustomed activity and energy led the people to believe

---

* Rapin ; Henry ; Holinshed ; Biondi.
† Holinshed ; Hall ; Pol. Vergil ; Rapin.

that, without her consent, the enemies of the Duke could not have dared to take his life.[*] That it should be said the Queen was implicated in such a crime, merely on account of her natural temperament, seems unjust. Still more surprising it appears, on reflection, that one of our historians, who in relating other facts has been remarkably circumstantial, should on this subject have contented himself with bare insinuations as the foundation for this opinion.

But historians differ much with regard to the part Queen Margaret took in this transaction. Some of them, by asserting that the Duke died a natural death, clear the Queen of this imputation altogether, and also all her ministers;[†] another boldly declares that the Queen first plotted the death of the Duke, and devised the means for its accomplishment.[‡] The truth would seem to lie between these two extremes.

The opinion became general that the Queen gave her sanction to the measures of her ministers, who, without it, feared, or pretended to fear, to engage in this plot. Those historians may perhaps be most relied upon who represent this affair as transacted by the Cardinal and his party, *apparently* under the authority of the Queen.[§] All writers of the events of this period, however, with one exception, concur in saying that the *share Queen Margaret took* in this guilty transaction is *uncertain;* yet, without any proof of her criminality,—any evidence beyond the suspicions of a discontented and offended nation,—the character of the estimable and high-minded Margaret of Anjou has been aspersed, and, thus sullied and defamed, has been transmitted to succeeding generations.

The surprising courage and bold genius of this

---

[*] Hume; Rapin; Henry.

[†] Wethamstead; Lingard.   [‡] Rapin.

[§] Hall; Rapin; Henry; Hume; Sharon Turner.

Queen in her subsequent adversities has doubtless led many to conclude that she did not, at this period, hesitate in the adoption of any means her penetration suggested as expedient; but let it be remembered, that "adversity is the school of heroes; it is there that man learns to walk alone, to command himself, and to govern others."

Margaret, with all her talents and political dexterity, was still a young woman at this period; and although she was not marked by the peculiar foibles of her sex, she had led, as history portrays her, too pure and innocent a life to admit without reluctance the open contemplation of crime. Had it been otherwise, she had, long ere the death of Gloucester, suffered the slander passed upon her by the enemies of the House of Lancaster, or had it been in their power to prove her conduct in early life exceptionable. Nor is it probable that, having passed her youth without censure, she should have so suddenly changed—so corrupted by the vile atmosphere of a wicked court— as to have proposed of her own accord the execution of this wilful and horrid crime; human nature shrinks from the suspicion. Again, when we consider the youth and inexperience of the Queen and her prejudice against the Duke of Gloucester, it seems probable that she might have been deceived by the artifices of the Cardinal, and ensnared into concessions, or persuaded to give her sanction to some project of her ministers, without understanding the full extent of their purpose.

Queen Margaret and her counsellors are said to have treated the Duke with marked affability previous to the meeting of Parliament, which had been con-

1447.
Holinshed;
Henry;
Rapin.

vened for the month of February, 1447, at Bury St. Edmunds, where it was supposed the Duke of Gloucester had fewer friends than in London, and there-.

fore this place was judged to be more suitable to the sinister views of the ministers.

The precautions taken on this occasion caused much surprise, and gave rise to many conjectures. The knights of the shires were summoned to come there in arms, the men of Suffolk were arrayed, and the King's residence well guarded, while patrols watched the roads leading to this town during the night as well as the day, "so that many died of cold and waking."○

The favour shewn to Gloucester by the Queen and her ministers was not intended to win his confidence, but rather to inspire him with mistrust of their designs, in order to betray him into some step which might afford a handle against him. It was even hinted to him, by secret emissaries, that a plot was laid against him to impeach him of various crimes in the Parliament of Bury St. Edmunds, which place had been chosen as most favourable to the designs of his enemies. Upon this it was expected that the Duke would withdraw himself, and that thus an appearance of truth would be thrown on the charges which the ministers intended to bring forward.†

It was in vain, however, that this noble-minded prince was advertised of the machinations of his enemies. Conscious of his own innocence, and too proud to seek security in flight, which would have afforded a plausible ground for these accusations, his generous mind resolved upon boldly confronting his accusers, and proving the falsehood of their charges.‡ He came from his castle of Devizes to Bury St. Edmunds, in Suffolk, with only a small retinue, and as it was customary for noblemen to appear in the high court of Parliament with a numerous suite out of respect to the King, and Gloucester, not having in his retirement suf-

○ Stow; Lingard.

† Hall; Rapin; Barante.   ‡ Hall; Rapin; Villaret.

ficient attendants, sent orders to some of his retainers and servants at Deptford to meet him at Bury; when however, a number of these prepared to obey the Duke's orders, they were arrested and charged with a conspiracy.

King Henry having kept his Christmas at Bury St. Edmunds, remained there until Easter, 1447.

1447.
Stow ;
Baker ;
Speed ;
Hume ;
Fox.

Upon the first day of the meeting of Parliament as appointed (the 10th of February), the King presided in person, sitting in a chair of state in the refectory of the monastery.   On this day the Duke of Gloucester arrived at Bury and was lodged in the hospital, where soon after he was arrested by Lord Beaumont, the High Constable of England, the Dukes of Buckingham, Somerset, and others, who appointed certain of the King's household to attend upon him, none of his own domestics being permitted to wait upon him.

Thus was the Duke of Gloucester cast into prison upon a charge of high treason, and it was reported, in excuse for his committal, that he had formed a design to kill his sovereign, usurp the throne, and rescue his Duchess, who had been a long time confined in Kenilworth Castle.   The people gave no credit to the first of these charges, and great disturbances were made throughout the town on account of the Duke's imprisonment; but the clamours were soon appeased, because it was generally believed that Gloucester was innocent, therefore no one doubted that he would as easily clear himself upon this as he had done on the former occasion.*   The Duke was not, however, permitted the opportunity for his defence, being found dead in his bed on the morning after his arrest.†

* Hall ; Biondi ; Stow ; Carte ; W. of Worcester ; Howel's Med. Hist. Anglicanæ ; Rapin ; Milles's Catalogue ; Sandford ; Baker ; Dugdale's Baron. ; Holinshed ; Paston Letters ; Fox's Monasteries ; Peck's Stamford ; Allen's York ; Henry ; Barante ; Villaret ; Hume.

† Stow writes that "on the 14th day he died, for sorrow, that he might

The cause publicly assigned for the Duke's death was apoplexy; but his unpopularity at court and with the Queen's party, and the violence which characterized this period, seems to give a degree of probability to that which rests on *tradition only*, viz., that the Duke was murdered in an apartment of St. Saviour's Hospital, then an appendage to the monastery. Nor did the exposure of the Duke's body, on which no marks of violence were perceptible, serve to remove from the public mind the impression, which was general, that the Duke of Gloucester had met with his death by unlawful means. Various conjectures were formed as to the manner in which this horrid deed had been perpetrated, and universal was the detestation with which those persons were regarded who were judged to have been its authors.[*]

Such was the unfortunate end of Humphrey, Duke of Gloucester, one of the first princes of the blood, and a great favourite with the people, who, for his love of literature and the rank he held as patron of the genius and talent of his age, was justly styled the " Mæcenas of his times." He was a magnificent patron and benefactor of the University of Oxford (where he had been educated), and founded the Bodleian Library, to which he presented one hundred and twenty-nine fair volumes on the sciences, in the year 1440.

Gloucester was a skilful and upright governor; ever disposed to favour the poor, and, therefore, much beloved by them. He was also " learned and courteous," and if we cannot agree with the old chronicler, who

not come to his answer;" while other authors state that he died on the 14th or 17th day after his arrest, or assert that he was found dead on the 23rd or 28th of February.

[*] Hall; Baker; Biondi; Holinshed; Stow; Pol. Vergil; Sandford; Milles's Catalogue; Carte; W. of Worcester; Fabian; Paston Letters; Hist. of Bury St. Edmonds; Fox's Monasteries; Howel's Med. Hist. Ang.; Speed; Allen's York.

adds that "he was also devoid of pride and ambition," we must at least allow him many excellent qualities, and confess it might be truly said of him, that he was

"Virtute duce non sanguine nitor."

"Great by deeds of virtue, not of blood."[*]

On account of his many virtues and the care he took of the commonwealth, Gloucester obtained from the people the title of the "Good Duke," and for his love of justice he was also styled the "Father of his country." He had governed the kingdom during twenty-five years, as we are told, "with great commendations, so that neither good men had cause to complain of, nor bad men to find fault with, his regency." He had been idolized by the nation, and not without reason, for he had long shown a lively interest in the welfare of his country, and had, in support of those points which he deemed essential to its honour, sustained repeated indignities and affronts. He had shown that he inherited the spirit of his family, a spirit which, in his brother Henry V. and the Duke of Bedford, had been generally esteemed and admired; yet he differed from these relatives in the irritability of his temper and his impetuosity, which doubtless caused his frequent quarrels with Beaufort, and gave that prelate a political ascendency over him. It is probable that the Duke of Gloucester owed his fate to his active exertions to reform the Church, and to banish ecclesiastical statesmen from their inordinate share in the government. In these attempts he could not fail to humble his rival and to excite his enmity; add to which, we are told, that he had attempted to deprive Beaufort of the see of Winchester, which must

* Biondi; Paston Letters; Rapin; Hume; Sharon Turner; Leigh's Collections; Holinshed; Baker; Hall; Sandford.

have increased his rage against him. Upon this occasion, as on many others, fresh fuel was added to the flame of discord which burned between these two powerful individuals ; and their petty feuds, (otherwise unworthy of the notice of the historian,) become important, as being the fruitful source whence sprang many of the contests and desolating wars of King Henry's reign.

That the young King should have been early prejudiced against his uncle is not surprising, being of so easy a temper that it required little address to win his favour ; this Beaufort secured for himself, and employed it against his adversary. The Duke of Gloucester, however, had deserved better at his nephew's hands ; for he it was who, with more spirit than prudence, had resented King Henry's exclusion from the Cabinet, when, at the age of seventeen, he had requested admittance there ; and Henry's subsequent incapacity is mainly attributable to his arbitrary governors, and his exclusion from, and ignorance of, public affairs.*

The body of the Duke of Gloucester was interred in the Abbey of St. Albans, to which he had been a great benefactor. The Abbot Wethamstead, whom he much esteemed, says repeatedly that the Duke fell ill immediately after his arrest, and died of his illness. Wethamstead commends him in these two lines,—

1447.
Rapin,

> " Fidior in regno Regi, Duce non fuit isto
> " Plus ne fide stabilis, aut major, amator honoris."
>
> " Than Humphrey none of faithfulness had greater store,
> " Stood firmer by the King, or loved his honour more."

It was in the Abbey of St. Albans that the Duke detected a man, who pretended to work a miracle in restoring sight to the blind. Gloucester had a strong

* Holinshed ; Pol. Vergil ; Speed ; Sandford ; W. of Worcester ; Rapin ; Lingard.

predilection for the shrine of St. Albans. He had bestowed upon it rich vestments to the value of three thousand marks, and the manor of Pembroke, that the monks should pray for his soul; and he had directed that his remains should be deposited within those holy walls. The tomb of the Duke was adorned by his friend, Wethamstead, and part of the expenses borne by the convent. A monument of stone, of elaborate workmanship, was erected to his memory behind the altar, on the south side of the church, where was the shrine of the patron saint. In a vault beneath, the remains of this prince were deposited, and great care and expense were originally taken for their preservation: they were enclosed in a leaden coffin, in a kind of strong pickle, with an outer coffin of wood. A crucifix was painted on the wall at the east end of the vault, with a cup on each side of the head, another at the side, and a fourth at the feet. These four chalices were receiving the blood, and a hand pointing towards it, with a label inscribed "Lord, have mercy upon me."[*]

Several knights and esquires in the Duke's service on the day of his arrest assembled at Greenwich, and resolved to proceed to Bury to join him. They were taken prisoners, and accused of conspiring to kill the King, to raise the Duke of Gloucester to the throne, and to release Eleanor, his wife, from her prison. They were tried, and five of them—Sir Roger Chamberlaine, Richard Middleton, Thomas Herbert, Arthur Tursey, Esqrs., and Richard Nedham,—were condemned of

---

[*] Thus were the remains of the "Good Duke Humphrey" discovered in 1701 (except that the outer case of wood had perished); and since that period they have been frequently exhibited to gratify the public curiosity. The dry bones and soft, fair, silken tresses of hair were of deep interest to all acquainted with his character, and tragic end. The inscription and the title on the cross have been long obliterated.—*Stow; Pol. Vergil; Sandford; Rymer; Rapin; Pennant; Willis's Abbeys; Paston Letters; Weaver's Funereal Monuments; Blore's Monumental Remains; Lingard.*

high treason, and sentence of death passed upon them. Their judges were appointed by virtue of the King's commission, and of these the Marquis of Suffolk was the chief.[o] The King granted a pardon to these unfortunate men. His humanity would not allow them to suffer. This clemency on the part of King Henry, we are told, was caused by his attention to a sermon, which had much affected him, delivered by Dr. Worthington, a celebrated preacher, on the forgiveness of injuries; and his Majesty declared " that he could not better show his gratitude for the protection of the Almighty than by granting a pardon to those who, he believed, had intended his destruction." These persons were thirty-two in number when apprehended; the five on whom sentence of death had been passed were drawn to Tyburn for execution. There the hangman had actually performed his office—the vital spark was almost extinguished—when the Marquis of Suffolk produced the tardy pardon upon which these miserable beings had relied, for it was suspected that they had been bribed to an acknowledgment of guilt upon a promise of certain pardon.

This pardon was by some persons conjectured to be only an artifice by which Suffolk sought to lessen the odium which might attach to himself after the death of Gloucester.

No investigation took place as to the cause of the sudden death of this Duke. It was asserted that he died a natural death, brought on by apoplexy, or the effect of anxiety of mind.[†] This opinion was held by three contemporary writers, who were all his friends and eulogists—Hardyng, the Yorkist; William of Worcester, who in recording the meeting of Parlia-

---

* Hall; Holinshed; Baker; Sandford; Howel; Stow; Rapin; Henry; Hist. of Bury St. Edmonds; Lingard; Smollet.

† Pol. Vergil; Speed; Carte; Villaret; Hume.

ment at Bury says only, "there died Humphrey, the Good Duke of Gloucester, the lover of virtue and the State;" lastly, Wethamstead, his intimate friend, tells us that, "after being placed in strict confinement, he sank from sorrow."

The seeds of discontent had been long sown in this country, and the division of the chief rulers into two parties had much increased this growing evil, while the Queen preserved a select favoured party around her court. Many, very many, had rallied round this idolized and deservedly esteemed prince; and the sudden bereavement of their favourite called forth their utmost indignation. They could not penetrate the apparent mystery, the cause of his death, and regarded it as a crime, a murder, and sought to attach it to his different enemies; and, casting off their respect for the rank of their Queen, they even dared openly to charge her with this outrage.*

The death of Gloucester, from whatever cause, did not remove from him the imputation of treason; it was still pretended that he was guilty of the charges laid against him, and for which some of his servants had been led to execution. These persons had never been confronted with him, neither were they of the chief of the Duke's household; nor were they such persons as he would probably have chosen to intrust with a secret so important, had he really entertained any treasonable projects.

Those individuals who were universally considered as the authors of Gloucester's death, were of too high a rank in the kingdom for anyone to have courage enough to accuse them, much more to inflict the punishment which, it was believed, they had so justly deserved.† When, however, hatred and malice had

* Holinshed ; Rapin
† Biondi ; Hume ; Rapin ; Henry.

effected their direful purpose, when no human authority could call the culprits to the bar of justice, the unerring will of the Almighty, whose omnipresent eye had regarded this secret deed, so disposed the chain of succeeding events, that this cruel murder became the source of continued trials and misfortunes throughout the lives of its authors.

In whatever manner effected, Gloucester's death certainly was, as an old historian expresses it, "like the stroke of an evil angel sent to punish England, and to make way for the practices of Richard, Duke of York, who, immediately after the death of Duke Humphrey, (that grand prop of the red rose-tree,) began to set on foot his royal title." *

The Duke of Gloucester most probably came by his death through the inveterate malice of his enemies, who had preconcerted the destruction of his power. These were the chief ministers of the Queen, the Cardinal of Winchester, the Archbishop of York, the Duke of Buckingham, and the Marquis of Suffolk. These four individuals consequently became the particular objects of popular hatred, and the impression made by this affair was never afterwards removed from the public mind. †

The attempts of these ministers to deceive the nation were fruitless and unworthy artifices. The arrest of the Duke's servants was a base subterfuge, which did not answer their purpose, (viz., to screen themselves from popular resentment); but it produced a contrary effect, in convincing the people by the favour shown to these unhappy men, that they were, as well as the Duke, altogether innocent of the charges laid against them.‡

---

* Sandford ; Holinshed ; Hall ; Smollet ; Peck's Stamford.
† Speed ; Allen's York.
‡ Villaret.

the impeachment of Suffolk, with one exception, which brings her before us as the enlightened patroness of literature.

King Henry VI., previous to his marriage with Margaret of Anjou, has been described as "advancing in virtue as he increased in age." He gave himself up to religious duties, and the worship of God and the blessed Virgin Mary. He took no share in the political affairs of his kingdom, committing them to his Council, neither would he participate in any worldly pleasures. He took a lively interest in the advancement of religion and the promotion of learning. In the year 1440 he had laid the foundation of Eton School, near Windsor, intending it as a nursery for his college in Cambridge, which he founded soon after. Eton College had a provost, ten priests, four clerks, six choristers, twenty-five poor grammar scholars, and twenty-five poor men.*

A little later in the year 1443, King Henry had founded a college at Cambridge to Our Lady and St. Nicholas, which was called the College Royal, or King's College. Truly royal and magnificent was the original plan of this foundation, if we may judge of it by the chapel, which has called forth universal admiration as one of the finest specimens of architecture in the world. The misfortunes, however, of the founder, unhappily prevented the completion of that plan. At its commencement, the King ordered that the ancient castle of Cambridge should be pulled down to supply materials for this great work. King Henry also translated to this place a certain hostle near Clare Hall, called the "House of God," (which had been erected by William Bingham, rector of St. John Zacchary, in London, in the year 1442, for grammarians), placing therein a pro-

* The supporters to the arms of King Henry on Eton College gate were two antelopes.

vost, four fellows, and scholars.   This building having been taken into the bounds of King's College, the King would have increased the number of scholars to sixty, had not the subsequent fatal wars obstructed his pious design.   To the maintenance of this college and that of Eton King Henry gave annually £3,400.   He also bestowed 120 volumes on the library at Cambridge. Henry, Duke of Warwick, (who had continued until his death the especial favourite of Henry VI.), was enrolled as one of the benefactors of this college.[*]

The same care and beneficence were bestowed by the King on certain colleges at Oxford.   The New College there, within the walls, received from this monarch certain possessions, and likewise the College of Oriel. Henry VI. was also a magnificent benefactor to Pembroke Hall, which was called the "*King's Adopted Daughter*," and King's College, Cambridge, his "*True and First-begotten Daughter*."   This magnificent plan [†] of King Henry called forth the poetic effusions of Walpole, who thus exclaims :—

" When Henry bade the pompous temple rise,
" Nor with presumption emulate the skies,
" Art and Paladio had not reach'd the land
" Nor methodiz'd the Vandal builder's hands :
" Wonders unknown to rule these piles disclose,
" The walls, as if by inspiration rose;
" The edifice, continued by his care,
" With equal pride had form'd the sumptuous square,
" Had not th' assassin disappointed part,
" And stabb'd the growing fabric in his heart."[‡]

* Howel ; John Rous of Warwick ; Carter's Cambridge ; Toplis ; Baker; Rapin ; Parker's Cambridge ; Henry ; Magna Britannica ; Gough's Sepul. Monuments.

† The intentions of King Henry were long afterwards effected by his pious relative Margaret, Countess of Richmond, the mother of Henry VII., who obtained from her son a licence, and plentifully endowed the college out of her own lands and possessions, that the revenues afforded maintenance for a master, 12 fellows, and 47 scholars.   The original plan is still to be seen in the library of the college.

‡ Walpole's Fugitive Pieces.

We are informed that Queen Margaret, observing the singular piety of her husband which led him to become founder of King's College, Cambridge, resolved on the establishing of another college close to it, and which obtained from its foundress the name of Queen's College. This building was erected on the borders of the monastery of the Carmelites. The chapel was dedicated to St. Margaret and St. Bernard, and Sir John Wenlock, Knight, laid the first stone, in the name of the foundress, on the 15th of April, 1448. On the corner stone was engraved, at the express desire of Queen Margaret, "*Erit Dominæ nostræ Reginæ Margaretæ Dominus in refugium, et lapis iste in signum*" ("The Lord will be a refuge to our Lady Queen Margaret, and this stone shall be the sign, or monument thereof"). The college was richly endowed by the Queen bestowing on it to the value of £200 a year, to maintain a master and four fellows. King Henry also conferred additional gifts upon it. This edifice was involved in the calamities incidental to the reign of this Queen, and which, even while it was in its infancy, caused it to be near perishing. It was, however, preserved by the care and diligence of Andrew Ducket, who had been appointed its first president by the foundress; and during forty years, while he continued in that office, he procured for it many benefactors through his solicitations, so that he might even be esteemed its preserver or second founder.*

1448.
Henry;
Carter's
Cambridge.

* When the civil wars compelled Queen Margaret, at the head of the Lancastrian party, to defend her husband's rights, this noble work of the college was suspended, until King Edward's queen, Elizabeth Woodville, animated, it would seem, by the good example of her predecessor, sought to emulate her fame in the completion of this noble building. This was happily accomplished in 1465, and many privileges granted it by King Edward. It was, however, chiefly owing to the active zeal of the president, Andrew Ducket, that the queen of Edward IV. took such interest in this undertaking; and it was through his persuasions, also, that the Countess of Richmond became so noble a patroness to King's College. He was appointed by this lady to the mastership, in which he continued thirty-six years, and prevailed on the

In the chapel of Queen's College was a curious altar-piece, on three panels, representing "Judas betraying Christ," "The Resurrection," and "Christ appearing to the Apostles after the Resurrection." These fine paintings, supposed to have been presented by the foundress, Margaret of Anjou, were afterwards removed to the president's lodge. *

The distracted state of the public affairs, and the discontents of the people, first inspired Richard, Duke of York and Lord of Stamford, with the hope of one day being able to establish his right to the crown. He had of late risen in power and popularity, and was a prince of great valour and abilities; he was also prudent in his conduct, and mild in his disposition. He was the only heir to the House of Mortimer, or March, and was descended, on his mother's side, from Lionel, the second son of Edward III., and elder brother of John of Ghent, whose descendant was Henry VI., the monarch at this period occupying the throne.†

When the truce with France had been prolonged, in 1445, the Duke of York had returned to England, after his regency there, and had been graciously received at court, and many acknowledgments made to him for his services. The King, to show in an especial manner his gratitude, appointed him again Regent of France for

most generous of the nobility to furnish large sums of money; and amongst these we find the Duke of Clarence, Cicely Duchess of York, Marmaduke Lumley, and others, who became great benefactors to this college. Andrew Ducket, a worthy and discreet man, died on the 6th of November, 1484.— *Sandford; Toplis; Henry; Rapin; Leland; Baker; Carter's Cambridge; Lysson's Cambridge; Parker's Cambridge.*

* This college, with the general title of "Queen's College," bears her hereditary arms. In the president's lodge is still to be seen a portrait of Queen Margaret of Anjou, and near to it that of her successor on the throne, Elizabeth Woodville. At the invitation of Bishop Fisher, Erasmus visited Cambridge many years later, and took up his residence in a tower of this college.

† Sandford ; Baker ; Hume ; Rapin ; Biondi.

the ensuing five years. Before this period had expired, however, the Duke became an object of serious mistrust to the Queen and her ministers, who, had they preserved the good opinion of the nation, or had the "Good Duke of Gloucester" been alive to maintain his rights, would not have had reason to fear these projects, as, in either case, it is highly improbable that the Duke of York would have ever asserted his claim.*

The Duke did not at first openly assert his pretensions; it would have been dangerous to him to do so, while he was as yet ignorant of the dispositions of the people. He therefore proceeded with such caution that his intentions could not be discovered. He contented himself with making his right known to the people by secret agents. It was circulated that the House of Lancaster had usurped the throne, and that, although the usurpation had been tolerated whilst its kings were men of ability and virtue, and governed to the satisfaction of the nation; yet, having now no longer that expectation in their present king, they were unwilling to maintain it for the sake of a queen, a foreigner, and one whose arbitrary government was so much to their disadvantage. That the House of March had been unjustly deprived of the succession, and that the Duke of York, as sole heir of that distinguished house, ought to be acknowledged king, and advanced to a dignity to which his virtues, talents, and the services he had rendered his country, justly entitled him. By these secret intimations, the Duke soon obtained a party amongst the people; but he did not himself appear, his friends only exerted their influence in his favour.

In support of the present administration there were still many persons of great power and influence in the

* Holinshed; Speed; Henry.

kingdom; of these were the Earl of Northumberland, the Duke of Somerset and his brother, the Dukes of Exeter and Buckingham, the Earl of Shrewsbury, the Lords Stafford, Clifford, Dudley, Scales, Audley, and others.[*]

The late reports had not passed unheeded by the Queen and her Council; and they were not slow in attributing them to their true author, who, if concealed from others, could not easily deceive such quick-sighted persons as those who were themselves so interested in making this discovery. These parties came at once to the resolution, if possible, to lessen the credit of the Duke of York. They were more desirous of doing this, as they suspected the Duke would, as Regent of France, obstruct the surrender of Maine and Anjou, promised to Charles of Anjou at the treaty of 1444.[†]

The desired opportunity soon presented itself.

The Duke of Somerset, whose family interests were ever opposed to those of York, had endeavoured to hinder the dispatch of this Duke on his first appointment to the Regency of France. He became again so envious of the distinction of his rival, that he prevailed on the King to repeal the grant he had made to the Duke of York; and, assisted by the Marquis of Suffolk, he obtained the same grant for himself.

This treatment was highly resented by the Duke of York, and gradually the mutual enmity of these two nobles led to their ruin, and also that of many others who became involved with them.

The Duke of Somerset, who had upon his brother's death succeeded to the family title, was dismissed to France to take upon him the office of Regent in the place of York, who was thus removed previous to the expiration of the period for which it had been be-

---

[*] Baker; Holinshed; Hume; Rapin; Henry; Villaret.
[†] Rapin.

stowed upon him.* York resolved to be revenged,
but for a time dissembled his resentment. The
haughty disposition of Somerset gave him great
offence also, and he became his determined enemy.

We shall soon have occasion to observe how private
pique, and the irritating sense of injustice, contributed
to increase the general dissatisfaction of the nation.
Discontent is a growing evil, which oft takes its rise
from some trivial cause; it needs the skilful hand of a
physician to eradicate its earliest symptoms, or it will
not fail to grow into an incurable disease.

Queen Margaret knew not how to stem the torrent
of dissatisfaction to which her conduct had given rise.
She seemed, at this time, as if she braved the people
by lavishing favours on the object of their aversion.
She caused the King, who submitted entirely to her
guidance, to create the Marquis of Suffolk a duke, and
by this a new pretext was afforded to the enemies of
Queen Margaret to stir up the people against her.

1448.
Speed;
Rapin;
Paston
Letters.

The King's weakness becoming daily more apparent, the nation seemed at this period to be wholly
ruled by the Queen and Suffolk. The great power of
this minister is thus set forth by a writer of that day,
who tells us, " There shall be no man so hardy to do,
neither say, against my lord of Suffolk, nor none that
longeth to him, and all that have done and said against
him, they shall soon repent them." †

It is doubtless an error in the ruler of a state to
listen only to the nobility, or to those courtiers who
immediately surround the throne. The voice of the
people should never be totally disregarded; and there
are, at times, concessions necessary to be made, even
to the meanest subjects in the realm.

* Sandford; Holinshed; Baker; Stow; Carte; Speed; Rapin; Lingard; Barante; Villaret; Leland's Ireland.

† Holinshed; Baker; Hall; Stow; Speed; Pol. Vergil; Rapin; Paston Letters; Villaret; Allen's York.

The honour lately conferred upon Suffolk was probably not intended to offend the people, but solely as a compensation to the Duke for the complaints to which he had been subjected; and possibly given to add weight to the King's declaration, and apparent conviction, of the Duke's innocence. Surely it could not have been expected that the Queen would pass censure on the conduct of Suffolk in the affair of her marriage, or be offended with a treaty by which she became Queen of England! This treaty, too, having been signed, and the conditions agreed to, would it be honourable not to fulfil them? Doubtless the Queen and her minister reasoned thus; and we have seen that they were influenced by it to remove the Duke of York from his Regency, that he might not obstruct the surrender of Maine and Anjou.

For this surrender, which appeared to them as an act of justice, they were severely blamed; and the more so, because these territories, being given up to Charles of Anjou, the uncle of Queen Margaret, it seemed to be done to favour the interests of her family.

CHAPTER VI.

(*Lord Say.*)   " Tell me wherein I have offended most ?
   " Have I affected wealth or honour, speak ?
   " Are my chests fill'd with extorted gold ?
   " Is my apparel sumptuous to behold ?
   " Whom have I injur'd, that ye seek my death."—Shakespeare.

(*Duke of York.*)   " T'was men I lack'd and you will give them me,
   " I take it kindly ; yet be well assured,
   " You put sharp weapons in a madman's hands,
   " Whiles I in Ireland nourish a mighty band,
   " 'Twill stir up in England some black storm
   " Shall blow ten thousand souls to heaven or hell,
   " And this fell tempest shall not cease to rage
   " Until the golden circuit on my head,
   " Like to the glorious sun's transparent beams,
   " Do calm the fury of this mad-bred flaw."—Shakespeare.

The surrender of Maine and Anjou—Losses in France—Complaints of the English—The arrest of York prevented—An affray at Coventry—Rebellion in Ireland—York is dismissed thither—Parliament meets—Suffolk accused of treason—His defence—He is sent to the Tower, and then banished the kingdom—His departure—His death—His character and enemies—The merits of the Duke of York—Reinforcements are sent to Somerset—Loss of Caen—The conduct of Sir David Hall—Somerset returns to England—Cade's rebellion and death.

It had been stipulated at the treaty of Tours, that the counties of Maine and Anjou should be surrendered to the French ; but Le Mans was still garrisoned by the English, who, unwilling to quit so important a city, had repeatedly delayed the restitution ; at first, on account of the opposition made to this measure by the Duke of Gloucester, and afterwards, by the Duke of York.*

King Charles demanded the full restitution which

* Rapin ; Barante ; Daniel ; Villaret.

had been promised him; and, at length, grown impatient of the delay, he dismissed Count Dunois with a powerful army, to lay siege to Le Mans. Upon this, King Henry commanded that the city should be given up; but, at the same time, he declared that it was but during the time of the truce, and that he reserved to himself the right of sovereignty.* The surrender was accordingly made in the year 1448.

1448.
Barante;
Rapin;
Hume

The feebleness of the English ministry at this period, while it served to encourage the discontents of the people, inspired their enemies, the French, with hopes of recovering their kingdom. Although they had again prolonged the truce, it was but to prepare for a renewal of war on the part of France. An unexpected circumstance, however, put an end to the truce sooner than was anticipated by any of the parties. The town of Fougiers, in Brittany, was suddenly seized upon by an Arragonese, named Surienne, who had been many years in the service of the English, and who had been governor of Le Mans at the time of its surrender to King Charles. He had, at first, refused compliance with the orders for this surrender, either doubting their authority, or anxious to retain his government as his only fortune; but, upon being compelled to yield it to the French, under Count Dunois, he withdrew with his troops, amounting to 2,500 men,† into Normandy, expecting to be quartered in some other town by the Duke of Somerset, who was Governor of Normandy. In this he failed, for Somerset refused to receive him, not being able to provide for his numerous followers, and displeased at his late disobedience.

Surienne, upon this, committed many ravages in Brittany, took the town of Fougiers, and supported his troops by his depredations.

* Holinshed; Barante; Hume; Carte; Villaret; Rapin; Monstrelet.
† Monstrelet says Surienne had only 700 men.

Y 2

The Duke of Brittany laid his complaints before King Charles, and this monarch required from Somerset compensation for these injuries. It was in vain that the latter represented that these depredations were committed without his privity, and that he had no power to restrain these adventurers; equally vain was his promise of affording satisfaction to the Duke of Brittany. The King of France rendered an accommodation impossible. He insisted on the recall of the plunderers, and that reparation should be made for the damages, which he caused to be estimated at the exorbitant sum of 1,600,000 crowns. This monarch had been occupied during the truce in establishing discipline in his army, in suppressing faction, repairing his finances, and promoting order and justice in his kingdom. Thinking this a fit opportunity for the renewal of the war, and conscious of his own superiority over the English, he dismissed two ambassadors to England to demand satisfaction for the insult offered to the Duke of Brittany; and should he even obtain this reparation, the King was prepared with another pretext to occasion a rupture with England. His ally, the King of Scots, had been engaged in a conflict with the English, who were charged by King Charles with having broken the truce with that monarch; but King James had not sought an advocate in his quarrel, and it was only because the French King had resolved on war that he made use of these pretexts.*

In England nothing but discord prevailed; the court was divided into factions, ever contending against each other, and exhibiting their mutual animosity; the people, displeased with their government, were full of complaints. In the midst of these dissensions the conquests in France were no longer attended to.

* Holinshed; Hall; Barante; Baker; Monfaucon; Hume; Pol. Vergil; Speed; Villaret; Ridpath.

The Queen and her counsellors did not even seem to think of preserving the acquisitions of Henry V.

The truces with France and Scotland had both been broken through, and there was much pillaging on the coasts, which were greatly exposed to such attempts. All these circumstances led to such great disorders, that men began to apprehend a rebellion. In the Paston Letters we find this, and similar expressions, "God save the King, and send us peace," which seem to imply a fear for the King's safety at this time, and alarm lest the discord so prevalent throughout the country should lead to civil war.*

The condition of England at this period, (when the 1448. Queen, and her chief minister, Suffolk, directed all public affairs, and when the discontents of the Yorkists were becoming more manifest,) render it highly probable that the hostilities on the northern borders originated, rather with the ambition and animosity of the chieftains of the Marches than from any public commands. The Scotch writers affirm that the English first violated the truce. The Earls of Northumberland and Salisbury, who were the Wardens of the East and West Marches, invaded Scotland, at the head of two different armies, and destroyed the towns of Dunbar and Dumfries.

A speedy revenge was taken by James Douglas, Lord of Balveny, (a brother of the Earl of Douglas,) by spoiling and laying waste the county of Cumberland, and burning the town of Alnwick. The English retaliated, and a considerable army marched against the Scotch, led over the Western March by the Earl of Northumberland, who encountered, near the River Sark in Annandale, the Scotch army, commanded by Hugh, Earl of Ormond, another brother of Earl Douglas. A bloody battle ensued, in which the Scots were

---

* Holinshed ; Hall ; Rapin ; Villaret ; Milles's Catalogue ; Paston Letters.

triumphant, and 3,000 English were killed, or, in their flight, were drowned in the Frith of Solway. Many were likewise taken prisoners, and amongst them Lord Percy, while bravely endeavouring to rescue his father from a similar fate. The Scots lost 600 men, and their chief, Sir Thomas Wallace, of Craigie, to whose prowess they were much indebted for their success. A short truce, the next year, was entered into, which ended these hostilities.* The King of Scots at this time celebrated his marriage with Mary of Gueldres.

In France, the Duke of Somerset was so ill-supplied with money, that he was obliged to disband great part of his army, and was unable to keep his towns and castles in repair; his exactions, too, in Normandy, rendered him hateful to the people of that province. In this unhappy position of affairs, he was at once attacked by four different armies, well disciplined and commanded; one of them by the King of France, another by the Duke of Brittany, and the other two by the Duke of Alençon, and Count Dunois. These forces no sooner appeared before the different cities than their inhabitants submitted. The French thus obtained possession of Verneuil, Nogent, Chateau Galliard, Ponteau de Mer, Gisors, Mantes, Vernon, Argentin, Liseaux, Fecamp, Coutances, Belesme, and Pont de l'Arche. So far from being able to lead his army into the field to oppose the enemy, the Duke of Somerset had not even the means of garrisoning the towns, or of furnishing them with provisions. He, therefore, had the mortification of beholding all the chief cities of this province fall successively into the hands of the French, while he retired with a few troops to Rouen, to endeavour to preserve this city from the general fate, and to await the arrival of succours from England;

1449.
Monstrelet;
Pinkerton.

1449.
Speed;
Hume.

* Ridpath ; Paston Letters ; Holinshed ; Pinkerton ; Monstrelet.

but even in Rouen the English could not long hope to maintain their ground, and they were soon besieged there. The Counts Dunois and St. Pol first encamped before the city, and as their heralds were not permitted to enter, they failed in their object of getting the people to declare for them. There were, however, numbers of the inhabitants already disposed to mutiny.*

The first assault failed; and King Charles, (who, accompanied by René of Anjou, arrived at this time at the camp,) thought it prudent to withdraw to Pont de l'Arche. Meanwhile Somerset, who, from the distracted state of affairs in England, could have but little hope of receiving succours, thought proper to treat with King Charles. Having obtained a safe conduct from the French King, the Archbishop and the chief citizens of Rouen, accompanied by several of the English generals deputed by Somerset, met, and conferred with Count Dunois, the Chancellor of France, and others. The Archbishop and his citizens accepted the terms offered by the French King, and engaged to use their endeavours for the surrender of the city; but with the English nothing was concluded.

The former kept their engagement, and the French troops were introduced into the city, amidst the universal joy of the inhabitants; while the Duke of Somerset and the Earl of Shrewsbury, with only 800 men, were compelled to withdraw to the palace, the castle, the gates, and other parts, for security.†

The Duke of Somerset demanded an interview with the King; and when conducted to him, he found him in the midst of his Council. Somerset required the same terms for the English as had been granted to the

* Barante; Monfaucon; Holinshed; Hall; Pol. Vergil; Rapin; Hume; Monstrelet.

† Baker; Rapin; Hume; Henry; Barante; Monfaucon; Anquetil; Villaret.

citizens, viz., permission to depart the city without molestation. To this request King Charles would not accede; but added, that he now required the surrender of Harfleur, and of all the fortresses in the Pays de Caux.

"Ah!" exclaimed Somerset, "give up Harfleur; "that can never be! It was the first city which sur-"rendered to our glorious King Henry V., five-and-"thirty years ago." He then left the Council, and with melancholy forebodings retraced his way to the castle, amidst shouts of "*Vive le Roi!*" and other demonstrations of the joy of the people.[*]

The siege was renewed by the French, and the Duke being unable, for want of provisions, to hold out many days, was, at last, compelled to capitulate. Somerset surrendered his artillery and six of the chief cities of the province, and made a payment of 50,000 crowns; he was also obliged to leave the Earl of Shrewsbury and Lord Butler as hostages for the performance of these conditions, and was then permitted to depart the city.[†] It was believed that the city would not have been lost if the citizens had remained faithful to the English; but the deficiency of supplies from England caused the Duke of Somerset to make large exactions on the people, and thus excited their ill-will.

Some authors, in speaking of the losses in France, assure us that the English were so weakened, that they could no longer resist the power of the French; while others blame the Duke of Somerset because he neglected to maintain a sufficient number of soldiers. It is certain, however, that the only true reason of all the evil was the divisions in England, where every

---

[*] Barante ; Monstrelet.

[†] Holinshed ; Baker ; Monfaucon ; Rapin ; Stow ; Henry ; Villaret ; Speed ; Pol. Vergil.

one was seeking his private revenge, instead of
uniting to resist their foreign enemies. Whilst there
seemed to prevail a kind of stupor in the English
Cabinet, and no attention was paid to the earnest
entreaties of Somerset, and others, for supplies for
the war, the whole realm was torn and distracted by
contentions.

The misrule of the Queen and her ministers, the
pride and hatred amongst the nobility, and the complaints of the people, all these were sufficient, even
more than sufficient, to paralyse any political power or
healthy action. It was the early manifestation of a
morbid condition which preceded the terrific scenes of
the civil war which speedily followed.

The Queen's inactivity about this time made it
almost appear that she was in league with her
husband's enemies; but it is evident that the English
were totally unprepared for war, and, therefore, that
Surienne acted independently in taking Fougiers;
yet, if the English were unable to continue the war,
and could not furnish the means for preserving their
acquisitions in France, some effectual step ought to
have been taken to establish peace.*

The conduct of the English ministers was faulty in
the extreme; they suffered King Charles to amuse them
with fruitless negotiations while he prepared for war;
and, on their own part, they neither contrived to
observe the truce, by making restitution to the Duke
of Brittany, nor did they take any measures for defence. Inexcusable as were these faults of the ministers, yet an accommodation with France would have
proved impossible, since King Charles was bent on
war, taking advantage of the dissensions in England.
These dissensions were rather aggravated than allayed

---

* Holinshed; Hume; Milles's Catalogue; Rapin; Villaret.

by King Henry and his Queen, the former not heeding them, and the latter being influenced by bad counsellors.

While the ministers were selected rather to favour the interests of the Queen, and to be subservient to her views and those of Suffolk, persons without talent and incompetent to rule the state were appointed, and others who had courage to oppose this party, (often men of merit and ability,) were dismissed from favour and excluded from any share in the administration. The people even complained that persons devoid of religion and without principle were chosen, in order that there might be fewer scruples in the way of any measure proposed by this party.

The Queen's government, as well as her choice of improper ministers, caused bitter complaints; and the people, impatient at the evident neglect of foreign affairs, became angry against the Duke of Suffolk, who, they said, had, by the surrender of Maine, been the cause of the losses in Normandy. They accused him of the murder of the Duke of Gloucester, whose memory was still cherished by the nation, and this served to throw a greater odium on all who were suspected of his death. Suffolk was likewise considered to have wasted the King's treasure, and to have removed from the royal presence his good and virtuous counsellors, and to have substituted persons of doubtful character, and enemies of the country. They even asserted that he had assisted in the removal of Gloucester, in order that this prince might not, with his wonted spirit and activity, penetrate or obstruct his designs.*

The Queen, too, became very obnoxious to the people; for, at this time, looking on Suffolk as the author of her power, she seemed to adopt his passions

---

* Holinshed; Sandford; Pol. Vergil; Allen's York; Rapin; Baker; Hume.

as her own; and, using her authority over the King, she found means to load the Duke with favours, following his advice in all things, and appearing to treat him as her confidant.[*]

This conduct was very unwise on the part of Queen Margaret, and highly prejudicial to her. It could only have been occasioned by her youth and inexperience. Yet the consequent imputations cast upon the Duke of Suffolk and Queen Margaret were not only untrue, but absurd and ridiculous, as may be believed when we consider the family of Suffolk, his character in private life, and his great age. Suffolk had attained his fiftieth year before the death of his great patron and friend, the Cardinal of Winchester, who had, as well as the Queen, shown him especial favour, yet exhibiting it towards him with the most judicious care.

The aspersions cast upon herself and Suffolk were not unnoticed by the Queen, who began to fear they tended to the destruction of the Duke, and perhaps might even be fatal to herself. It is said that Queen Margaret adjourned the Parliament, assembled at that time at Blackfriars, to Leicester, and again from thence to Westminster.[†]

Many private dissensions originated at this period of our history; and some of them still remain involved in mystery. Amongst them may be named the enmity between Lord Bonville and the Earl of Devon. In 1449 the latter nobleman was engaged in besieging Lord Bonville in his castle of Taunton, which caused a great disturbance throughout the West of England. Assistance was most unexpectedly rendered to the besieged by Richard, Duke of York, Lord Molines, William Herbert, and others; and we are informed that Bonville delivered himself up to the Duke of York. The origin of this quarrel does not appear, but

1449.

---

[*] Carte.   [†] Baker.

Lord Bonville from this period espoused the interests of the House of York; and even at this time Richard aimed at the crown.*

1449.

There were many changes also in the high offices of the kingdom. In this year the Bishop of Lincoln died; and, through the intercession of Suffolk, this bishopric was given to Marmaduke Lumley, Bishop of Carlisle.† John, Lord Beauchamp was made Treasurer, and Lord Cromwell, Chamberlain. Somewhat later the former was driven from office, and John Tiptoff, Earl of Worcester, was made Treasurer in his place; and, although Cromwell continued to be Chamberlain, we are told that the kingdom was ruled by the party of Somerset. This Duke was, indeed, sharing the royal favour. He was made Captain of Calais by King Henry, upon the occasion of the celebration of the festival of Christmas, held by this monarch at Greenwich in 1449.†

During the preceding summer a marriage had taken place, which had proved the unhappy source of contention. Thomas Neville, the son of the Earl of Salisbury, was united to the granddaughter‡ of Lord Cromwell, at Tattersalls, in Lincolnshire; and in returning from these nuptials a quarrel arose between the bridegroom and Thomas Percy, Lord Egremont, near York; which, adds the historian, " gave rise to the greatest trouble in England."§ This, and many other dissensions, like the gathering clouds in the distance, were portentous of the approaching political storms of this realm.

1449.

Amidst the confusion which prevailed at this period, a lawyer's apprentice, named Brystall, moved that the King, having no heir to give security to his title, an heir apparent should be elected; and he proposed the

* Toulmin's Taunton; Lingard.　　† W. of Worcester.
‡ Or niece, as others say.　　§ Lingard.

Duke of York. But for this offence Brystall was afterwards committed to the Tower.*

The Duke of York, at this time, first began to afford Queen Margaret cause for serious inquietude. At a meeting between this nobleman and the King he made some demands on the royal favour, to which, if this monarch was, by his meek and yielding temper, disposed to listen, we are informed that Queen Margaret was decidedly opposed ; and the Duke departed in satisfaction with his sovereign, but not in the same " good conceit" with his royal mistress. It was, indeed, rumoured that if the Duke of Buckingham had not, by his interference, prevented it, the Duke of York would have been arrested. The part which Buckingham took on this occasion was caused by the offence he had taken at the sudden dismissal of his two brothers from their offices of Chancellor and Treasurer, for this Duke usually sided with the Queen.†
He was also the friend of Somerset, whose part he took during an affray at Coventry, in which two or three townsmen were killed and the alarm-bell rung, when a general insurrection took place, to the annoyance of the nobility ; and " all this arose from the general hatred of the Duke of Somerset."‡

The aversion was even more general against the Duke of Suffolk, who upon one occasion (in 1449) was, with Lord Cromwell and others, in the Star Chamber, when William Taylboys, with a numerous party of his attendants—who were all secretly armed—surrounded the door of Westminster Hall and the Star Chamber, as Cromwell asserted, with intent to kill him. This was denied by Taylboys, and Suffolk admitted his excuses ; yet the Council committed him to the Tower.

1449.

* W. of Worcester.
† Paston Letters ; W. of Worcester.
‡ Lingard ; Paston Letters.

Lord Cromwell afterwards obtained a verdict against him; and, although it was against the wish of Suffolk, Taylboys was thrown into prison. Lord Cromwell also caused Suffolk to be called to account by the Commons for his disloyalty.

1449.
Stow.

On the 6th of November in this year John, Viscount Beaumont was made Lord Chamberlain of England; Henry de Bromefield was created Lord Vesey; and William Bonville was created Lord Bonville. William Beauchamp was also created Lord St. Amaraud, and Thomas Percy, Lord Egremont. John Stafford, Archbishop of Canterbury, dying in this year, he was succeeded by John Kemp, Cardinal of York.*

A rebellion in Ireland at this time added to the troubles in which the English Court was involved; but it afforded Queen Margaret an opportunity of dismissing the Duke of York from her presence, who had made himself particularly obnoxious to her by the rumours lately circulated respecting his pretensions to the crown. He was created Lord Lieutenant of Ireland, and dismissed to quell the insurrection, for which office, it was pretended, no one else was so well qualified. Only a few troops were, however, furnished him; and it is said that his enemies hoped he would, by a failure in this enterprise, forfeit his reputation with the people, or, that the chance of war would for ever remove this object of their mistrust.†

The Duke was keen enough to penetrate their designs; but he was so skilful that, by his condescension and mildness, he gained the good opinion of the Irish; and it must, in justice to the Duke, be said, that the Acts he passed during his administration were very creditable to his memory. He brought them back to their

---

* W. of Worcester; Stow; Paston Letters; Collinson's Somersetshire; Lysson's Mag. Brit.

† Baker; Stow; Rapin; Burdy's Ireland.

duty; and, without having recourse to arms, he accommodated their differences : nay, he did more than this, for he so won their affections that they ever afterwards remained faithful to his interests, and those of his family, even in their greatest troubles.[*] It was thus the Duke of York became all-powerful amongst this people; add to which, his vast possessions in Ireland increased his importance. He was Earl of Ulster and Cork, Lord of Connaught, Clare, Trim, and Meath, including at least a third of the kingdom in his inheritance.

In accepting the office of Lord Lieutenant of Ireland, the Duke had taken care that it should be attended with all the honours and power which his most distinguished predecessors had enjoyed. He had stipulated to hold his government for ten years; to receive the whole revenue of Ireland without account; with a pension annually of two thousand marks, and the same sum in advance. He was also empowered to let the King's lands, to dispose of all offices, to levy all such forces as he might consider necessary, to name his own Deputy, and to return to England at his pleasure.[†]

Two rival powers at this time contended for supremacy amongst the Irish, at the head of which were the Earls of Desmond and Ormond. Of these it may be observed, that the former was a powerful leader, although his authority had been acquired by a kind of usurpation of the rights of his nephew.

The Earl of Ormond, struggling amidst many difficulties and troubles, had been twice unjustly accused to Henry VI., whose lenity and kindness to this nobleman seems to have originated the lasting attachment

[*] Stow; Speed; Leland's Ireland; Moore's Ireland; Lingard; Burdy's Ireland; Rapin; Hume; Ellis's Orig. Letters.

[†] Leland's Ireland.

of the family of Butlers to the House of Lancaster.*
The leaders of the two opposing factions were chosen
by the Duke of York, upon the birth of his son, George,
Duke of Clarence, in the Castle of Dublin, to be the
sponsors for the child; which incident had its full
effect on Desmond, who became confirmed in his ad-
herence to the House of York; and by the use
which the Duke of York made of his power, he enabled
his party, in the subsequent contests with the Lancas-
trians, to draw forces from Ireland to maintain their
cause. It is also said that the zeal of the Irish was
much augmented by the flattery of the Duke whenever
called upon to support his cause in the subsequent
wars.

The use of the English bow was much encouraged
by the Duke in Ireland, and it was enacted that every
one holding lands or possessions to the value of 20*l.*
should entertain an archer, arrayed and horsed after
the English manner. This provision, though apparently designed for the Irish, was really intended to
maintain the Duke's cause in England, whenever he
should openly assert his claims to the Crown.*

During the absence of Duke Richard in Ireland the
dissensions at home continued, and no attempt was
made to accommodate them. Three predominant evils
still harassed the country, and seemed to threaten its
ruin. First, the misgovernment of the Queen and her
ministers; secondly, the pride and evil passions, especially covetousness, of the lords spiritual and temporal;
and lastly, the discontents of the people, occasioned by
the said misgovernment. There were many changes
in the rulers, and frequent commotions throughout
England, which could scarcely be allayed; the aristo-
cracy, growing more and more powerful, contended
against each other, and while yielding to their hatred

* Leland's Ireland.

and private animosities, the national welfare was forgotten.

To add to the murmurings of the people at this time, a considerable tax was laid upon the citizens of London.

The Bishop of Chichester, possibly discerning the coming disasters, resigned his seat in the Cabinet, and retired to Portsmouth, where, on the 9th of January, 1450, he was cruelly murdered by some sailors, said to have been hired for that purpose by Richard, Duke of York. Indeed the Duke's guilt was so apparent, that King Henry, two years afterwards, in his reply to the Duke of York's letter of complaint, confidently alluded to it. It has been suggested by some writers, that the Duke's hatred to all who were either wise or valiant enough to uphold King Henry, prompted him to this despicable action, and the sincerity of the Bishop could not fail to be a crime in the eyes of York. This was but one of many perfidious acts done by the adherents or accomplices of Richard, while he remained in Ireland. The people generally, however, appear to have taken part in this cruel deed, since they cried out that the Bishop was " a traitor to the King and Queen, and one of the " barterers of Normandy."

1450.
Speed.

Adam Moleyns, Bishop of Chichester, who was of the baronial family of Moleyns, was also Dean of Salisbury. The old chroniclers call him "a wise and "stout man." He was one of the ambassadors who, conjointly with Sir Robert Roos and others, had agreed for the cession of Maine and Anjou.*

In the same year, though somewhat later, the great power of Richard, Duke of York, was again made

1450.
Stow.

---

* Adam Moleyns was succeeded by Sir Reginald Peacock in the bishopric of Chichester.—*Stow; Speed; Carte; W. of Worcester; Toulmin; Howel's Med. Hist. Ang.*

apparent. In the city of Gloucester he took Reginald, Abbot of St. Peter's, and sent him, with others, to the castle of Gloucester. This act was immediately on the Duke's return from Ireland.[*]

1450. The annals of this year were filled with tragical events, which exhibited the ferocious spirit of the times, and seemed to be precursors of the coming national calamities. One dark and mysterious page relates the cruel destruction of William Ascough, Bishop of Salisbury. He was descended from an ancient family, seated at Kelsey, in Lincolnshire. On the 26th of July, 1438, he had been consecrated to the above see, in the chapel of Windsor, and soon after appointed the King's confessor; this being the first instance of a bishop fulfilling this office.

Having occupied this see nearly twelve years, he had become obnoxious to the Commons of Leicester, who pointed him out as an object of public resentment, and when the rebel Jack Cade and his followers came to Edginton, in Lincolnshire, where the Bishop then was, some of this prelate's own tenants joined the rebels, and falling upon his carriages, plundered them, carrying off no less than 10,000 marks in money. They assaulted the Bishop himself on the following day, the 29th of June, 1450, even whilst officiating at the altar in his vestments; and dragging him away to a neighbouring hill, they barbarously murdered him. While kneeling down and offering his last prayer, one of the party clove his skull with a bill; then tearing his bloody shirt in pieces, *to be preserved in memory of the action*, they left his body naked on the spot.[†]

* Stow; Fosbroke's Gloucestershire.
† Stow; Fabian Speed; W. of Worcester; Baker; Lingard; Fuller's Worthies.

Dr. Fuller, in speaking of this tragedy, gives this distich :—

> " By people's fury mitre thus cast down
> " We pray henceforward God preserve the crown."

The motive for this cruel treatment is not at first apparent. Bishop Godwin cannot account for it; but Dr. Fuller imagines it was because the Bishop of Salisbury was "learned, pious, and rich," three capital crimes in a clergyman; and the last of these sufficiently accounted for the horrid tragedy, it being very probable, that, having robbed the good Bishop, they afterwards murdered him to secure his riches.

When we again consider the *tearing of the bloody shirt to pieces, to be borne away as a trophy* of the act, it does not appear that it was *avarice* which actuated the murderers. The circumstance of the Bishop's own tenants having joined in the attack would seem to show that he was, though perhaps unjustly, held to be a haughty or cruel master.[*]

Amidst the general dissatisfaction, which extended itself even to the members of the Council, Parliament met to arrange the affairs of France, and to devise some means for the recovery of their losses. The Queen perceived the necessity of their assistance to prosecute the war in France, lest they should be compelled to withdraw from that kingdom, and thus afford fresh cause for displeasure to the nation.

The divisions in the Cabinet suggested to the mind of Queen Margaret that she might obtain her object with more facility by the removal of the Parliament to Leicester, where she hoped to find herself more popular than in London; but her design was so earnestly opposed by the Lords, that she was compelled to abandon it, and the meeting was held at West-

1450.
Rapin.

---

[*] Fuller's Worthies ; Biograph. Britannica.

consort to follow up his success by the pursuit of the insurgents. Yielding rather to feminine weakness, or fear, she entreated that the King would not place himself in personal peril, but resign to his lieutenants this easy victory.

The prayers of Margaret prevailed, and Henry, giving Sir Humphrey Stafford charge of his forces, retired with the Queen to the castle of Kenilworth.

Surely in the midst of the troubles and difficulties with which Queen Margaret had so lately been surrounded, it can hardly be doubted, that she must have greatly required the skill and experience of the several nobles and statesmen of whose services she had, in so brief a period, been deprived. Her indignation had been excited by the cruel murder of the Duke of Suffolk, whom she had vainly endeavoured to protect; and while deploring the loss of her earliest friend in England (who had brought her hither, and had braved with her the public enmity and hatred), how painful must it have been to her to endure alone these trials!

Even more than Suffolk must the youthful Queen have missed the talented Cardinal of Winchester, whose skill and discernment had, for so many years, been employed in the direction of political affairs. He might indeed, like the helm, have guided safely the tempest-tossed vessel in the late rebellion, during which, it may even be believed that the saving hand of a Gloucester would have been welcome!

At such a time as this, the return of the Duke of Somerset was considered fortunate, and we are told that the royal pair "hailed his arrival as a blessing." Somerset was indeed the nearest relative of the King; and at this moment, when the court was beginning to be distracted by the pretensions of the Duke of York, it was hoped that the services and attachment of one whose interests were allied to those of the crown, would successfully oppose the ambitious projects of that nobleman. By some historians, Somerset has been considered as the only faithful minister of Henry VI., who, by his care, watchfulness, and good counsels, sought to deliver the kingdom from factions, and preserve peace. The Duke of York, therefore, justly anticipated the opposition he would raise to his projects, and determined to excite against him the hatred of the people and the envy of the nobility.

Certain it is, that the presence of Somerset was attended with new troubles to the Queen. The people immediately raised clamours against the Duke; they accused him of not having done his duty in Normandy, and blamed him for the loss of that province, but especially for his conduct at the siege of Caen. The Commons, adopting these complaints, presented a petition to the King, praying that the conduct of Somerset might be investigated, and that, in the meantime, he should be sent to the Tower. Their request was granted, for Henry was unwilling to offend the House of Commons.* Upon receiving the news of the imprisonment of the Duke, the populace evinced such transports of delight that they immediately attacked and plundered his palace; and in spite of the exertions of the King's officers, they created such a tumult as could not be appeased until one of the ringleaders had been despatched.

At the breaking up of Parliament the Duke was liberated, and placed in the same situation at court as the Duke of Suffolk had occupied. He was created Prime Minister, and the Queen showed him great

1451.
Paston
Letters.

---

* This arrest of Somerset appears, according to some authors, to have been by the advice of the lords of the King's council, for the safety of his person, and to prevent his falling into the hands of his adversary; besides, that the power of the Lancastrian party was sufficiently strong to prevent his being brought to trial. His imprisonment was only for fourteen months. *Paston Letters; Rapin; Lingard; Villaret; Daniel.*

Duke as to the support he would be likely to obtain from the people; for, if such vast numbers were disposed to support the pretensions of one who had such slight claims to their notice, what might not be expected when the true heir of the House of March should step forward to demand their support?[*] The general discontent at the Queen's conduct, and that of her ministers, also warranted his hopes, and encouraged him in the first steps of his ambitious career.

This nobleman held a consultation with his friends and adherents, with whom it was determined that the Duke should retire into Wales, where he had many partisans, and there secretly secure an army to support his pretensions.[†]

1451.
Rapin;
Holinshed.

The Duke lost no time in executing his designs. When he had raised an army of 10,000 men in Wales, he addressed, from his castle of Ludlow, a monitory letter to the King, previously to his taking any steps which might be construed into rebellion. He therein complained, that during his stay in Ireland, he had been calumniated to the King; and that certain persons, set as spies, had been lying in wait in six several places to seize him, with intent to convey him to Conway Castle. Also, that his landing in England had been opposed by the King's officers; and that letters had been despatched to Chester, Shrewsbury, and other places, to prevent his reception. He also complained of the malicious attempts of certain persons to indict him for treason, to his great injury, and that of his family, and "for all this, he required, that justice should be done him." The Duke also complained of the general disaffection to the ministry, and especially

---

[*] Pol. Vergil; Rapin; Henry.

[†] Holinshed; Baker; Sandford; Pol. Vergil; Milles's Catalogue; Lingard.

towards the Duke of Somerset, whose conduct, he prayed, might be inquired into, and satisfaction afforded to the nation.   He offered his assistance in the execution of this purpose; and further complained, of Somerset's restoration to favour without being subjected to any examination.*

It was evident to the ministers that the Duke of York sought to quarrel with them; but, in the present position of affairs, they dared not show him any resentment.   King Henry, in his reply to the Duke's letter, alluded to the fact of the Duke having unlawfully slain the Bishop of Chester, as one of the causes of the frequent complaints against him; also, that the rumours of the ambitious sayings of the Duke had led the court, although uncertain of their truth, to act on the defensive, by placing troops to oppose his landing; but that the manner of the Duke's appearing, being unarmed, had sufficiently evinced his loyalty; and that his reception by the King would have been different had not the suddenness of his coming, without previous notice, occasioned the servants of the crown to act on their former orders.   The King wrote also to this effect, viz., that he had some time since resolved to reform the government; and that for this purpose he intended to appoint certain counsellors of talent and virtue, amongst whom the Duke should be included; that it required some deliberation before he could bring to justice the traitors, of whom the Duke had complained; but that he would not permit them to go unpunished, not even the Duke of Somerset.†

This moderate reply, which was altogether unexpected by the Duke of York, took from him every pretence for rebellion; yet he resolved that the King's refusal to punish the ministers immediately should

---

* Hall; Fabian; Rapin; Hume; Phillips's Shrewsbury.
† Holinshed.

furnish him with a pretext for employing an army already prepared; and that he would not be turned from his purpose by a moderation which might be real, or designed to deceive him.*

Thus it was that ambition stifled the dictates of reason, and led on to civil warfare.

The Duke of York marched at the head of his new army towards London; but he had not proceeded far before he learnt that the royal forces were prepared to oppose him.

The Queen, who had anticipated his design, had been more active than he expected. She had raised, in the King's name, a body of troops, but without informing them for what purpose; and thus, while the Duke had retired into Wales, she had been engaged in preparing an army to advance against him.†

It was not the Duke's object to risk a battle yet, without a better pretence to win the people to his side, and to justify his rebellion. He well knew also that the citizens of London were of themselves sufficiently powerful to incline the balance in favour of either party, and therefore he resolved to gain that city over to his interests. On a sudden, therefore, he altered his course on hearing of the King's approach, although he was not deficient in courage, or in experience.‡ He endeavoured, by a rapid march, to get before the King, and expected on reaching the capital to be well received there; but, to his great disappointment, he found the gates shut, the citizens being unwilling to declare for him, while their King was so near at hand, with a much larger army. The Duke of York was therefore obliged to cross the Thames, at Kingston. He encamped at Brent Heath, near Dartford, twelve miles from London, whither the King followed him,

* Rapin; Pol. Vergil.

† Baker.   ‡ Rapin.

and pitched his camp at a distance of four miles from the insurgents. An engagement seemed inevitable; but the King dismissed the Bishops of Winchester and Ely to demand the reason of the Duke of York taking up arms; and the latter finding it expedient, at this juncture, to make his peace at court, for fear of ruining his affairs by precipitation, alleged that it had never been his intention to desert his sovereign; but that he only desired to remove from the Council certain evil-disposed persons, of whom the Duke of Somerset was the chief; and that he was willing to disband his troops, if the King would consent to the imprisonment of Somerset, so long as Parliament should decree.

King Henry's compliance with this request occasioned no less surprise to the Duke than he had before felt at his moderation, in the answer to his letter. He knew that both the King and Queen were guided by the advice of Somerset, whose interest it was to reject these demands; and for whose sake (as York wished it to appear) the ministers did not hesitate to involve the country in a civil war. The King not only engaged to comply with the Duke's request, but immediately caused the Duke of Somerset to be apprehended. Then would York gladly have retracted his word; but he was thus compelled to disband his forces, which he preferred doing to the risk of losing the favour of the people.[*]

Upon this the Duke boldly appeared in court, without taking any precautions for his own safety; nay, he even ventured, in the presence of the King, to accuse the Duke of Somerset, with much vehemence, of having sacrificed the interests of his country to his own ambitious and sordid views. At this moment, whilst he was boldly proclaiming his enemy to be a traitor,

* Sandford; Baker; Milles's Catalogue; Daniel; Stow; Pol. Vergil; Rapin; Hume; Henry; Lingard; Birch's Illus. Persons of Great Britain.

Vaudemont. Queen Margaret, although not able to share these duties, was deeply afflicted, and sympathized in the grief of René, who for a time appeared inconsolable.

If it be true that highly gifted intellects are apt to grasp at the probable future, and to guide their actions thereby, we may suppose that Queen Margaret, observing the passing clouds which oft overshadowed the reasoning faculties of her husband, formed some anticipation, that by a more heavy oppression he might be visited. She felt the urgent need of judging and acting for him when he was unable to decide on public affairs which perplexed and excited him. She therefore adopted the course of leading him to pass his time in peaceful occupations and amusements. Some have blamed this prudence, saying these pursuits were more suitable for a monk than for a king. Yet the Queen evinced in this her gentleness and affection for her consort no less than the correctness of her judgment.

It was during this unhappy position of affairs that Queen Margaret gave birth to her only child, Prince Edward. This summer the Queen had been residing at the Palace of Westminster, and here it was that her son, the heir of King Henry's now disputed throne, first saw the light, on the 13th of October, (St. Edward's day,) in 1453. The Queen was attended by the Duchess of Somerset, to whom she was much attached.

1453.
Holinshed;
Sandford;
Pol. Vergil;
Hume;
Lingard;
Rapin.

The nation rejoiced greatly at the birth of their prince. The little infant was baptized in Westminster Abbey, the ceremony being performed, with great splendour, by the pious William Waynfleet, Bishop of Winchester,* who was King Henry's most beloved

---

* This prelate immediately afterwards confirmed the infant prince, according to the Roman Catholic rites.

friend and counsellor; and the Duke of Somerset, the Archbishop of Canterbury, and the Duchess of Buckingham were the sponsors. The font was arrayed in russet cloth of gold, and surrounded by a blaze of tapers. The "Crysome" or king's mantle, in which the royal babe was received after his immersion, with other accessories, cost the sum of £554 16s. 8d. This mantle was very rich with embroidery of pearls and precious stones, and was lined with a fine white linen wrapper, to prevent the brocade and gems from coming in contact with the delicate skin of the new-born prince.*

On the 18th of November the ceremony of the churching of the Queen took place at the Palace of Westminster, a writ of summons under the privy seal having been issued to command the attendance of ladies of the highest rank in England. On this occasion were present ten duchesses, eight countesses, one viscountess, and sixteen baronesses.†

1453.

King Henry was still suffering under his severe mental malady, and in such a state of aberration of mind that he could not notice his little son. The condition of the King, at this time, is portrayed in an interesting passage in a letter addressed to the Duke of Norfolk, as follows:—"As touchyng tythynges, "please it you to wite, that at the Princes comyng to "Wyndesore, the Duke of Buk' toke hym in his armes, "and presented hym to the Kyng in godely wise, be-"sechyng the Kyng to blisse him; and the Kyng gave "no maner answere. Natheles the Duk abode stille "wit the Prince by the Kyng; and whan he coude "no maner answere have, the Queene come in, and "toke the Prince in hir armes, and presented hym in

---

* Issue Rolls; Fabian; Milles's Catalogue.

† Five hundred and forty "brown sable backs" adorned the Queen's churching-robe. See Appendix, p. 435.

" Panynges, Clyfford, Egremond, and Bonvile, are get-
" ting all the forces they can to come hither with them."

" Tresham, Joseph, Daniel, and Trevilian, have
" made a bill to the Lords, desiring to have a garrison
" kept at Windsor for the safeguard of the King and
" Prince, and that they may have money for wages of
" them, and other, that shall keep the garrison. Thorp
" of the Exchequer, articulethe fast against the Duke
" of York, but what his articles were is unknown. The
" Duke of Somerset's herbergeour hath taken up all
" the lodgings that might be had near the Tower, in
" Thames Street, Mark Lane, St. Katherine's, Tower
" Hill, and thereabout."

" The Queen has made a bill of five articles, which
" she desires to be granted her. First, that she desires
" to have the whole rule of this land ; the second, that
" she may appoint the Chancellor, Treasurer, Privy
" Seal, and all other officers of this land, with sheriffs,
" and all other officers that the King should make ;
" the third is, that she may give all the bishoprics of
" this land, and all other benefices belonging to the
" King's gift ; the fourth is, that she may have suffi-
" cient livelihood assigned her for the King, the Prince,
" and herself ; the fifth article was omitted."

In continuance, the writer describes the coming, on
the 25th January, of the Duke of York to London,
with his friends, Salisbury, Warwick, the Earls of
March, Richmond, and Pembroke, each one of them
with a formidable array of armed retainers. Next, he
adds ;—" Every one who is of the opinion of the Duke
" of Somerset makes himself ready to be as strong as
" he can make him."

Then follows a caution to York to watch and beware of the snares of his enemies ; for, he adds, " the
" Duke of Somerset has spies going in every lord's
" house of this land ; some go as brothers, some as

" shipmen and otherwise, which make known to him
" all that they see or hear relating to the Duke;
" therefore," he repeats, " beware and watch." *

According to the information conveyed in this
letter,† the Duke of York made his appearance in the
metropolis, accompanied by his most powerful adherents and friends, each of them bringing a numerous
retinue. The Court took alarm; and to prevent dissensions and warfare, which they apprehended, the
Queen reluctantly consented to admit the Duke of
York, and the Earls of Salisbury and Warwick, to the
Council.

The Parliament which had been summoned to meet
at Reading on the 12th of November, 1453, was, in
consequence of the King's illness, adjourned until the
11th of the February following, and again until the
14th of the same month in 1454, when the meeting
was appointed to be held at Westminster.

Previous to the events of this year, 1454, York had
taken the resolution to remove the unfavourable im-
pressions inspired by his former conduct, by adopting
a mild and submissive course, at the same time seeking to win the public favour. His willingness to disband his troops, and his oath of fidelity to the King,
were, he well knew, likely to remove any suspicions of
his evil intentions.‡

The King's malady was at its height in the year 1453,
and the government was then chiefly administered
by the aged Chancellor Kemp. It is true Queen
Margaret herself exercised the regal authority in the

* Egerton MSS.

† The object of the writer appears to have been to convey information
privately, which had been collected by several persons belonging to the
household of John Mowbray, Duke of Norfolk, one of the lords of the Yorkists' party, that their master might be acquainted with the events passing
in London, and other places, before his arrival in the capital.

‡ Rapin.

These all encamped the night before their encounter at Watford, and the following morning entered St. Albans.[*]

[*] Baker ; Holinshed ; Stow ; Sandford ; Carte ; Phillips's Shrewsbury ; Howel ; Hume ; Pol. Vergil ; Rapin ; Lingard ; Henry.

APPENDIX
TO THE FIRST VOLUME.

(Rymer's Fœdera, vol. xi.) A.D. 1444. 22 Henry VI.

For the Earl of Suffolk upon his scruples in the execution of the Embassy entrusted to him.

The King to all, &c. :—

Know that, as we have commissioned our dearly beloved cousin, William de la Pole, Earl of Suffolk, Great Seneschall of our Household, our Ambassador, and others in his suite in our kingdom of France, to our Uncle and Adversary of France, upon certain matters touching Us, our Kingdom, our dominions and the quiet of our subjects.

And as our cousin fears to exceed the bounds of his commission as granted by Act of our Council under our own hand and Seal.

We, wishing to remove all occasion of fear and scruple from our aforesaid cousin, and all doubt in the execution of our laws and commands, and every like feeling in the hearts of our subjects.

To all and every we wish to be known, in our great desire for peace, the matrimony of our person, and the quiet and tranquillity of our faithful English subjects, &c., &c.

Here follows a declaration exonerating the Ambassador and his heirs for ever and ever from any consequences resulting from the discharge of his embassy, and freeing him and his heirs from all molestation, or demands on the part of the King, his heirs or successors.

Witness the King at Westminster,
Feb. 25.

Mandate for the Payment of Moneys for the expenses of the Queen's journey into England.

Henri, by the grace of God, kyng of Englande and of Fraunce, and lord of Irlande, to the tresorere and chamberlains of oure Eschequier, greting,

We, by the advice of oure counsail, have maade certain advisamentz of dispenses and coustages that by estinacione wolde suffise for the bringing oute of our reaume of Fraunce unto oure presence of oure mooste beste beloved wyf the quene, as by ij copies of the said advises, the whiche we sende unto you closed withinne thees, it may appere unto you more at plain. We wol therefore, by thadvis of oure saide counsail, and charge you that yedeliver, by way of apprest, unto oure welbeloved servantz Johne Breknoke and to Johne Everdone, clercs in oure householde, or to the oon of theim, whom we have assigned to entende for and aboute the said expenses, the sommes conteigned in the said cedules after the tenour of theim, to paie the same sommes after the teneure of the said advises.

Yevene undre oure Prive Seal, at Westminster, the xix day of Augst, the yere of oure regne xxij.

BENET.

(The Second Schedule.)

Five barons and baronesses, each four shillings and sixpence the day, and three esquires, each at twenty-three pence the day, two valets, each at sixpence the day for ninety-one days.

The controuller at two shillings and sixpence the day, and one esquire at eighteen pence the day, two valets each at sixpence the day, for ninety-one days.

Thirteen knights, each at two shillings and sixpence the day, and six valets, each at sixpence the day, for ninety-one days.

Forty-seven esquires, each at eighteen pence the day, and one valet, each at sixpence the day, for ninety-one days.

Eighty-two valets, each at sixpence the day, for ninety-one days.

Twenty sumptermen and others, each at four pence the day, for ninety-one days.

BENET.

On Safe Conduct to see the Coronation of the Queen.

The King, by his letters patent to remain in force the next half year, doth take under his especial protection, safe keeping, and defence, for safe and sure conduct, William Monypeny, Esqr., and Master Donald Motmulon, Clerk, Scotsmen, and their sixteen servants, in their journey in the Kingdom of the King of England, by land or by sea, by water, on foot or on horseback, with their gold and silver in bars and wallets, and all other goods whatever, on their coming to see the solemnity of the Coronation of the Queen.

Here follows permission to come to any place within his Majesty's dominions, Territories, and Jurisdiction, to abide and to go backwards and forwards as often, and in what way they please, during the term of the

Safe Conduct, without let, hindrance, or obstruction from the servants and officers of the King.

Provided always, that they conduct themselves well and honestly towards the King and his people, and that neither by word or deed they say, or attempt anything that may tend to the prejudice of the King or people—provided always, that they do not enter into any Castle, Fortress, or fortified Town of the King, without shewing to the proper Authorities the letters of Safe Conduct.

Witness the King at Westminster,
Dec. 5.

(Ibid.) A.D. 1445. 23 Henry VI.

Concerning the ring with which the King was sacred on the day of his Coronation at Paris, to be remade for the marriage of the Queen, and of various presents.

Right trusty and well-beloved,

For, as moch as oure Trusty and well beloved Squire John Merston, Tresorier of oure Chamber and Keeper of our Jewels, hath by oure special commandement delivered these jewelles under written; that is to say :—

A Ryng of Gold garnished with a fayr rubie, somtyme yeven unto us by our Bel oncle the Cardinal of Englande, with the which we were sacred in the day of our Coronation at Parys, delivered unto Matthew Philip to Breke and thereof to make another ryng for the Queen's wedding ring.

Here follows an enumeration of various articles of gold and jewellery with their prices, presents from the King to various persons, on the New Year's day previous.

A Tabulet of Gold with an Ymage of the Pite of Our Lord, Garnished with Stones and Perle, bought of Matthew Philip, and yeven unto oure bel oncle, the Duc of Gloucester, by us on Neweyere's Day last passed, price xc *lib.*

A Cuppe of Golde covered and chased, bought of John Pattesley, goldsmith of London, and yeven by us to oure bel oncle the Cardinale of England, on the said Neweyere's Day, price xc *lib.* vij *s.*

An Ouche of Gold Garnished with a Balys, a Saphyr, and a great Perle, bought of the said Mathew, and yeven by us unto the Duc of Exeter on the said Neweyere's Day, price lx *l.*

A Tabulet of Gold garnished with stones and perle, Bought of the said John Pattesley, and Yeven by Us unto the Archebishop of Canterbury on the said Neweyere's Day, price l *lib.*

A Tabulet of Gold with an Ymage of Our Lady, garnished with stonys and perle, Bought of the said John, and Yeven by Us unto the Duchesse of Buckingham on the said Neweyere's Day, price xxxiii *l.* vi *s.* viij *d.*

An Ouche of Gold made in manner of a Gentil-woman, garnished with stones and perle, bought of the said Mathew, and Yeven by Us unto the Earl of Warwick on the said Neweyere's Day, price xxx *l.*

A Tabulet of Gold with an Ymage of St. Katerine, garnished with stonys and perle. Bought of the same Mathew and Yeven unto the Bishop of Sarum on the said Neweyere's Day, price xxvi*l*. xiii*s*. and iiij *d*.

A Gipser of Gold, garnished with Rubies and perle, bought of the said Mathew, and Yeven by Us unto oure Cousin, the Viscount Beaumont, on the said Neweyere's Day, price xx *l*.

An Ouche of Gold made in manner of a parc, garnished with Stonys and Perle, and bought of the said Mathew, and Yeven by us unto the Lord of Sydeley, on the sayd Neweyere's Day, price xx *l*.

An Ouche, garnished with a Balys, a Saphyr, and six Perles, bought of the said Mathew, and Yeven by Us unto Sir James Fenys, Knight, on the same Neweyere's Day.

An Ouche of Gold made in manner of a Peche, garnished, bought of the said Mathew, and Yeven by Us unto Sir John Beauchamp, Knight, Steward of our Howshold, on the same Neweyere's Day.

An Ouche of Gold and in the middes a Flour de Lyes, bought of the said Mathew, and Yeven to Sir Roger Fenys, Knight, Tresorier of oure household on the same Neweyere's Day.

And an Ouche of Gold garnished with a greet Perle, a Rubie, and a Diamond playn, taken of the Stuff of our Jewelhows, and Yeven by Us unto Rose Merston on the sayd Neweyere's Day.

We wol and Charge you, that, under our Prive Seal, being in your Warde, ye do make oure Letters of Warrant sufficient and in due forme unto oure said Squire for his discharge for the deliverance of the Jewelles aforesaid, and theese our Letters shall be your Warrant.

Yeven under our Signet at our Castle of Wyndesore the xij day of January the yere of oure Regne xxiii.

Dors.

To our Right Trusty and Well beloved Clerc, Maister Adam Moleyns, Keper of oure Prive Sele.

Concerning the jewels prepared for the Coronation of the Queen, &c., &c.

(Ibid.) A.D. 1445. 23 Henry VI.

R.

To the Tresorer and Chamberleins, &c., Greting.

We Wol and Charge you that ye Deliver sufficient assignement of the Half XVth Graunted unto Us by the Lay People of this oure Reaume in this oure present Parlement of Four Thousand Marc, as for Monnoye Lent unto Us in manere and fourme as foloweth; that is for to sey,

Of Two Thousand Marc to Us into oure Chambre by the Handes of John Merston, Keper of oure Jewells, for a Jewell of Saint George the whiche we have Bought of oure trusty and welbeloved Knight, William Estfeld.

And of the other Two Thousand Marc, for Two Thousand Marc the whiche oure said Knight hath lent nowe unto Us in Prest Money at the Contemplacion of our moost best beloved Wief the Queene for hir commyng nowe unto oure Presence.

Yeven, &c., at Wyndesore the Sext Day of Aprill, the Yere, &c., xxiii.

R., &c.

To the Tresorer and Chamberleins of oure Eschequier Greting.

We Wol and Charge you that, for such things as oure right entierly Welbeloved Wyf the Queene most necessaryly have for the Solempnitee of hir Coronation, ye Deliver, of oure Tresour, unto oure trusty and welbeloved squier John Merston, Keper of oure Jewell, a Pusan of Golde, called Ilkyngton Coler, Garnished with iv Rubees, iv greet Sapphurs, xxxii greet Perles, and liii other Perles. And also a Pectoral of Golde Garnished with Rubees, Perles, and Diamonds, and also with a greet Owche Garnished with Diamondes, Rubees, and Perles, sometyme bought of a Marchant of Couleyn for the Price of Two Thousand Marc,

He as wel to Deliver the saide Pusan as the said Pectoral unto oure saide Wyf of oure Guft.

Yeven, &c., at Southwyk the xviii Day of Aprill, the Yere, &c., xxiii.

(Ibid.) A.D. 1445.   23 Henry VI.

Concerning the attendance of the Queen to England.

The King to all greeting :—

Be it known that we, in consideration of the great care, trouble, and expense, which our trusty and faithful Secretary, Richard Andrew, in our business, as our Ambassador, and especially in his attendance on our well-beloved Consort, on her departure from our Kingdom of France, and on her coming to our presence, has had and sustained, and also of the valuable, acceptable, and praiseworthy services which he has rendered us, and will render to us in future, in our especial favor, we have granted him One hundred pounds, to be received every year from the last past Festival of St. Michael.

To wit—Sixty Pounds from our Customs on Wool, Tan, and Skins in the port of our Town of Southampton, to be paid by the Collectors of those duties for the time being, at the Easter and Michaelmas Quarters, in equal portions of forty pounds from our Customs on Wool, Tan, and Skins, in our port of London, to be paid by the Collectors of those duties for the time being at the aforesaid periods in equal portions.

Confirming all other grants and gifts formerly made by us to the said Richard, all and every statute, act, ordonance, restriction, on any cause or matter whatever otherwise made or provided notwithstanding.

In virtue whereof, &c.,

Witness the King at Westminster,
15th day of May.

R E 2

(Ibid.) A.D. 1445. 23 Henry VI.

Concerning the customary gifts for the Master of the Ship who brought the Queen to England.

The King to all, &c., greeting :—

Know that, as we have been informed that it has always been a custom on those occasions, when Queens have arrived in this our kingdom, that certain gifts should be granted to the masters of those vessels in which they have crossed the seas.

We, therefore, in consideration of the good and faithful services which our trusty Thomas Adam, late master of the Ship called Cok John of Cherbourg, in which our well-beloved and chosen Queen voyaged to our said kingdom, rendered to our aforesaid Consort on her passage, in our especial favor do grant him 20 marks annually to the end of his life, on the death of John Williams, seaman, of our Customs, in port of our Town of Southampton, to be paid by the Collectors of Customs for the time being, at Michaelmas and Easter, in equal portions.

In virtue whereof, &c., &c.,

Witness the King at Westminster,
June 10.

Issue Roll, 23 Henry VI.

18th June.—To five minstrels of the King of Sicily, who lately came to England to witness the state and grand solemnity on the day of the Queen's coronation, and to make a report thereof abroad. In money paid to them in discharge of £50, viz. :—to each of them £10 which the Lord the King commanded to be paid, to be had of his gift by way of reward. By writ, &c. £50.

To two minstrels of the Duke of Milan, who came to England to witness the solemnization of the Queen's coronation, and report the same to the princes and people in their country. In money paid to them by the hands of Edward Grymeston, in discharge of 10 marks ; viz. :—to each of them 5 marks, which the Lord the King, with the advice and assent of his Council, commanded to be paid to the said minstrels, to be had of his gift. By writ, &c. £6 13s. 4d.

To John de Surenceurt, an esquire of the King of Sicily, and steward of the Queen's household abroad, who came previously to the Queen's reception, to witness the solemnization of her coronation, and to report the same as above. In money paid to him by the hands of Edward Grymeston, in discharge of 50 marks, which the Lord the King, with the advice and assent of his Council, commanded to be paid to the said John, &c. By writ, &c. £33 6s. 8d.

To John d'Escoce, an esquire of the King of Sicily, who, as a true subject of the Queen's father, left his own occupations abroad and came in the Queen's retinue to witness the solemnity on the day of her coronation. In money paid to him, &c. By writ, &c. £66 13s. 4d.

19*th June.*—To Sir Almeric Chaperon, knight, and Charles de Castelion, clerk, Ambassadors from the King of Sicily, lately sent to the Lord the King, in the Queen's retinue, upon certain affairs on behalf of the said Lord, the King of Sicily. In money paid to them in discharge of 200 marks, which the said Lord the King commanded to be paid to the said Almeric and Charles; viz.:—to each 100 marks, to have of his gift by way of reward.   By writ, &c., £133 6*s.* 8*d.*

Issue Roll. 27 Henry VI.

14*th Nov.*—To William Flour, of London, goldsmith. In money paid to him by assignment made this day, in discharge of 20 marks, which the Lord the King commanded to be paid to the said William, to be had by way of reward, because the said Lord the King stayed in the house of the said William on the day that Queen Margaret, his consort, set out from the Tower of London for her coronation at Westminster. By writ of privy seal amongst the mandates of Michaelmas Term, in the 24th year of the said King.   £13 6*s.* 8*d.*

PETITIONS IN PARLIAMENT IN THE TWENTY-THIRD YEAR OF HENRY VI.

(From original Documents in the Tower of London.)

So it baille as Srs.

     Grace be to the Lord.

" Henry by the grace of God, King of England and France, and Lord of Ireland, to all the present members of his Parliament Saluting.

Ye know how, when the honour of high rank of King took its first origin, and to which we have attained, it was disposed of by God to be administered by his rule, that the subordinate powers might be bestowed on all those needing and deserving the Royal munificence. In like manner it is fitting that the King's Majesty should be the more studious to provide for the Queen, as relating to her dowry; and since the ineffable providence of the Eternal King, ever bestowing his favours upon us, decided wisely on both sides; he has taken in marriage the most illustrious daughter of the King of Naples and Jerusalem, and Grand Duke of Lorraine, the Queen Margaret, born of Isabella, according to the agreement of our nuptials.

We do therefore tenderly solicit your wills and custom in the dowry of the Consort herself of Henry; following nobly the recorded works of our ancestors, the titles of her right, declaring that it should be given her at this demand in the following form; by the advisement and assent of the Lords present and temporal, and of the authority of King Henry of England in the present Parliament at Westminster; begun and held

A.D. 1444.

The Queen's Dower

on the twenty-fifth day of February, in the twenty-third year of King
Henry's reign, and until the twenty-ninth day of April then next following, adjourned and prorogued ; and afterwards until the twentieth day
of October then next following, adjourned ; and from the said twentieth
day of October, until the twenty-fourth day of January then next following, adjourned and prorogued ; by authority of those belonging to
the said Parliament : "We do give and concede to the said consort of
Henry, the castle, town, possessions and honours of Leicester, with its
members and dependencies in the county of Leicester, namely the Manor
of Desseford, the Bale of Desseford, the Manor of Shulton, the Bale of Shulton, the Manor of Hinkeley, the Borough of Hinkeley from without the Bale
of Hynkeley ; the Bale of Glenfeld, the Bale of Belgrave, and Syleby, with
40 marks per annum from the fruitful farm of the town of Gunthorp in the
county of Nottingham, the Bale of Curleton, the Manor of Stapulford, the
Bale of Stapulford, Hethelye, with the deed of the thrifty Frith, the Bale
of the Honor of Leicester in the Counties of Northampton, Warwick, and
Leicester, the Manor of Swannington, the farm and Mills of the town
of Leicester, the Manor of Fouston, the Manor of Sweton, and the Manor
of Langton in the County of Leicester, fixed at the value of 250l. 8s. 0¾d.
per annum.   The Castle, the Manor, and Honor of Tudbury, with their
members and appurtenances, viz., the Manor of Rolleston, the Manor of
Barton, the Manor of Marchington, Manor of Uttoxhatter, Manor of
Adgarseley, the Bale of one part, called Anard, of the other part, called
Rodman, the Bale lately freed in the County of Stafford, the Ward of
Tudbury, Ward of Barton, Ward of Yoxhale, the Ward of Marching-
ton, and the Ward of Uttoxhatter, in the County of Stafford ; and in the
County of Derby, the Manor of Duffeld, the Manor of Beaurepaire, Manor
of Holbrok, Manor of Allerwassle, Manor of Southwode, Manor of
Heighege, the Hundreds of Gresley, the Manor of Edrichay, Manor of
Holand, Manor of Byggyng, Manor of Irtonwode, Manor of Bonteshale,
Manor of Brassington, Manor of Matloke, Manor of Hertington, Manor
of Spondon, Manor of Scropton, the Hundreds of Appaltre, the Bale for
filling up lately freed in the County of Derby ; the Ward of Duffeld,
the Ward of Holand, the Ward of Colbrok, Ward of Beaurepare, the
Castle and Manor of Melbourne, the farm Querrere of Rouclif, the
Castle and estate of Alti Pecci, the Landsend called Wynnclondes, the
new freedom in Pecco in the County of Derby, fixed at the value of
927l. 17s. 7¼d. per annum.   The Manor of Yerkhull in the county of
Hereford, at the value of 6l. 13s. 4d. per annum.   The Manor of Croudon
in the County of Bucks, at the value of 20l. 11s. 4d. per annum.   The
Manor of Haseley, Manor of Kirtelington, Manor of Dadington, Manor
of Firyton, and the Manor of Ascot in the County of Oxfordshire, to the
value of 155l. 7s. 10½d. per annum.   The Castle and Estate of Plecy, the
Manor of Heighestre, Manor of Waltham, Manor of Masshebury, Manor
of Badewe,. Manor of Dunmowe; Manor of Lighes, Manor of Wykes,
Manor of Walden, Manor of Dependen, Manor of Quenden, Manor of
Northampstede, Manor of Farnham, Manor of Shenfeld, the Bale of the
Honor of Tudbury, Lancaster and Leicester, in the Counties of Essex,

Hertford, Middlesex, London and Surrey, the Manor of Enfeld, and a building called Hackeys, in the County of Middlesex, an Hotel in the city of London, called Blanch Appleton, with a house, called Steward's Inn, in the parish of St. Olive's in that city; the Castle and town of Hertford, the Manor of Hertfordingbury, Manor of Esgudeu, and the Manor of Bayford in the County of Hertfordshire; and the Manor of Walton in the county of Surrey, to the value of 555l. 16s. 0½d. per annum. The Estate in the County of Essex, to the value of 40l. 10s. 10d. per annum. The Manor of Wathersfield, in the County of Essex, to the value of 27l. 10s. 7d. per annum; and the Castle and possessions of Kenelworth, with dependencies in the County of Warwick, to the value of 15l. 4s. 6½d. per year. And certain Castles, Towns and honours, domaines, manors, lands and houses, and other things pertaining to Duke Henry of Lancaster, are promised and are held per annum at the value of 2,000l. To be had, held and kept of the said Consort of Henry, all the appointed Castles, Honours, Towns, Domains, Manors, Wapentaches, Bales, county estates, sites of France, carriages, landed farms, renewed yearly, the lands, houses, possessions and other things promised, with all their members and dependencies, together with the lands of the Military, Ecclesiastic advocacies, Abbotcies, Priories, Deaneries, Colleges, Capellaries, singing academies, Hospitals, and of other religious houses, by wards, marriages, reliefs, food, iron, merchandize, liberties, free customs, franchise, royalties, fees of honour, returned in a short time, and other our commands, given in our presence, and by executions on the same things by outlets, boundaries, and amercements, forests, chaises, parks, woods, meadows, fields, pastures, warrens, vivaries, ponds, fish waters, mills, mulberry trees, fig trees, and all other things pertaining to the same Castles, Honours, Towns, Estates, Manors, Possessions, lands, houses, and other things promised; however they may tend, or pertain to them; together with such returns of lands and tenements in the dowry, to the end of her life, or years; and by all other returns made to the appointed Castles, Towns, Honours, Possessions, Manors, Wapentaches, Bales, Lands, Houses, and other things promised however, tending, or pertaining thereto; to be given at the feast of the sacred Michael the Archangel, in the 24th year of King Henry, to the end of her life, in respect of her dowry, and so freely and honestly, until some restoring or making over to Us, or the heirs of Henry, so that we may inherit them, or be indebted to his heir if we hold them at the hands of Henry. And if it should happen that some of the appointed Castles, Honours, Towns, Dominions, Manors, Wappentaches, Bales, County Estates, Annuities, sites of France, carriages, landed Farmes, Restoration Lands, Tenements, possessions, or other things promised, should so be assigned through us to the said Consort of Henry in respect to her dowry, or some parcel of the same, that they shall be shown and recovered out of the hands of the said Consort of Henry, or that she herself shall be lawfully expelled from thence, or from some parcel of thence; then We will and concede, that the said Consort of Henry do receive the necessary satisfaction, and recompence of us, the heirs and successors of Henry, having so shown or recovered them by this means. And that the same Consort of Henry, when her authority is allowed, shall have and coerce for her whole life, through herself and her ministers, all things and all such like privileges, franchises, liberties, state affairs, with executions, for grant and proclamation of the same, concerning the Castles, Honoures, Towns, Dominions, Manors, Bales, and other things promised, assigned, and conceded, to the same Consort of Henry in the form appointed, such as we have appointed to Duke Henry in the said ways. And since diverse annuities to the amount of 324*l.* 11*s.* 3*d.* annually accruing, conceded to different persons before these times, to the end of the life of the same separately, of Castles, Dominions, Manors, Lands, Tenements, and other things promised, pertaining to the Duke Henry of Lancaster, are ended ; that it is appointed that such should be assigned to the Consort of Henry in respect to her dowry. We have conceded, and we do concede, when her authority is allowed, to the said Consort of Henry, 324*l.* 11*s.* 3*d.* to be had and held of the said Consort of Henry annually, from the said feast of the Sacred Michael to the end of her life ; on account of the issues, profits and returns of Henry, Duke of Cornwall, and on account of the issues, profits and returns of the Tin Coinages in the Counties of Cornwall and Devon, through the hands of the General Receiver, the said Duke Henry, our heirs and successors, and of whatever other Receivers, Occupiers, or Holders of the said profits, issues, and returns, for the time being, in recompense for the appointed 324*l.* 11*s.* 3*d.* of the appointed Castles, Dominions, Manors, Lands, Tenements, and other Possessions appointed, in the annuities being ended, which were given to the end of the lives of the divers persons separately. Provided always, that after that, it should happen, that any person inheriting any annuity by concession or confirmation of Henry, whether of any one of our progenitors, or ancestors, in the said Castles, Dominions, Lands, Tenements, and other possessions of the said Consort of Henry in respect to her dowry, above assigned, shall retire, whilst the appointed Consort of Henry is living ; that then such a sum as the same person may thus receive per annum from thence, or from some parcel thence, shall be annually deduced and cut off, during the life of the said Consort of Henry, for the use of Henry and our heirs, from the appointed 324*l.* 11*s.* 3*d.* conceded by the same Consort of Henry, as is appointed in recompense, and so singly during the life of the said Consort of Henry, after the decease of whose person some annuity in the appointed Castles, Dominions, Manors, Lands, Tenements and possessions appointed, shall be assigned to the said Consort of Henry, in the appointed form, as part of her dowry, by concession or confirmation of Henry, or of our fore fathers, or ancestors, as it is appointed, the heir dying, such a sum as the said person in his life may receive of the appointed 324*l.* 11*s.* 3*d.* annually, above repeated, during the life of the said Consort of Henry, shall be deduced and cut off, for the use of Henry and our heirs. We will also, and by granted authority ordain that the Chancellor, Duke Henry of Lancaster, for the time being, in writing under the seals of the same acknowledged Duke, shall certify before the Saint Henry to the Treaturers and Barons of the same Saint for the time being, other men, and single persons, for the said annuities of the said Castles, Dominions, Manors, and other things promised, pertaining to the same Duke, as part of the dowry that is promised to be assigned, or of some parcel of the same, inherited in whatever manner, besides the sums and quantity of this annuity of the same persons, that the same Treasurer and Barons may be able particularly to receive nothing in deducing and cutting off the said 324*l.* 11*s.* 3*d.* in recompense of the things conceded. And that all those who inherit, or are now about to inherit any farms belonging to the specified Castles, Manors, Honours, Lands, Tenements, Possessions, Profits, Emoluments, or commodities of whatever kind belonging to the Duke Henry of Cornwall through the said Royal patents of the great seal of Henry, or otherwise are held, or shall be held, to return, or pay whatever gains they themselves make through us for those farms, that they pay, and are compelled and held to pay, such gains to the Receiver-General, Henry, Duke of Cornwall, and not to the Reception of St. Henry, nor any others by any means. And that the same Dwellers on the soils of this said Receiver Henry, called Duke Henry for the time being, his farms made and appointed through the acquaintance or acquaintances of the Receiver himself, with St. Henry, and of our heirs, do testify the sum, or sums of monies received and paid of this same, to us, Henry's heirs and successors, that they may inherit the allowed allocation, and live quiet and free, and without pretext of any other payment, or by other means done. We concede also, and by granted authority of the said Consort of Henry we concede, a thousand pounds to be had and received of the same Consort of Henry, to the end of her life, annually, from the said feast of St. Michael, to the end of the Passover and St. Michael, in respect of her dowry, or marriage portion, from the issues, profits and returns of other remains of Castles, Dominions, Manors, Lands, Tenements, Honours, Services, Possessions and Heritages, and other emoluments of whatever kind belonging to Duke Henry of Lancaster, as in England, so in Wales existing and remaining in the hands of Henry, beyond the said Castles, Dominions, Manors, Lands, Tenements, and other things promised, pertaining to the Duke aforesaid, in respect of the dowry assigned, by the hands of the General Receiver, Henry, our heirs and successors, of the same Duke Henry of Lancaster for the time being. And if the said annual return of a thousand pounds or any part pertaining thereto, on the contrary should not be paid to the same Consort of Henry to any end aforesaid, then we will and concede, by authority and assent of the aforesaid, that it shall be held well lawful for the same Consort of Henry, through her officials and ministers in all the Castles, Dominions, Manors, Lands, and Tenements of Henry remaining appointed to the said Duke Henry of Lancaster, existing and remaining in the hands of Henry, to bind fast, and to carry off, the bond thus taken, to escape and hold back themselves from punishment until it is satisfied and paid to the same Consort of Henry by the same return and arrangements of the same party. And moreover lest perhaps the said possessions, and other things promised belonging to the Duke Henry of Lancaster remaining in the hands of Henry, should be diminished or accumulated by imposition, through which it might be likely that the said Consort of Henry should be retarded by any one from receiving payment of her said annual return of £1,000, by the said assent and authority we ordain and establish, that if any person of whatever rank or station he may be, shall adopt and receive any of the said patent royalties, under Seal of Duke Henry of Lancaster, or any other seal of Henry or of our heirs, or successors, in diminution, accumulation, or lessening of the same possessions and other things promised, after the Feast of Pentecost which will be in the year of our Lord 1446, that these said patents shall be deprived of vigour and authority in his cause. And moreover by the said authority We will, concede, and ordain, that all donations and concessions given after the said Feast of Pentecost henceforward through us to any person, or persons, by the said Henry, under the Seal of the Duke Henry of Lancaster, or any other seal of Henry, of any Dominions, Manors, Lands, Tenements, Restorations, and Services, of the said Duke Henry of Lancaster, or of any annuity proceeding from the same, made in any manner, shall be void in law, and that all that so given or conceded and contained in the said Henry's patents then finished, made known or specified, forthwith and immediately after the donation or concession of the same as is appointed to be done, shall remain to the said Consort of Henry, to be held to the end of her life, as part of the deduction of the said £1,000 assigned and conceded to the same Consort of Henry as is appointed in respect to her dowry or marriage portion. Provided always, that the true annual value of this thing so given or conceded, be annually deducted and pruned out of the said £1,000 for the use of Henry and our heirs: and in order that for better security it be paid annually to the same Consort of Henry out of her said annuity of £1,000 through us, as it is appointed to be conceded to her, by the hands of the General Receiver Henry for the time being, we will and ordain, by the aforesaid authority, that no particular Receiver for any one of the Castles, Dominions, Manors, Honors, Grounds, and other things promised of the Duke Henry of Lancaster remaining in the hands of Henry, shall have any demand in his computations henceforth returned through the Auditors of the same Duke Henry, of any sums of money whatever out of the issues of his office through any other person except that to be paid by Henry the Receiver-General, the said Duke Henry, during the life of the said Consort of Henry ; always excepted whatever sums of money are inherited by any persons as any annuities, by the concession, or confirmation of Henry before these times, received by any person of the said Duke Henry, through such his annuities, and through the grounds and walks of the Officials and Ministers of Henry, by and under the said Duke Henry paid annually, besides by the necessary Keepers and repairers of the Castles, Dominions, Manors, Lands, and Tenements of the said Duke Henry, existing in the hands of Henry, and by other repairers and rebuilders of the same. And if any such particular Receiver should make any payment out of the issues of his office otherwise than as it is ap-

pointed by the Receiver-General Henry, the said Duke Henry, he shall
be burdened still in his computation by sums so paid through him to us.
We concede also, and by the said authority moreover we assign to the
same Consort of Henry, £3,666 13s. 4d. to be had and received of the
same Consort of Henry, annually, to the end of her life, from the
said Feast of St. Michael the Archangel, to the end of the Passover
and St. Michael, by equal portions, as a part of her dowry, in the
subsequent form, viz., £1,000 thence annually to the end of the aforesaid time, both from the small and great Customs of Henry, our heirs
and successors in the Port of the Town of Southampton belonging
to Henry, through the hands of the Collector of the same Customs
for the time being. And £1,008 15s. 5d. thence per annum, to the
end of the said time, from the issues, returns, and profits of the said
Duke Henry of Cornwall, and from the issues, profits, and returns of
the Pewter and Tin Coinage in the Counties of Cornwall and Devon,
through the hands of the Receiver-General Henry, heirs and successors of the same Duke, and of whatever other Receivers, occupiers,
or Dwellers of the same Profits, issues, and returns for the time being.
And £1,657 17s. 11d. thence per annum, to the same end, to the Saint
Henry, our heirs and successors through the hands of the Treasurers and
Chamberlains of the same Saint for the time being, as well from the first
monies proceeding from the advances of our Vice-Counsellor and Com-
missary, our heirs and successors, as from whatever other issues, profits,
farms, debts, and returns are paid to the said Saint, until We, the heirs
and successors of Henry, shall have made provision and recompense to
the same Consort of Henry, from the Lands, Tenements, Returns, and
other possessions to the value of the said £3,666 13s. 4d. per annum,
within Henry's kingdom of England, as part of her dowry, or other
things to be held to the end of her life. And moreover by the said
authority, We will and concede, that the aforesaid Consort of Henry
shall be provided and recompensed out of the lands, tenements, returns,
and possessions, which first come or fall into the hands of Henry, or of
our heirs through us, and the said heirs of Henry, according to
the deduction and satisfaction of the said £3,666 13s. 4d. to be held
as part of her said dowry. And by the aforesaid assent and authority,
We will and concede that the said Consort of Henry shall have so many
and such Baronial fees as may be allowed by Law, and unemployed,
by demand, and other Baronial fees and other Warrants so many
and such as may be necessary and opportune to be conceded and
assigned to her in this part, for the payment of sums and annuities
to her, as it is promised, and for the execution of the promised things.
And that the Chancellor, Henry of England, and the Keeper of the
private Seal of Henry, besides the Chancellor, Duke Henry of Lancaster,
We, being heirs and successors for the time being, do make, without
delation from the tenor of those presents, such Baronial fees and
Warrants, from time to time whensoever and wheresoever on the part of
the Consort of Henry *ronabiliter*, they may be requisite. Save whatever
things are bound to the state of Henry, or his possession, right, title and

interest, in the customs, issues, profits, and returns of the said Duke of
Cornwall, the Pewter and Tin Coinages, and in the said Castles, Towns,
Dominions, Manors, Honors, Bales, Grounds, Lands, Tenements, Wapentaches, sleek cattle, Hundreds, Franchises, Liberties, Farms, Returns,
profits, Commodities, Possessions, and other things promised to the same
Consort of Henry in the said form conceded and assigned both in the
said Dukedom of Henry of Lancaster, and in Grounds, Roads, Annuities,
Custodies, Offices, and Farms whatever in or about the Dukedom of Henry
of Lancaster, or other parcels of the things promised, if such are contained
in the same.

We concede moreover to the said most beloved Consort of Henry, that
she shall by no means whatever be burdened or compelled to return to Us
or the heirs of Henry, any computation of any issues, profits, or returns
of the said Castles, Dominions, Lands, Tenements, and other things promised, or of any one of the same : so that she may be quiet and un-
annoyed in any manner by any computation and other burdens whatever
thence, regarding Us and the heirs of Henry. · But all these things
are through Us, by the said authority, confided, given, conceded, and
assigned, on the 19th day of March, in the Twenty Fourth year of
Henry's reign, by the said Parliament of Henry then sitting."

" In whose reign," &c., &c.

Issue Roll.   24 Henry VI.

30th May.—To Margaret, Queen of England.   In money paid to her
by assignment made this day by the hands of John Norrys, in discharge
of £1,000 which the lord the King commanded to be paid to the said
Queen, as well for the daily expenses of her chamber as in relief of the
great charges which the said Queen incurred on the day of the Circum-
cision of our Lord last past.   By writ, &c., £1,000.

Amidst the agitation caused by the disastrous public events, and
whilst the spirit of resistance to the government was beginning to manifest itself, songs and poetry, as a means of promoting the general discontent, were much used, and even assumed a bold character.   Some of
these, which have happily been preserved, are most valuable.   There
are many allusions in one of them to persons of rank and influence, each
of whom is described by his badge.   It appears that this poem was
written after 1447, as Cardinal Beaufort, who died in that year, is
spoken of as having " his velvet hat closed."

The deaths of the Dukes of Bedford, Gloucester, Exeter, and Somerset,
and of Cardinal Beaufort, are first enumerated, and the commencement
of the troubles in England is dated from the capture of Rouen in 1417.
The Duke of Norfolk "laid to sleep," meaning bribed by Suffolk, who

envied him. The gallant Talbot, Earl of Shrewsbury, in reference to his name and badge, "our good dog," was perhaps "bounden" by the grant of the Earldom of Waterford, &c., in 1446. By Lord Fauconberg having "lost his angle-hook," his capture by the French is implied. Lord Willoughby de Eresby seems accused of indolence, and by the bear being "bound that was so wild, for he had lost his ragged staff," allusion was intended to Richard Neville having been created Earl of Warwick, which distinction may have satisfied his wishes, and thus, to use the metaphor, the bear was deprived of his staff. The Duke of Buckingham's "wheel" became spokeless from his having taken offence at the dismissal of his brothers, (the Chancellor and Treasurer,) by Suffolk; and also from having induced the King to receive with kindness, the Duke of York. Thomas Daniel, John Norreys, and John Trevilian are particularly mentioned, since the last-named is said "often to have blinded the King," and their names appear among those indicted by the Commons, in 1451, "for mysbehaving about the King's roiall persone." The Earl of Arundel having refused to support Suffolk's power, became popular in Sussex and Kent. Bourchier, and some other noble, who is described as the wine bottle, (possibly the Earl of Oxford, since a long-necked silver bottle was one of his badges,) and the Prior of St. John's, are mentioned as having united with the Bishop of Exeter. The Earl of Devonshire is related to have retired into his own country, instead of helping "with shield and spear" the attempt then contemplated to overthrow the obnoxious minister; while the Duke of York's anxiety and irresolution are admirably described under his cognizance, a falcon, flying hither and thither, uncertain where to build her nest.

ON THE POPULAR DISCONTENT AT THE DISASTERS IN FRANCE.[1]

Bedfords[2]   Gloucester[3]
"The Rote is ded, the Swanne is goone
            Excetter[4]
" The firy Cressett hath lost his lyght ;
" Therfore Inglond may make gret mone,
    " Were not the helpe of Godde almyght.
        Roone[5]
" The castelle is wonne where care begowne
        Somerset[6]
    " The Portecolys is leyde adowne
                Cardinalle[7]
" Iclosid we have oure welevette hatte
    " That keveryed us from mony stormys browne,

---

[1] Verses in the Cotton. Rolls, ii. 23.
[2] John Plantagenet, Duke of Bedford, third son of Henry IV. Badge,—the Root of a tree.
[3] Humphrey Plantagenet, Duke of Gloucester, fourth son of Henry IV. Badge,—the Swan.
[4] John Holland, Duke of Exeter. "A Cressett with burning fire," i.e., a fire beacon, said to have been the badge of the Admiralty.
[5] Rouen, surrendered to the French in 1447.
[6] John Beaufort, Duke of Somerset. Badge,—a Portcullis.
[7] Henry Beaufort, Bishop of Winchester "Cardinal of England."

Northfolke[1]
" The White Lioun is leyde to slepe
Southfolk[2]
" Thorouz the envy of the Ape clogge,
" And he is bownden that oure dore shuld kepe,
" That is Talbott oure goode dogge[3]
Fawkenberge[4]
" The Fisshere hathe lost his hangulhooke ;[5]
" Gete theym agayne when it wolle be,
Wylloby[6]
" Oure Mylle-saylle wille not abowte,
" Hit hath so longe goone emptye.
Warwick[7]
" The Bere is bound that was so wild,
" Ffor he hath lost his ragged staffe,
Bokynghame[8]
" The Carte nathe[9] is spokeless,
" For the counseille that he gaffe,
Danyelle[10]
" The Lily is both faire and grene ;
Norreys[11]
" The Coundite rennyth not, as I wene,
Trevilian[12]
" The Cornysshe Chowgh [13] offt with his trayne
Rex
" Hath made oure Egulle blynde.
Arundelle[14]
" The White Harde is put out of mynde,
" Because he wolle not to hem consent ;
" Therfore the commyns saith is both trew and kynde,
" Bothe in Southesex and in Kent.
Bowser[15]
" The Water-Bowge and the Wyne-Botelle,
Prior of Saint Johanis
" With the Vetturlockes cheyne bene fast.
Excettur
" The Whete-yere wolle theym susteyne
" As longe as he may endure and last.

[1] John de Mowbray, Duke of Norfolk.   Badge,—a White Lion.

[2] William de la Pole, Duke of Suffolk.   Badge, — the Clog argent and Chain or.

[3] John Talbot, Earl of Shrewsbury, who had been recalled from active service in France.

[4] William Neville, Lord Fauconberg, one of the heroes of the French wars. Badge,—the " fysshe hoke."

[5] A hook for angling, or a fish-hook.

[6] Robert, Lord Willoughby, another hero of the French wars.   Badge,—the Mill-sail.

[7] Richard Neville, Earl of Warwick.   Badge,—the Bear and ragged staff.

[8] Humphrey de Stafford, Duke of Buckingham.   Badge,—a Cart-wheel.

[9] The nave of a cart.

[10] Thomas Daniel, "armiger," or esquier, one of the unpopular courtiers.

[11] John Norris, one of the officers of the household to Henry VI.

[12] Daniel Trevilian.   Badge,—a Cornish Chough.

[13] The bird.

[14] William Fitz-Alan, Earl of Arundel.   Badge,—the White Horse, here signified by the "White Harde."

[15] Henry, Lord Bourchier, whose arms were argent a cross, ingrailed gules, between four water bougets.

Devynshire[1]
" The Boore is farre into the west, ·
  " That shold us helpe with shilde and spere,'
Yorke[2]
" The Fawkoun fleyth, and hath no rest,
  " Till he witte where to bigge[3] his nest."

Another of these compositions is addressed to the lords of the court, and contains a warning for the King himself. The courtiers, who ruled the King, are called upon to restore the grants they had obtained from him, for they had reduced him to such poverty that he was obliged " to beg from door to door " through his tax gatherers. Untruth, oppression, and evil-doing prevailed throughout the land much more than the King knew ; but vengeance was at hand. So poor a King and such rich nobles were never seen before ; while the Commons could support their burdens no longer, in spite of the resolution of the Lord Say to tread them under foot. The Earl of Suffolk had sold Normandy, and now sought to make the King take the blame of his treason.

A WARNING TO KING HENRY.[4]

" Ye that have the kyng to demene[5]
" And ffrauncheses gif theyme ageyne,
  " Or els I rede[6] ye fle ;
" Ffor ye have made the kyng so pore,
" That now he beggeth fro dore to dore ;
  " Alas, hit shuld so be.

" Tome of Saye[7] and Danielle bothe,
" To begyn be not to lothe ;
  " Then shalle ye have no shame.
" Who wille not, he shalle not chese,[8]
" And his life he shalle lese,[9]
  " No resoun wille us blame.

" Trowthe and pore men ben appressede
" And myscheff is nothyng redressede ;
  " The kyng knowith not alle.
" Thorowout alle Englande,
" On tho that holdene the fals bonde
  " Vengeaunce will cry and calle.

" The traytours wene[10] they ben so sly,
" That no mane can hem aspy ;
  " We cane do theme no griffe.

---

[1] Thomas Courtenay, Earl of Devonshire.
[2] Richard Plantagenet, Duke of York.   Badge,—a Falcon.
[3] To build.   [4] Cotton. Charters.   [5] To direct or lead.
[6] To counsel or advise.
[7] James Fienes, Lord Saye and Sele, lord treasurer, one of the unpopular statesmen of the day. This song was written before this nobleman was thrown into the Tower.   [8] To choose.
    [9] To lose.   [10] To think.

" We swere by hym that hairwede[1] helle
" They shalle no lenger in eresy dwelle
    " Ne in ther fals beleve.

" So pore a kyng was never seene,
" Nor richere lordes alle bydene ;[2]
    " The communes may no more.
" The lorde Saye biddeth holde hem downe,
" That worthy dastarde of renowne,
    " He techithe a fals loore.

" Suffolk Normandy hath swolde,[3]
" To gete heyt agayne he is bolde,
    " How acordeth these to in one ;
" And he wynethe,[4] withouten drede,
" To make the kyng to avowe his dede,
    " And calle hit no tresoun.

" We trow the kyng be to leere,[5]
" To selle bothe menne and lond in feere ;
    " Hit is agayne resoun.
" But yef the commyns of Englonde
" Helpe the kyng in his fonde,[6]
    " Suffolk wolle bere the crowne.

" Be ware, kynge Henré, how thou doos ;
" Let no lenger thy traitours go loos ;
    " They wille never be trewe.
" The traytours are sworne alle togedere
" To holde fast as they were brether ;[7]
    " Let them drynk as they hanne[8] brewe."

    " O rex, si rex es, rege te, vel eris sine re rex;
    " Nomen habes sine re, nisi te recte regas."

The following extract is from a spirited ballad on the death of the Duke of Suffolk. It commemorates how, in the month of May, Jack Napes, as the favourite is here termed, had gone to sea as a mariner, but was arrested on the way by death ; and that Nicholas (possibly the name of the ship's commander) offered to be his confessor.

    " In the monthe of Maij, when gresse groweth grene,
    " Flagrant[9] in her floures, w* swet savour,
    " Jack Napes[10] wolde ouer the see, a maryner to ben,
    " With his cloge,[11] and his cheyn, to seke more tresour,
    " Syche a payn prikkede hym, he asked a confessour.
    " Nicholas said, ' I am redi, this confessour to be.'
    " He was holden so, that he ne passede that hour,
    " For Jack Napes soul, Placebo and Dirige".[12]

[1] Harrowed.   [2] At once, or at the same time.   [3] Sold.
[4] Thinketh.   [5] Empty or weak.   [6] Dilemma.
[7] Brethren.   [8] Have.   [9] Fragrant.
[10] A nickname for William de la Pole, Duke of Suffolk.
A Clog argent with a Chain or, the badge of Suffolk.   [12] Cottonian MS.

A poem more general in satire was written, just before the civil wars commenced, on the troubles arising in the land.

"HOW MYSCHAUNCE REGNETH IN INGLONDE.

"Now God, that syttyst an hyghe in trone,
"Help thy peple in here greet nede,
"That trowthe and resoun regne may sone
"For thanne schal they leve owt of drede.
"In that wyse conscience schal hem lede,
"Hem to brynge onto good governaunce ;
"That yt may sone be doon in dede ;
"Of alle oure synnys, God, make a delyveraunce.

"Meed¹ and falscheed assocyed are ;
"Trowthe bannyd ys, the blynde may not se ;
"Manye a man they make fulle bare,|
"A strange compleynt ther ys of every degré,
"The way is now past of tranquyllyté,
"The wyche causyth a full greet varyaunce ;
"Amange the comunys ther ys no game nor gle ;
"Of alle oure synnys, God, make a delyveraunce.

"Murder medelythe ful ofte, as men say ;
"Usure and rapyne stefly dothe stande,
"Here abydyne ys wythe her that goon ful gay ;
"For whanne they wele they have hem in hande,
"Ful manye they brynge to myschaunce.
"Wyse men, beholden, be wayr al afore hande ;
"Of alle our synnys, God, make a delyveraunce.

"Wyght ys blak, as many men seye,
"And blak ys wyght, but summe men sey nay ;
"Auctoryteys for hem they toleye ;²
"Large conscience causyth they croked way,
"In thys reame they make a foul aray,
"Whanne the dyse renne, ther lakkythe a chaunce
"Clene conscience bakward goth alway ;
"Of alle our synnys, God, make a delyveraunce.

"Myscheef mengid³ ys, and that in every syde ;
"Dyscord medelythe ful fast amonge ;
"The gate's of glaterye⁴ standen up wyde,
"Hem semythe that al ys ryghte and no wronge,
"Thus endurid they have al to longe ;
"Crosse and pyle standen in balaunce ;
"Trowthe and resoun be no thynge stronge ;
"Of alle our synnys, God, make a delyveraunce.

---

¹ Mede,—reward or bribe.   ² Toleye,—to put forward.
³ Mengid,—reminded.   ⁴ Glaterye,—flattery.

" Rychesse renewyd causith the perdicioun
" Of trowthe, that scholde stande in prosperyté
" Between here and hope ys mayd a divisioun,
" And that ys al for lak of charyté ;
" Wherefore ther regnethe no tranquillyté :
" Thys mateer causith the fool ignoraunce,
" That the peple may not in eese be ;
" Of alle our synnys, God, make a delyveraunce.

" Now, God, that art ful of al pletevousnesse ;[1]
" Of al vertuys grace and charyté,
" Putte from us al thys unsekyrnesse,[2]
" That we stande in grete necessyté,
" That agayn trowthe no varyeng be.
" Al tymes that art founteyne of al felycité,
" Of al oure synnys, thou make a delyveraunce."[3]

In a curious metrical prophecy, still more obscure, we are told that disastrous occurrences are to take place, and among them a battle on the banks of the Humber, " when Rome shall be removed into England, and every priest shall have the Pope's power in hand." Another poem describes England as in a state of universal contention ; that there were much people of light consciences ; many knights possessing little power ; many laws with little justice ; little charity but much flattery ; great show of living on small wages, and many gentlemen but few servants ; &c.

ON THE TIMES.

" Now ys Yngland alle in fyght ;
" Moche peple of consyens lyght ;
" Many knyghtes, and lytyll myght ;
" Many lawys, and lytylle ryght ;
" Many actes of parlament,
" And few kept wyth tru entent ;
" Lytylle charyté, and fayne to plese ;
" Many a galant penyles ;
" And many a wonderfulle dysgyzyng[4]
" By unprudent and myssavyzyng ;[5]
" Grete countenanse and smalle wages ;
" Many gentyllemen, and few pages ;
" Wyde gownys, and large slevys ;
" Wele besene, and strong thevys ;
" Moch bost of there clothys,
" But wele I wot[6] they lake[7] none othys. [b]

[1] Plentevousness,—abundance. [2] Unsekyrnesse,—insecurity.
[3] MSS. in the University Library, Cambridge, in a handwriting of the reign of Henry VI.
[4] Disguising. [5] Bad counsel. [6] Know. [7] Lack.
[b] MSS. in Corpus Christi College, Oxford.

Issue Roll. 32 Henry VI.

To Humphrey, Duke of Buckingham, who, by the King's command, n the month of September, in the 29th year of his reign, went to the said Lord the King at his castle of Kyllyngworth, and to his city of Coventry, with a strong guard ; also attended at great costs and expenses about the King's person. In money paid to him by assignment made this day by the hands of John Andrew, £400, which the Lord the King commanded to be paid him, &c. By writ, &c., £400.

Issue Roll, Easter. 32 Henry VI.

17*th July.*—To Margaret Queen of England. In money paid to her by assignment made this day, by the hands of Robert Tunfield, for divers sums of money paid by the said Queen for an embroidered cloth, called "*Crisome,*" for the baptism of the Prince, the King's son, and for 20 yards of russet cloth of gold, called "tisshu," and "540 brown sable bakkes," worth altogether £554 16*s.* 8*d.* The said Queen to have the same by the King's command of his gift. By writ, &c., £554 16*s.* 8*d.*

Issue Roll, Michaelmas. 33 Henry VI.

19*th February.*—To the Prior and Convent of the Blessed Peter, Westminster. In money paid to them by the hands of John Wode in discharge of £10, which the Lord the King, with the advice of his Council, commanded to be paid to the said Prior and Convent, for the wax lights burnt at the baptism of Edward, the son of our Lord the King. By writ of privy seal amongst the mandates of this term. £10.

21*st February.*—To Margaret, Duchess of Somerset, who, by the King's command, resided and remained in attendance in the city of London and suburbs thereof from the feast of Lent, in the 31st year, to the 11th of August then next following, at her great cost and charge. In money paid to her, &c., in discharge of £100, which the said Lord the King commanded to be paid to the said Duchess, of his gift, &c.

By writ of privy seal, £100.

END OF VOLUME I.

BRADBURY, EVANS, AND CO., PRINTERS, WHITEFRIARS

RY

1 on

Lightning Source UK Ltd.
Milton Keynes UK
UKOW05f2327260717

306081UK00001B/73/P